Conflict, Cooperation and Leadership in the Mediterranean

Ivan Ureta

# Conflict, Cooperation and Leadership in the Mediterranean

European Political Entrepreneurs from
the 1980s to the Arab Spring

## PETER LANG

Lausanne - Berlin -Bruxelles - Chennai - New York - Oxford

Bibliographic Information published by the Deutsche Nationalbibliothek
The Deutsche Nationalbibliothek lists this publication in the Deutsche Nationalbibliografie; detailed bibliographic data is available online at http://dnb.d-nb.de.

Library of Congress Cataloging-in-Publication Data
A CIP catalog record for this book has been applied for at the Library of Congress

ISBN 978-3-0343-4345-9
ePDF 978-3-0343-4828-7
ePUB 978-3-0343-4829-4
DOI 10.3726/b21588

© 2024 Peter Lang Group AG, Lausanne
Published by Peter Lang Group AG, Lausanne, Switzerland

info@peterlang.com - www.peterlang.com

All rights reserved.
All parts of this publication are protected by copyright.
Any utilization outside the strict limits of the copyright law, without the permission of the publisher, is forbidden and liable to prosecution.
This applies in particular to reproductions, translations, microfilming, and storage and processing in electronic retrieval systems.

This publication has been peer reviewed.

# Acknowledgements

I would like to thank the many friends, colleagues, diplomats, journalists, politicians and organizations who have made it possible for the author to work and understand the maze of data and research material. Especially I want to thank Cristina Gallach who opened me the doors of the not easily penetrable diplomatic world. Her kindness and readiness facilitated the gathering of first-hand information as well. I would like also to thank to all the interviewees who accepted to help me with this research. Despite their very busy schedules they all received me with openness and familiarity. I cannot forget my family. They have represented a fundamental pillar due to their constant support. Finally I thank to Rory Miller, who has provided invaluable guidance, attention and support over the last years.

Locarno, 21 March 2023

# Table of Contents

List of Abbreviations .................................................................. 11

Graphics and Tables ................................................................... 13

Introduction .............................................................................. 15
   Mediterranean Politics ............................................................. 16
      EEC/EU Foreign Policy and the Global
      Mediterranean Policy ........................................................... 17
      The 5+5 Dialogue ................................................................. 18
      The Euro-Mediterranean Partnership (EMP) ......................... 18
      The European Neighbourhood Policy (ENP) ......................... 20
      The Alliance of Civilizations (AoC) ....................................... 22
      The Union for the Mediterranean (UfM) .............................. 22
   Framing Euro-Mediterranean Politics, Political
   Entrepreneurs and Brokers ...................................................... 23
      Realist-Constructivism ........................................................... 26
   Political Entrepreneurship and Brokerage ................................ 29
      Political Entrepreneurs .......................................................... 29
      Political Brokers .................................................................... 31
      The Mediterranean: A Profitable Opportunity ..................... 32
   Unveiling Political Entrepreneurs and Brokers ........................ 38
      Corpus Linguistics and Critical Discourse Analysis .... 38
      Corpus Linguistics (CL) ........................................................ 38
      Critical Discourse Analysis (CDA) ....................................... 39
      CL and CDA as Complementary Approaches ..................... 40
   Contents ................................................................................... 41

1 Spain and the Great Gallop: Strategies of a Political
   Entrepreneur ............................................................................ 45
   1.1 Spain's European Ambitions and the
      French Response ................................................................. 45
   1.2 Trying to Build a New Image ............................................ 48
   1.3 French Reactions ................................................................ 50

1.4 Amateur Government Paving the Road for the Next Steps ............ 51
1.5 A Political Entrepreneur Looking for a Strategy ......... 53
1.6 The Spanish Gallopade: Looking for International Acknowledgement ............ 54
1.7 The Mediterranean Card ............ 55
1.8 The French Attitude ............ 59
1.9 Spain: Achieving Objectives ............ 60
1.10 Spain Sells the Mediterranean: A Threatening Political Discourse ............ 61

## 2 Lights and Shadows The Assertion of Spanish Leadership in the International Arena during the Aznar Era, 1996–2004 ............ 69

2.1 Discussing the Paternity of Spain's Foreign Policy ........ 69
2.2 The Baseline of Spain's New Foreign Policy ............ 73
2.3 Aznar and the Mediterranean: The First Step ............ 75
2.4 Aznar's New Foreign Policy: Changing Methodology ............ 79
2.5 Mutating Axes: The Atlantic- Mediterranean Approach ............ 81
2.6 Aznar *versus* the EU? A Converging Attitude, Different Approaches ............ 87
2.7 Aznar's Strong Political Stances and the End of His Mandate ............ 94

## 3 Zapatero's Attempt to Reposition Spain in the Mediterraean ............ 97

3.1 Back to the Mediterranean. Back to the Roots ............ 98
3.2 The Alliance of Civilizations: Building on the Sand ............ 103
3.3 A Political Broker Managing an Abstract Political Opportunity ............ 107
3.4 Lack of Clarity and a Fainted Strategy: Missed Opportunities? ............ 109
3.5 European Reactions ............ 116

## 4 The Presidency of Nicolas Sarkozy and the Mediterranean Frustrated Ambitions, Failed Leadership ............ 121
4.1 Jacques Chirac's Foreign Policy and the Arab World ............ 121
4.2 Sarkozy and the Mediterranean Window: Launching the Mediterranean Union ............ 124
4.3 European Reactions ............ 128
4.4 Europeanizing the Project: Rebuilding Trust ............ 131
4.5 Initial Reactions from the South ............ 135
4.6 Spain Becomes Home to the UfM ............ 136
4.7 The Benefits of the Union for the Mediterranean or for the South? ............ 137
4.8 Europe and the Future of the UfM ............ 142

## 5 Migration, Security and Public Opinion in the Euro-Mediterranean Region Challenging Political Entrepreneurs and Brokers ............ 145
5.1 General Migratory Trends ............ 150
  5.1.1 Migration in the Mediterranean ............ 150
5.2 Gambling on the Needs and Problems of Southern Mediterranean Countries ............ 155
5.3 Trying to Manage Migration: The Fundamental Gap ............ 157
5.4 Migration and the Economic Cycle: Triggering National Fears, Evidencing Multilateral Deficiencies ............ 159
5.5 Migration and Public Opinion: National Politics Challenging International Projects ............ 161

## 6 The Long Cultivation of the Arab Spring ............ 171
6.1 Making Friends by Securing the House ............ 172
6.2 Understanding "center/s-periphery/ies" Relations and Interactions ............ 174
6.3 Heirs, Political Mortgages and "forced" Allies ............ 177
  6.3.1 Libya ............ 178
  6.3.2 Tunisia ............ 180
6.4 A Surprising Arab Spring? ............ 181

6.4.1 Revolutions Propelled by the International
  Financial System ................................................ 183
6.5 EU's Response, Scope and Outcomes ........................ 184
**Conclusions** .................................................................. 189
Political Entrepreneurship Cycle (PEC) ............................ 194
Creation ............................................................................ 195
  Design ............................................................................ 195
  Implementation ............................................................. 195
  Institutionalization ....................................................... 196
  Evaluation ..................................................................... 196

**References** .................................................................. 201

**Appendix** .................................................................... 257

# List of Abbreviations

| | |
|---|---|
| AP | Alianza Popular (Spain) |
| ALN | Armée de Libération Nationale (Algeria) |
| AMU | Arab Maghreb Union |
| BMENA | Broader Middle East and North Africa |
| CAP | Common Agricultural Policy |
| CDI | Christian Democrat International –Later – Centrist Democrat International |
| CDSP | Common Security and Defense Policy |
| CFSP | Common Foreign Policy and Security Policy |
| CSCM | Conference for Security and Cooperation in the Mediterranean |
| CRUA | Comité Révolutionnaire d'Unité et d'Action (Algeria) |
| EC | European Commission |
| EAEC | European Atomic Energy Community |
| EAP | Economically Active Population |
| ECSC | European Coal and Steel Community |
| EEC | European Economic Community |
| EMFTA | Euro-Mediterranean Free Trade Area |
| EMP | Euro-Mediterranean Partnership |
| EMPA | Euro-Mediterranean Parliamentary Assembly |
| ENP | European Neighbourhood Policy |
| ETA | Euskadi Ta' Askatasuna |
| EU | European Union |
| FLN | Front de Liberation National |
| FRAP | Frente Revolucionario Antifascista y Patriota |
| GATT | General Agreement on Tariffs and Trade |
| GCIM | Global Commission on International Migration |
| GDR | German Democratic Republic |
| GMP | Global Mediterranean Policy |

| | |
|---|---|
| IEE | Instituto Español de Emigración (Spanish Institute of Immigration) |
| IEMED | European Institute of the Mediterranean (Catalonia) |
| IPEMED | Institute de Prospective Économique du Monde Méditerranéen (France) |
| JDP | Justice and Development Party (Turkey) |
| JHA | Justice and Home Affairs |
| MEG | Maghreb Europe Gas (Pipeline) |
| MENA | Middle East and North Africa |
| MEPI | Middle East Partnership |
| OIC | Organization of Islamic Countries |
| ODA | Overseas Development Aid |
| PA | Palestinian Authority |
| PACE | Parliamentary Assembly of the Council of Europe |
| PP | Partido Popular |
| PSOE | Partido Socialista Obrero Español |
| SMIC | Salaire Minimum Interprofessionel de Croissance (Minimum Interprofessional Growth Salary) |
| NATO | North Atlantic Treaty Organization |
| OPEC | Organization of the Petroleum Exporting Countries |
| UFM | Union for the Mediterranean |
| UN | United Nations |
| UNAOC | United Nations Alliance of Civilizations |
| UNCD | United Nations Conference on Disarmament |
| UNHDR | United Nations Human Development Report |
| USA | United States of America |
| WMD | Weapons of Mass Destruction |

# Graphics and Tables

## (A) Graphics

| | | |
|---|---|---|
| Graphic 1. | European Councils. Conclusions of the Presidency, 1993–1995. | 63 |
| Graphic 2. | European Councils. Conclusions of the Presidency. 1996–2000. | 77 |
| Graphic 3. | José María Aznar. Discourses. 1983–2013. | 88 |
| Graphic 4. | European Councils. Conclusions of the Presidency. 2001–2004. | 92 |
| Graphic 5. | PSOE 2008–2011. Electoral Program. | 111 |
| Graphic 6. | AoC Madrid 2008–Istanbul 2009. | 112 |
| Graphic 7. | European Councils. Conclusions of the Presidency. 2005–2008. | 117 |
| Graphic 8. | Strategic Partnership between the EU and the Mediterranean and the ME. | 119 |
| Graphic 9. | Sarkozy. Discourse. Toulon. 2007. | 125 |
| Graphic 10. | Declaration of Marseille. Variables. | 135 |
| Graphic 11. | European Council. Conclusions of the Presidency. 2009–2013. | 142 |
| Graphic 12. | International Migrants as a Percentage of the Population. | 153 |
| Graphic 13. | Annual Rate of Change. Migrant Stock % in Spain, Italy, France and Malta. | 154 |
| Graphic 14. | Annual Rate of Change. Migrant Stock % in Europe. | 155 |
| Graphic 15. | International Migrants as a Percentage of the Population in Europe. | 155 |
| Graphic 16. | Spain. Public Opinion. | 164 |
| Graphic 17. | Italy. Public Opinion. | 165 |
| Graphic 18. | France. Public Opinion. | 166 |
| Graphic 19. | Malta. Public Opinion. | 166 |
| Graphic 20. | Compared Migration. Spain, Italy, France and Malta. | 167 |
| Graphic 21. | Aggregated EU. | 168 |

Graphic 22. Trend-lines, Europe. ............................................. 168
Graphic 23. Ideal Political Entrepreneur. ................................ 192
Graphic 24. Leaders. Behavior and Characteristics. .............. 193
Graphic 25. Long-Term Comparative Analysis. CE
Public Speech. 1993–2013. .................................. 197
Graphic 26. Trend-Line. Evolution. Public Opinion.
1997–2011. .......................................................... 198

**(B) Tables**

Tables 1.   Distribution and Status. UfM Projects.
August 2012. ........................................................ 141

**(C) Figures**

Figure 1.   Political Entrepreneurship Cycle. ....................... 194

# Introduction

The so-called "Arab Spring" exploded amid incredulous eyes. Politicians, scholars and the public opinion alike reacted with surprise – seemingly these uprisings were unexpected. In actual fact Western governments reacted slowly and cautiously prioritising maintaining a certain order where long-term collaboration, business cooperation and strategic alliances were needed. Almost from one day to the next, the slant of newspaper headlines and optimistic socio-economic forecasts changed; heads of state of North African countries like Ben Ali, Mubarak and Ghadafi began to be described as dictators by Western Media.

European countries were very aware of two important facts of the region: these governments and their leaders were not adhering to democratic principles in the way that they are applied and understood in Western societies, and their economic structures as well as their unbalanced and divided societies were posing big challenges to the future. Already in 1999 *Le Monde Diplomatique* published an article titled: Notre ami Ben Ali: Dictature à la Tunisienne (LB, 1999). The potential for conflict was therefore very high but strengthening economic and diplomatic relations with dubious regimes were crucial to ensure Europe's prosperity and security.

In order to better understand and demonstrate this I embarked upon a difficult path aimed at identifying and interviewing some of the politicians and diplomats who were most involved in the designing and developing of Euro-Mediterranean political and diplomatic relations. In the following chapters, most of those interviewed recognised that realism was the strongest element driving political and economic decisions *vis-à-vis* the southern rim of the Mediterranean. Idealism was put behind when important decisions were about to be taken.

In acknowledging the rampant socio-economic deficiencies and long-standing struggles experienced by North African countries since the achievement of their "independence", one question arises: How did these revolts not start earlier? The script was not written. The outcomes were foreseeable.

The central research question that I want to address is the following: Was the Arab Spring somehow induced by long-term forces led by Western geo-political and economic interests and initiatives in coalition with North African elites?

In line with the precedent research question, this book aims more specifically at understanding how Spain, and to a lesser extent France, have been implementing and managing policies and mechanisms to lead Euro-Mediterranean politics in order to achieve greater diplomatic influence, regional power and strategic leadership within the EU and the southern Mediterranean rim.

I consider these stakeholders as political brokers and entrepreneurs, whose natural market is the Mediterranean. Though I accept the rich cultural, historical, social and political values of the Mediterranean, I consider these factors to have been used and manipulated in order to construct a fictitious sphere of cooperation and achieve economic and security objectives. Accordingly, in this context, I view the Mediterranean as a transactional good that has been used and traded multi-directionally for political, economic and diplomatic goals.

## Mediterranean Politics

Representative scholarly work on Mediterranean politics is readily available and covers a wide array of topics. However for the purpose of framing this book I have decided to summarise the following policies and mechanisms: the Mediterranean Global Policy, the 5+5 Dialogue, the Barcelona Process or Euro-Mediterranean Partnership (EMP), the European Neighbourhood Policy (ENP), the Alliance of Civilizations (AoC) and the Union for the Mediterranean (UfM). My thesis will also analyse other parallel Euro-Mediterranean initiatives such as the Common Agricultural Policy (CAP), the Conference on Security and Cooperation in the Mediterranean (CSCM), the Mediterranean Forum, the Eurofor and Euromarfor and the MEDA programme.

With regard to the operational point of view of these six policies and mechanisms I agree on the following points. Firstly, Gómez has stated that these policies have demonstrated the EU's ability and capacity ["to embark upon strategic foreign policy behaviour but that the ability to consistently translate strategic objectives into effective action is not yet in evidence"] (Gómez, 2003). Secondly, as Monar has stressed, the EU's policy in the Mediterranean ("suffers from the gap between its apparent potential to act and its actual performance") (Monar, 1998). Thirdly, as Schimmelfennig, Sasse and Gänzle have highlighted, EU policies and mechanisms, in agreement with union member's needs, ambitions and strategic interests through the different enlargements, face two kinds of entrapments: a rhetorical entrapment and a procedural entrapment

(Schimmelfennig, 2001; Sasse, 2008; Gänzle, 2009). These three aspects will drive the rationale of my position.

## EEC/EU Foreign Policy and the Global Mediterranean Policy

The development of EU foreign policy corresponds to the EU institutional building process. Therefore the development of such a policy has corresponded and evolved according to the needs and strategic interests of member states. National needs, preferences and interests marked the way that EU foreign policy has evolved, as studied by Bulmer and Moravcsik (Schimmelfennig, 2001).

This idea will be valuable in understanding the role that political entrepreneurs from certain countries, such as Spain and France, have played in designing and lobbying for new proposals, e.g. the Euro-Mediterranean policy, in order to define and develop a more integrative EU foreign policy. This has made defining EU foreign policy cumbersome.

As Smith has underlined, European co-operation with regards to both foreign policy and security was completed in its third decade (Smith, 2000). In 1970 the European-Political Co-Operation (EPC), was created and transitioned in 1991 to the Common Foreign and Security Policy (CFSP) before the defence integration within the framework of the European Council of Cologne and Helsinki took place in 1999 (Smith, 2000).

EU foreign policy towards the Mediterranean has followed its own dynamic. Bicchi has studied EU foreign policy towards the Mediterranean from 1957 to contemporary times (Bicchi, 2007). Joffé has explained that the beginning of the Mediterranean policy started in 1956 with the intention of decreasing the economic dependence and implications of North African countries towards Europe after the French decolonisation process (Joffè, 1997)

However, it is important to note that from 1957 to 1972 EU foreign policy was non-existent. Nevertheless, European foreign policy towards the Mediterranean rapidly integrated the political and diplomatic agenda due to the geo-strategic interest in the Middle East. In 1970 the six original members of the union gathered in Munich to discuss the framework that constituted European Political Cooperation.

By quoting Western European officials Calabrese reminds us that they have consistently asserted that European interests cannot be separated from the Mediterranean basin (Calabrese, 1997). This was also valid for the US approach and their own geo-strategic interests in the Mediterranean, as demonstrated by Pero in the 1968–1976 period (Pero, 2001).

As Tayfur has mentioned, the EEC's interest in developing a policy towards the Mediterranean was mostly motivated by the changing nature of security challenges (Tayfur, 2000). In fact two years after the constitution of the EPC, in 1972, it launched the Global Mediterranean Policy (GMP). Tsoulakis notes that the implementation of the GMP coincided with major political-economic events like the energy crisis and the empowerment of OPEC as well as southern countries (Tsoulakis, 1997).

## The 5+5 Dialogue

The availability of scholarly literature on the 5+5 Dialogue is limited and it is rarely examined as a stand-alone research topic. Most of the journal papers dealing with the issue embed it within topics related to the EMP and other policies and mechanisms. Joffé has explained that the 5+5 initiative was launched by President Francois Mitterrand at the beginning of the 1980s during a period when French politics was still very much focused on North Africa (Joffè, 1997).

Barbé, Mestre i Camps and Soler i Lecha have studied how after French interest in the Mediterranean started to fade during the second half of 1989, Bettino Craxi, Prime Minister of Italy, looking to strengthen the socialist alliance with Spanish President Felipe González re-launched the 5+5 dialogue (Barbè, Camps and Soler i Lecha, 1997).

## The Euro-Mediterranean Partnership (EMP)

The launch of the Euro-Mediterranean Partnership (EMP), or Barcelona Process, in 1995 resulted in an increase of scholarly work related to Euro-Mediterranean issues. As Joffé has stated, the EMP represented the culmination of European political, diplomatic and economic attempts to design and implement a common policy towards the Mediterranean during and following the Cold War (Joffè, 1997). Gomez and Barbé have examined the first stages of the partnership and how it was negotiated (Barbè, 1996 and Gòmez, 2003)

Joffé, Branch, Marquina, Brad, Liotta, Hahn, Montanari and Guillespie among others have studied the implications, limitations and challenges of the EMP since its inception in 1995 focusing on issues including politics, development, economics and trade (Joffè, 1999; Brauch et Al., 2000; Gillespie, 1997; Hahn, 2009; Montanari, 2007).

Gillespie has studied how the architecture and philosophy of the Barcelona Process was challenged by the events of September 11th 2001 (Gillespie, 2003) while authors like Suzan have looked into the new security approach adopted by both the Barcelona Process and the EU to fight terrorism (Suzan, 2002).

Another very important part of the literature has concentrated on analysing the role and influence of the EMP in dealing with the Arab-Israeli conflict (Tovias, 2003; Peters 1998; Alpher, 1998). Assenburg has identified the Middle East conflict as the main obstacle challenging the entire EMP almost since its launch despite initial optimism (Assenburg, 2003).

Nevertheless, the European Commission, along with scholars like Joffé and Vasconcelos, has been making efforts to show the positive impacts of the Barcelona Process (European Commission, 2011; Joffè and Vasconcellos, 2000). On the economic and trade side, Bensassi, Márquez Ramos and Martínez Zarzano have concluded that within the Barcelona Process framework southern Mediterranean economies have benefited due to an increase of their exports into the EU (Bensassi et Al., 2012).

Most of these works, however, provide a northern Mediterranean or European perspective sometimes lacking in reflective criticism. Examples of this can be found in Marks who stated that global economic liberalisation would incur greater instability in the south. He also argued that any potential success would not depend upon the EU's actions but rather upon how Southern Mediterranean countries would be able to address and deal with their own instability (Marks, 1996).

This issue has become the most important and relevant factor of contemporary Euro-Mediterranean politics. On the other hand, authors like Khader have been working to re-evaluate a Southern point of view and have been criticising Euro-Mediterranean policies and mechanisms for to their lack of consistency, coherence and their attempt to verticalize Euro-Mediterranean relations (Khader, 2001).

Moreover, having been a place of competition and strategic interest for a number of stakeholders, the Mediterranean has ended up with the design and implementation of a number of parallel initiatives and mechanisms. These have contributed to making the panorama more confusing and the policies less efficient. From this perspective, Ünven Noi has examined how the EMP clashed with the Broader Middle East and North Africa (BMENA) initiative of the US (Noi, 2011).

The BMENA was launched in Rabat, Morocco in 2004 after a meeting called the Forum for the Future. It was conceived by the George W. Bush administration in an attempt to foster democracy in the Arab and non-Arab Muslim world through political and economic liberation following a neo-liberal approach (Sharp, 2005). As pointed out by Dalacoura, the objectives were heavily concentrated on economic issues rather than on political reforms or on activating and strengthening non-governmental and civil society organisations. (Dalacoura, 2005)

### The European Neighbourhood Policy (ENP)

As Del Sarto and Schumacher have outlined, until 2004 the UMP was the most important mechanism channelling the relations between the EU and southern Mediterranean countries (Del Sarto and Schumacher, 2005). However, the international context between 1995 and 2005 challenged the EMP's philosophy and hypotheses. On one hand the Middle East peace talks did not evolve as the EMP would have desired. In the same way that 9/11 altered the global landscape with the US promoted intervention in Iraq, the 2004 Madrid and the 2005 London bombings contributed to deepening the tensions between the West and the Arab world (Pace, 2005). Furthermore, as Smith has mentioned, in 2004 the EU was enlarged by 10 countries – a move that resulted in new neighbours and new external borders that required new policies and mechanisms (Smith, 2005).

It was with this backdrop that the European Neighbourhood Policy (ENP) was proposed and launched in 2004. The European Commission's Benita Ferrero-Waldmer explained that the ENP was designed to allow each country to determine the level and strength of collaboration that they desired with the EU (Ferrero-Waldmer, 2007). This principally represents the development of a bilateral policy between the EU and partner countries (EC, 2003). This policy was built upon Romano Prodi's 2002 proposal to bring the EU's foreign policy up to speed based on the idea of a ["wider Europe"] surrounded by a ["circle of friends"] (Prodi, 2002) This project was described by Prodi as "sharing everything with the Union but institutions" (Prodi, 2002). Basically this meant developing a Common European Economic Space where bilateral relations with neighbouring countries would follow mostly economic and not political or institutional procedures.

As soon as it was launched some authors expressed their doubts and criticism over the ENP. Sasse emphasised that when measured against a rationalist conditionality model the ENP was both conceptually and empirically was weak (Sasse, 2008). The lack of institutional commitment was one of the most obvious points to be criticised. Lavenex put forth that the EU was seeking to expand legal boundaries by restricting openings of institutional boundaries (Lavenex, 2004). Fostering economic reforms without considering political and institutional transformations is not realistic. Kelley wondered whether ["the potential of 'everything without institutions' [would] motivate democratic and human rights reforms"] (Kelley, 2006).

This asymmetric relationship has also been noticed by Smith who stated that the ENP was demanding too much from neighbours while only giving a number of vague incentives (Smith, 2005). Following this thinking, Gänzle noted that the ENP aimed at integrating non-EU countries into policy-taking instead of policy-making processes (Gänzle, 2005). This perspective clashes with the initial hypothesis that the ENP would increase the sense of co-ownership.

Within the Mediterranean the ENP was intended to strengthen the EMP, not to substitute it. However, as Natorski has stressed, even with the adoption of the ENP initiatives and the objectives proposed by the EMP the relations with the Middle East would remain unclear (Natorski, 2007). Youngs has pointed out that the ENP faced number of challenges: the redistribution of funds among new member states; an increasing bilateralism that clashed with the EMP's multilateral approach and objectives towards the Arab world; and the increasing claims from Arab countries to be considered according to their particular specificities. According to Johansson-Nogués, this bilateralism represented a step backwards because it increased the possibilities of developing asymmetric relations (Johansson-Nogués, 2004).

In addition, this initiative entailed modern political and diplomatic dynamics within the region and increased competition among states. As Bicchi and Natorski have assessed, by acting like entrepreneurs EU member states attempted to find alternative ways to increase their influence and new leadership (Bicchi, 2002). One of the most prevalent problems of southern Mediterranean countries is related to political and democratic reforms. The EMP was inefficient in proposing such changes. With regards to the ENP, as Emerson and Noutcheva have described, the new mechanisms would prioritise economic issues over political reforms (Emerson and Noutcheva, 2005). Therefore stability problems of the region as well as the promotion of democracy remained unsolved, as explaied by Schimmelfennig and Scholtz (Schimmelfennig and Scholtz, 2008). These elements would undermine the entire argument, rationale and value of the ENP (Youngs, 2005).

## The Alliance of Civilizations (AoC)

Even though the Alliance of Civilizations (AoC) was adopted in 2007–2008, the scholarly debate on this topic basically coincides with the celebration of the tenth anniversary of the EMP and the proposal of the ENP (2004–2005). Naïr has argued that an AoC would help to soften the increasing tensions between the West and the Arab world (Näir, 2005). However, this initiative immediately generated negative reactions, controversies and contributed to political polarisation. Bardají and Kamen claimed that this political initiative was inaccurately designed and proposed from a political, budgetary and conceptual point of view (Kamen, 2004; Bardají, 2005).

Conceptually speaking, Balci has defined the AoC as a clash/alliance dichotomy and as an initiative that was represented by a reactionary identity (Balci, 2009). Vallespín, following a similar critical approach, analysed the role future stakeholders would play within such a complex mechanism, recognising that this factor would determine the success or the failure of such an initiative (Vallespín, 2005).

Despite these criticisms, authors like Petito have considered that the AoC could aid in defining the limits of a global political discourse that could contribute to the elaboration of an international political theory (Petito, 2007). Barreñada dubbed the AoC as one of Spain's most innovative proposals due to its cultural and political impulse to fight against global security problems (Barreñada, 2006). Cajal added that the AoC was ["a Spanish ethical initiative for a lasting world peace"] (Cajal, 2009). Both authors consider the AoC to be a major success of Spanish diplomacy. Celso has insisted that this policy and multilateral diplomatic effort ensured Spain's strategy to define a national, post 3/11 antiterrorist policy (Celso, 2009).

## The Union for the Mediterranean (UfM)

The Union for the Mediterranean (UfM) was adopted by the EU in 2008 after Nicolas Sarkozy introduced the idea of a Mediterranean union during a speech in Toulon, France in 2007. The scholarly literature on the UfM, its inception and its developments has followed the same trend as the other policies commented on earlier – strong criticism mixed with positive reviews. Emerson has pointed out that Sarkozy's initial proposal was poorly conceived and ["awkwardly presented politically"] (Emerson, 2008). Soler i Lecha contends that the proposal of a Mediterranean Union was the initiative that revolutionised most Euro-Mediterranean politics since 2005 (Soler I Lecha, 2008).

However it also revolutionised European politics. As Balfour and Schmid have commented, Sarkozy's proposal provoked strong opposition and criticism from Germany through Angela Merkel as the initiative did not take into account the EU's existing communitarian efforts, policies and mechanisms to deal with southern Mediterranean partners. (Balfour and Schmid, 2008). Balfour mentions that the concepts of Mediterranean Union, Barcelona Process: Union for the Mediterranean and the final Union for the Mediterranean, have not been semantic evolutions. These definitions have been coined in order to be accepted by all EU member states (Balfour, 2009). Gillespie has described and studied how tensions with European and non-European states challenged an initiative that aimed at placing France as a leader, promoter and centre of a new Mediterranean political, diplomatic and economic reality (Gillespie, 2008).

With regards to Franco-Spanish relations and Spain's reactions to Sarkozy's initiatives, Soler i Lecha has commented that Spain, as the former political leader in the Mediterranean, had to react in order to either minimise the impact of the French proposal against the existing EMP or, on the contrary, try to strength it (Soler i Lecha, 2008). The main question however remains: Do these new mechanisms and policies overlap or complement existing initiatives? Authors like Aliboni, Joffé, Lannon, Mahjoub, Saaf, Vasconcelos or Ammor describe the final formula and design of the UfM as a continuation of the UMP and argue that there is more room for initiatives that may strengthen Euro-Mediterranean relations.

## Framing Euro-Mediterranean Politics, Political Entrepreneurs and Brokers

Building on the above, in my effort to understand and explain how brokers and entrepreneurs have acted and shaped Euro-Mediterranean politics, I have tried to define and use a multidisciplinary theoretical approach. I have done so because I do not believe that one single theory can explain complex processes, like these, that most usually present opposing elements and characteristics. The analysis I present in this book is an attempt to make sense of the maze of contradictions that have constructed the Euro-Mediterranean reality.

Traditionally it is possible to classify theories of international relations into four different families. First, authors like Waltz, Copeland and Mearsheimer among others, have examined the variables that configure the distribution of power among states (Waltz, 1979; Mearsheimer, 1989). Within this category Deutsch, Ruggie or Rosencrance have devoted scholarly efforts to assess trade, financial flows as well as interstate communication (Deutsch, 1969; Ruggier, 1983; Rosencrance, 1986). Other authors like Keohane and Martin have studied the degree of institutionalisation among different countries (Keohane and Martin, 2003).

Second, as Walt has enumerated, there is a group of theories that concentrate their attention on (Walt, 2005): The study of different types of regimes (Fearon, 1994); the characteristics of bureaucratic and organisational politics, a group of theories that are relevant to this volume (Halperin, 1972); the level of internal cohesion (Levy, 1989); as well as the analysis of ideas and doctrines, are central to this book (Goldstein and Keohane, 1993).

Third, authors like Jervis, Mercer or Byman and Pollack among others, have concentrated their study in assessing both individual and group psychology (Jervis, 1976; Mercer, 1996; Byman and Pollack, 2001). Within this group of theories and considering a systemic approach it is important to mention decision theory. Applying this theory to international relations it is possible to explain and assess the levels of rationality, coherence and achievement of objectives by studying the behaviour of groups, agents and individuals and how it shapes the decision-making process. This approach is also relevant to this book because I accept the transformative and influencing capacity of political actors such as political brokers and entrepreneurs. Therefore, this approach overcomes structural perspectives, which are shared in contradictory ways by neo-realists and scholars working on world-system theory. As Wendt has put forth, these two theories fail to recognise the ["mutually constitutive nature of human agents and system structures"] (Wendt, 1987). Finally, research developed by Finnemore, Ruggie and Wendt has been conducted to better grasp the interconnections between ideas, identities and socio-political discourse (Finnmore, 1996; Ruggie, 1998; Wendt, 1999).

The aforementioned groups of theories use a wide array of methods that can be borrowed from different disciplines. However, there are theories that might present higher or lower degrees of applicability and that are mostly descriptive. Realism and its variations represent the most relevant framework and it is widely accepted by policy and decision makers. Nevertheless, in considering big families of theories such as idealism, realism, Marxism, functionalism and critical theories, there is a marked trend amongst scholars and theorists to consider these theories as isolated compartments. This happens to the point that scholars and theorists tend to identify themselves, almost doctrinally, with their theoretical frameworks and therefore, interconnections or mixed approaches can be penalised by the scholastic, not scholarly, community.

As said before, I have preferred not to follow a closed theoretical program but to integrate theories and approaches that can better serve the purpose of the main objective, the specific objectives and the methodological design of this research. I have implemented an interdisciplinary approach that not only helps to evaluate complex situations and scenarios related to international affairs with a greater degree of precision, but also with aspects related to individual and collective behaviour, as well as communication processes as a baseline paradigm.

On one hand I recognise that the realist approach may be the most accurate of the group to understand state's interests, strategies and decision-making processes. They are guided first of all by their own interests, the perpetuation of their influence as well as their security. Their interests with regards to foreign policy remain –or should remain stable-, while their alliances might vary according to the context. On the other hand, however, as political entrepreneurs and brokers, their strategies as well as their decision-making processes and communicational strategies are more understandable using a complementary approach: constructivism. Constructivism helps to understand how ideas, myths and fears can mould the international system and how, for instance, public opinion can be shaped and manipulated to follow or support political postulates and strategies.

Considering the precedent comments, the philosophical backbone of this text is represented by the discussion and the understanding of how on one hand, theory can explain the way practitioners –diplomats and political brokers, opportunists or entrepreneurs – understand their daily tasks and how and why they act, responsibly or irresponsibly. Therefore, this theoretical approach aims to shed light and bridge the gap between theory and practice to better explain procedural aspects, decision-making processes and agenda setting. Walt has stated that

IR theorists have not been able to satisfy the demands of policy and decision-makers (Walt, 2005). A similar view has been defended by Jentleson and Wallace (Jentleson, 2002; Wallce, 1996).

### Realist-Constructivism

Linked to the aforementioned points, this book explores how states have been acting as political and diplomatic entrepreneurs, brokers and opportunists in order to achieve greater international diplomatic influence on the one hand and to address national interests on the other. In convincing other political and institutional stakeholders, political brokers and entrepreneurs have to start defining a particular communication strategy to persuade about the importance of their proposal. A successful communication strategy and rhetoric has to shape an existing shared imagination and construct a new one based on common values, needs and objectives. Besides this, they have to make sure that this communication strategy and speech remains linked to their permanent national interests and the defence of their objectives.

Therefore, operationally speaking, first, political entrepreneurs and brokers like Spain and France, have had to design and develop a communication strategy to shape and re-construct the aforementioned common imagination in order to gather consensus and after that implement and institutionalise the new policy. Second, once the EU has agreed to follow up with the proposal and given that Euro-Mediterranean proposals entailed the participation of southern Mediterranean countries, the EU has had to convince European public opinion and southern Mediterranean countries of the pertinence of the new policy in order to adhere to the proposal.

Theoretically speaking these strategies have to be explained by adopting a mixed approach. First, an approach based upon the prioritisation of security-related issues suggests a realist framework. Within the international system, the first priority of a state is to survive, as Waltz and the defensive realists suggest (Waltz, 1979). However, in considering political entrepreneurs and brokers, they mostly aim at maximising their relative power following an offensive realism (Mearsheimer, 1994, 2001). Political entrepreneurs and brokers that are small or medium powers would pursue an expansionist policy of increasing diplomatic and political weight in an international context – ["when and where the benefits of doing so outweigh the cost"] (Taliaferro, 2000).

Nevertheless, the realist approach does not fully explain the process of how political entrepreneurs and brokers define their strategies. According to my understanding, it is partially useful to describe foreign policy decision-making systems. In fact, as Waltz has stated, there is a difference between international politics and foreign policy (Waltz, 1996). That is why a more comprehensive and multidimensional theoretical approach is needed to explain these processes.

One answer can be offered by the post-realist approach (Beer and Hariman, 1996). As has been suggested earlier, communication strategies and public speech are fundamental parts of the methods used both by political entrepreneurs and brokers. As well as realism, post-realism accepts both logic and facts. Hariman and Beer characterise post-realism as an approach that by adopting a ["linguistic turn ...emphasizes narrative as an important means of persuasion. Post-realism relies on criticism and the formulation of alternatives. It involves deconstruction and reconstruction. Finally, post-realism combines strategy and ethics, power and prudence, cultural context and interpretation, and persuasion and psychology"] (Beer and Hariman, 1996).

These characteristics are relevant to explain and understand how political brokers and entrepreneurs behave, plan and lobby. Therefore, post-realism constitutes a good bridge between realism and other theoretical frameworks that focus their attention on socio-cultural and political processes like constructivism.

Realism, as Brown has argued, has dominated IR theories, but constructivism is increasingly developing as an oppositional theoretical framework (Brown, 2005). Barkin states that constructivism has been regarded as a theory opposing realism (Barkin, 2003). Rooted in the philosophical and sociological tradition, constructivism was applied to IR theory within the context of the end of the Cold War. Greenwood Onuf considered that states –and therefore political entrepreneurs and brokers – act equally as individuals and live in a ["world of our making"] (Greenwook Onuf, 1989). Social and political facts and power relations are constructed.

In looking at the social construction of power politics, a central element of realism, Wendt took the discourse a step further (Wendt, 1992). These initial discussions were later developed and paved the way for a more consistent constructivist approach within IR theories. It was consolidated as a stronger critic of realism where it was stressed that according to the constructivist approach structure is constructed by social practice (Wendt, 1999).

Following a similar theoretical framework, as Copeland has discussed, realism has been missing the ["intersubjectively shared ideas that shape behaviour by constituting the identities and interests of actors"] (Copeland, 2000). The application of this framework was not immediately adopted to explain how Europe has and is being constructed and integrated (Christiansen et Al., 1999). The works of Delanty, Christiansen, Knud and Wiener started to focus more on the social construction of Europe (Delanty, 1995). For them, ["crucial aspects of the integration process –polity formation through rules and norms, the transformation of identities, the role of ideas and the use of language –are thereby opened up to systematic inquiry"] (Christiansen, 1999).

Considering Europe as a collective construction, language and discourse play a very important role in defining new values and new sociocultural and political paradigms (Paasi, 2001). Language, rhetoric as well as narratives and their evolution over time, define communicational strategies of political entrepreneurs and brokers. They aim at re-shaping realities and collective perceptions in order to attain their political objectives. From this point of view, language and communication strategies, as well as the management of symbols, are the vehicles to transmit fresh ideas and replace old collective imaginations. This approach is not distant from radical constructivism. This framework insists on the relevance of language as one of the most important agents of social construction (Glaseerfeld, 1984).

Bearing in mind the characteristics of political brokers and entrepreneurs with the aim of better understanding and explaining how they behave and implement different strategies, it is evident that some theoretical aspects commented on above are useful.

Realism and constructivism might appear as contradictory theoretical frameworks, according to Jackson and Nexon (Jackson and Nexon, 2004). However, a combination of both approaches helps us to understand and explain how these political entrepreneurs and brokers behave. Some authors have aimed at combining these two theories, but Barkin was the first to successfully offer a consistent bridge between them (Sterling-Folker, 2002). As he claims, constructivist epistemology and classical realist theory are compatible. He argues ["not that constructivism is necessarily realist, but that constructivist research is as compatible with a realist worldview as with any other. Having a realist constructivism could prove useful in IR theory beyond clarifying methodological debates, including helping to specify the relationship between the study of power in international politics and the study of international relations as a social construction"] (Barkin, 2003).

In suggesting this, Barkin defines constructivism as a cluster of research methods and tools, (Jackson and Nexon, 2004) ["a set of assumptions about how to study world politics, rather than a set of assumptions about how politics work"] (Barkin, 2003). It is on these terms that this research considers a realist-constructivist approach.

## Political Entrepreneurship and Brokerage

After introducing and framing the theoretical elements that might help to explain how political brokers and entrepreneurs plan and behave, it is important to reflect on some of the theoretical considerations related to them.

### Political Entrepreneurs

According to Christopoulos, political entrepreneurs are similar to economic entrepreneurs given that they share ["intellectual ability, good knowledge of their domain, team building skills, reputation, extensive networks, strategic vision and tenacity"] (Christopoulos, 2006). However, the differences, he argues, are related to the fact of ["having a different incentive structure in attempting to control or exercise political power"] (Christopoulos, 2006). The other important operational element that is common to political entrepreneurs is that they are network-dependents and this implies that their ["ability for political action is network-contingent"] (Christopoulos, 2006).

As stated by Van der Steen and Gronewegen the literature on policy entrepreneurship is still in its infancy (Van der Steen and Groenewegn, 2008). The practical and theoretical understanding has been studied by Kingdon who elaborated the Policy Streams Approach (Kindgon, 1995). Kingdon explains policy design and formation as the product of the interaction between three streams: the problem stream, the policy stream and the politics stream (Guldbransson and Fossum, 2009). The first element, the problem stream, is related to public affairs requiring attention. As Guldbrandsson and Fossum have stressed ["some conditions are not even defined as problems until there is something to do about it, i.e. there is a solution (a policy) available and recognized by the politicians"] (Guldbrandsson and Fosum, 2009).

Second, the policy stream refers to proposals aimed at inciting changes. According to Guldbrandsson and Fossum, ["before a problem can reach the decision agenda, decision makers must be given at least on alternative solution, worked out and ready to put in place"] (Guldbransson and Fossum). Third, the politics stream is related to political issues, changes of public opinion or administration amongst other factors.

Normally these three streams evolve independently and are not necessarily linked. However, when a given problem has been recognised, a partial or total solution for it has been defined and the political environment welcomes changes as a policy window appears. This process facilitates the understanding of public policymaking. As Kingdon has noted, this system can be conceptualised as a set of processes: first, setting an agenda; second, specifying alternatives for such an agenda; third, an authoritative choosing process evaluating the existing alternatives: and fourth, the implementation of the decision or the law (Kingdon, 1995).

Prior to this, Polsby has added a fundamental preparatory process that is important to assess in order to better understand the mechanisms and the possible failures or strengths of a given agenda setting, policy or political process: policy initiation. It is defined as ["the politics of inventing, winnowing and finding and gaining adherents for policy alternatives before they are made part of a program"] (Polsby, 1984). Roberts and Kings have elaborated an interesting taxonomy that partially explains the characteristics of public entrepreneurs, listed below (Roberts and King, 1991):

- Advocacy of new ideas and development of innovative proposals;
- Define and reframe existing problems;
- Search for political alternatives;
- Brokering the new ideas and proposals among a number of representative political or policy actors;
- Mobilizing public opinion through strategies of political communication and public speech.
- Helping to set the decision-making agenda.

With regards to the functional aspects of public entrepreneurs, Roberts and King have identified 4 central stages:

- Creation: An innovative idea is developed and starts to emerge;
- Design: The innovative concept is perfected and is encapsulated into a formal statement or proposal;

- Implementation: The new concept or idea has been theoretically approved and is tested to constitute a new initiative or programme;
- Institutionalization: The idea becomes an established practice and is not any longer considered as something innovative.

These four functional and procedural stages developed by Roberts and King are going to be used as a framework to analyse, understand and explain the process that political entrepreneurs and brokers have used to design and implement Euro-Mediterranean politics. The virtue of this model is justified by the fact that it is measurable, replicable and empirically re-testable either in different socio-political and cultural contexts or in considering different issues and political problems.

Nevertheless, even though these four stages provide the most valid framework to achieve the objectives of this book, this model is not entirely satisfactory and it has to be developed further. The four stages – creation, design, implementation and institutionalisation – are relevant to analyse how the process evolves from the inception to the institutionalisation. However, it analyses a linear process and does not consider the possibility of understanding this process as a cycle.

It is key to understand the consequences of such policies and mechanisms beyond the linear description proposed by this framework. The framework can be completed by introducing a fifth variable: evaluation. By integrating this factor, it will be possible to analyse an entire cycle. This final vision will be provided in the conclusion. Therefore this design will allow for a dynamic framework that will permit to study and explain these dynamic processes. In considering these elements this dissertation will conclude with the proposal of the Political Entrepreneurship Cycle (PEC).

## Political Brokers

Traditionally, brokers are defined as middle-men mediating between buyers and sellers. This concept can be applied to policy and decision-making processes. However, the literature on political brokers is ample, diffused and not always clear. It started to develop during the 1950s. Pye studied the role of political brokers in non-Western societies (Pye, 1988). He defined political brokers as those ["seeking first to differentiate special interests within the society so as to be better able to aggregate those interests as a propagandist basis. The political broker tries to satisfy the largest possible number of people by discovering how their particular interests can be brought together and adjusted to each other"] (Pye, 1958).

According to this description political brokers provide ["a common symbolism by aggregating the separate interests of people"] (Pye, 1958). From this point of view, symbolism management will represent one of the most relevant actions of both political brokers and entrepreneurs. These two definitions will be applied in this book for the purposes of explaining the role of political brokers as entrepreneurs.

Over the 1970s and the 1980s authors like Valenzuela, Barbaro, and Smith applied a very similar understanding of political brokers by focusing their analyses on local, regional and national politics (Valenzuela, 1977; Barbaro, 1972; Smith, 1972). In the 1980s Mann researched the role of brokers as entrepreneurs (Mann, 1984). As it has been stated before, political entrepreneurs and brokers have to be differentiated, even though their roles can be interactive and can overlap operationally.

Since the 2000s a new wave of scholarly works on political brokers has been developing. Beyond the negative features –manipulation – offered by aforementioned works, Pielke wrote about the potential positive impact of ["honest brokers"] (Pielke, 2007). However, this positive approach is not shared by most authors focused on understanding how political brokers manipulate and manage common or scattered needs to get the desired consensus even trespassing moral and ethical limits in the process (Carty and Cross, 2010).

## The Mediterranean: A Profitable Opportunity

Normally, the differences between the roles and characteristics of entrepreneurs and brokers are not clearly specified. Therefore it should be necessary to disentangle this conceptual problem. Bicchi for instance has suggested that looking at entrepreneurial states as brokers would help to understand these dynamics. In fact, as she has stressed, ["once a policy window exists and a policy entrepreneur acts on it, the third factor that leads to development of European foreign policy making is the interaction among member states and EC/EU institutions"] (Bicchi, 2007).

This argument is very pragmatic and explains the role of the state as a broker. However, an initial critical point that may arise is related to the consistency and coherence of such speculative proposals beyond this pragmatism. In other words, to what extent are states acting as brokers – as the middle point between decision-makers and "political buyers" – conscious of an issue like political responsibility and the potential negative impacts and collateral damages of such policies? Which kind of reward would they expect from this transaction? What about the sustainability of such proposals that entail the mobilisation of important financial resources and hopes? This book will address these questions in the course of the following chapters, as there is a noticeable gap in the literature in terms of research dealing with foreign policy and bilateral relations from this perspective as well on the impacts on responsible political leadership.

In considering these facts, I will focus on differentiating when a political actor should be denominated as a political entrepreneur or as a political broker – or both simultaneously. This book will also explain how a political entrepreneur or broker is able to define a strategy to gather others' interest to join proposals. In order to operationally understand this objective, the consecutive chapters will explain how political entrepreneurs or brokers design, adapt and modify their political speech to gain consensus by understanding changing contexts and scenarios. In accepting that there might be two or more political entrepreneurs or brokers competing for the same political window, such is the case of Spain and France, this text will discuss and assess the mechanisms and strategies used by both competitors to attract consensus.

This point will help explain how alliances have been built and to what extent, beyond the fact of attracting consensus within the short and the medium term, political entrepreneurs or brokers considered the possible future consequences and sustainability of their proposals. Political entrepreneurs appear more far-sighted than political brokers who are prone to concentrate their energies on the short term.

As Tsoukalis has mentioned, the EEC began to be interested in putting the "Global Mediterranean Policy" (GMP) into effect in response to some major politico-economic events that significantly impacted EEC-Mediterranean relations (Tsoulakis, 1977). For instance, the oil crisis of 1973 brought more relative power to the Arab oil-producing members of OPEC, in turn ["provoking also a shift in the balance of power towards the south"] (Tsoulakis, 1977). The establishment of the Euro-Arab Dialogue from 1975 onward marked a very important milestone despite the initial hesitation among EEC members, oil producing countries and southern countries (Allen, 1977; Al Dajani, 1980). However, as with the Barcelona Process, two decades later the GMP was mostly limited to economic measures as has been explained above (Tsoulakis, 1977).

This approach is useful in explaining how economic, market and strategic interests drove and have been driving Euro-Mediterranean relations and why the Mediterranean was, and still is, considered as political window or opportunity for political entrepreneurs and brokers.

In analysing the 1970s, the EEC was already very interested in the Mediterranean due to both economic and trade objectives. By 1974, the 9.4 percent of EEC exports went to Mediterranean countries (Tsoulakis, 1977). The years of 1975, 1976 and 1977 were very active in terms of the signing of trade agreements between the EEC and Mediterranean countries (Commission of the European Communities, 1978). The focus on economics as well as the treatment of the 17 participating Mediterranean countries as a homogeneous bloc was a mistake (CEC, 1978). Arguably, as will be addressed later in the following chapters, this same mistake was repeated in the EMP from 1995 onward. Moreover, northern Mediterranean countries, such as Spain, Portugal, Italy and France, differed from Maghreb countries in political terms as according to Article 237 of the Treaty of Rome, they were eligible for full membership with the EEC and ["this has a definite influence on the attitudes and policies of both sides"] (CEC, 1978).

This structural problem was not solved with the EMP and the same restrictions were present during the Barcelona Process as well as parallel and subsequent initiatives as explained previously. Considering Europe-Arab relations, the question of attitudes probably represents the most important element that may allow or block any attempt of implementing sustainable policies.

This statement is central to this book. In considering Euro-Mediterranean politics and in assessing how political entrepreneurs, brokers and opportunists have been designing policies and mechanisms to increase their diplomatic and political power, it is important to understand how asymmetric politico-economic relations operate. The relationship between southern European countries – Portugal, Spain, France, Italy and later Malta and Greece – and Maghreb countries are a clear example of asymmetry. In analysing how political entrepreneurs operate and bearing in mind the four stages described above –creation, design, implementation and institutionalisation –it is implicitly assumed that political entrepreneurs prioritise their self-interest and design policy proposals according to their objectives. However, the introduction of the evaluation of the PEC model will help us understand the degree of coherence and political responsibility *vis-à-vis* southern Mediterranean partners.

This evaluation component of the PEC model assesses to what extent attitudes deployed by dominant political partners, lobbies or political entrepreneurs have really considered the interests and needs of Maghreb partners –and to a certain point Mashrek partners like Egypt – or if, on the contrary, their needs have been used and manipulated to impose the EU's ambitions and objectives. The evaluation component therefore analyses the issue of political responsibility, coherence and consistency that is not implicit in the four stages that were presented in the original model by Roberts and King.

The issue of responsibility would establish the difference between political entrepreneurs, political brokers and opportunists. From this point of view, political entrepreneurs and brokers would be those who integrate in their proposals an ethical concern aimed at producing and generating win-win solutions. Whereas political opportunists are those who design policies and mechanisms aimed at fulfilling and accomplishing their own objectives by manipulating and speculating on others' needs. The theoretical differentiation of both concepts is related to the principles that characterise industrial and financial capitalism and how market power is understood and applied to a wide array of decision-making processes as Chandler, Teece, Katz, Doucet, Stern and Neal, among others, have explained (Teece, 1993; Katz et Al., 2002; Neal, 1993).

With regards to networks, coalitions and the implementation of new political projects and policies within the Mediterranean, Bicchi has pointed out that ["the most effective policy entrepreneurship has come from a state member, state or from a coalition of actors guided by a member state"] (Bicchi, 2007). This concept is important in understanding the development and evolution of the Euro-Mediterranean political and diplomatic realm, as well as Franco-Spanish engagement and competition in the region.

The Euro-Mediterranean region raises deep challenges for policy makers. Political brokers and/or entrepreneurs have to evaluate and identify how these economic, social and cultural challenges may affect their proposals and therefore they must adapt their communication strategies in order first to identify the correct political window or opportunity, and second, to convey the message aimed at gathering political consensus.

Within the Mediterranean sphere and especially considering EU-Maghreb relations, sensitive problems like migration flows, security, crime, religion and labour define potential political windows or opportunities to be developed by political brokers and entrepreneurs. Though these categories also carry risks of altering north–south relations due to misconceptions generated by entrepreneurs or brokers when they design their communication strategies.

For the purpose of this book I consider that a political entrepreneur would act and communicate responsibly and would try to use these sensitive issues to promote positive changes and win-win solutions. Whereas political brokers would speculate with these sensitive issues in order to achieve short-term objectives that would entail unilateral benefits.

Euro-Mediterranean related issues, such as migration, mobility and security, represent some of the most acute obstacles that challenge a cooperative and responsible political communication. These elements have been central in the discourse of Euro-Mediterranean political entrepreneurs and brokers.

Southern European countries, such as Portugal, Spain, France, Italy, Malta and Greece, have to deal with a number of problems relating to international migration flows from the South of the Mediterranean. In the beginning of the 1990s, the likes of Siune and Treutzschler studied the existence of "media politics" in Western Europe (Siune and Treutzchler, 1992). Recent studies on the same region conducted by Ellinas have demonstrated that far-right parties from these countries are using the media to spread extremist, nationalistic and racist discourses (Ellinas, 2019).

This is why the EU has elevated the migratory question to that of security. Furthermore, it explains why the EU standardised migration policies with the Amsterdam Treaty (AT) in 1997, even though, as Hammar has shown, massive scepticism prevails around the degree of Europeanisation of those policies (Hammar, 1995).

Thus, the idea of a welfare state is very much rooted in European culture – despite its regional variations – and any potential threat which might jeopardise its continuity constitutes a very profitable excuse, politically speaking, to gain consensus and to maintain a certain social cohesion and balance. Hence, beyond an economic approach, I am very much inclined to a cultural-symbolic discourse and interpretation of this problem. Weiner wrote that the unwillingness of states to open borders transcends economic considerations (Weiner, 1993). The rationale behind these political decisions is much more bound to the fact that it *ensures* that an influx of economic migrants, refugees and asylum seekers may generate xenophobic sentiments and trigger conflicts between natives and migrants and, as a consequence, increase the appeal of right-wing political groups.

To what extent is this true? For instance, migratory policies in Spain have been much more damaging for immigrants during Zapatero's socialist government than during Aznar's conservative presidency. Thus, it is possible to repeat, that we face a socio-political realm where symbols and values are at stake and the subsequent political communication has been, and will remain, focused on managing these symbols and values through the generation of "branded concepts", or widely accepted paradigms, such as the migration-security nexus.

The case of migration highlights that current political communication is more strongly affected by the management of "branded concepts" than in the past. This might be related to the attempt to intentionally dislocate or change existing social norms and conventions as a way of gaining influence and dominance. The essence of this conflict resides in the will and necessity of artificially, though in a seemingly natural process, and paradoxically creating situations of imbalance –an unsettled cultural model –where precarious social balance has been achieved.

Media influence on public opinion regarding sensitive issues such as migration and security in the Euro-Mediterranean area has been studied with a focus on North Africa and central Europe (Ureta, 2010). Zapata and Lorite have concentrated on the Spanish case (Zapata and Van Dijk, 2007; Zapata, 2008; Lorite, 2002; Lorite, 2006). Tailleur and Blion have examined France (Tailleur, 2002; Blion, 2008). More generally, although still roughly addressing these issues, it would be interesting to underline the pioneering work done by King and Wood (King and Wood, 2001). In recent years, a collection of essays edited by Sabry continues this line of research (Sabry, 2004). It is also important to mention Mattelart's study on media, migration and transnationalism (Mattelart, 2007). All show that by accepting a bi-directional correlation between politics and media, we can carefully analyse ideas, values, myths, beliefs, images and stereotypes.

## Unveiling Political Entrepreneurs and Brokers

Given that this book aims at analysing how political entrepreneurs and brokers have been designing and managing Euro-Mediterranean politics, it is important to give special attention to the use of language and the rhetorical strategies these stakeholders have been following in order to achieve their objectives. This approach is fundamental in understanding the processes, dynamics and mechanisms of policy design and management as well as how these processes and mechanisms can be evaluated through the evolution of the socio-economic context and the reaction of the public opinion to them.

## Corpus Linguistics and Critical Discourse Analysis

To properly understand how political and diplomatic entrepreneurs and brokers conceptualise, plan, define and implement their proposals and projects, content analysis is a crucial research method. Content analysis is defined by Holsten as ["any technique for making inferences by systematically and objectively identifying special characteristics of messages"] (Holsti, 1968).

The way that diplomats and politicians have framed Euro-Mediterranean affairs is linked to their management style. As Semetko and Valkenburg have stressed, alongside content analysis and agenda-setting research, framing analysis ["shares (…) a focus on the relationships between public policy issues in the news and the public perceptions of these issues"] (Semetko and Valkenburg, 2000).

In order to analyse these strategies, I have decided to use Corpus Linguistics (CL) and critical discourse analysis (CDA). This methodological framework will be essential to characterise, differentiate and define the strategies and behaviours deployed by political entrepreneurs and brokers. It will also help the reader to understand: the mechanisms of agenda setting, the long-term analysis of political communication strategies on sensitive issues, the behaviour of public opinion according to different contexts and, finally, the policy-evaluation process necessary to understand the PEC.

### Corpus Linguistics (CL)

Corpus Linguistics (CL) is a recently developed discipline that attracts increasing attention among linguists (Aarts and Keijs, 1990). As Biber, Conrad and Reppen mention, studies of language have been classified into two areas: studies of structure and studies of use (Biber, Conrad and Reppen, 1998). CL emphasises language use and therefore it is possible to investigate the ways speakers, writers and in this case, politicians and diplomats, have been exploiting the resources of their language (Biber et Al., 1998).

MacEnery and Wilson highlight that a corpus is in principle [("any collection of more than one text"] (MacEnery and Wilson, 2001). However, and this is relevant to our understanding of the dynamics of CL, Butler has described that a corpus differs completely from any collection of texts or an archive because they are not necessarily ordered (Butler, 2004).

Nevertheless, as Biber, Conrad and Reppen point out, it is important to ["analyse a large amount of language collected from many speakers to make sure that we are not basing conclusions on a few speakers' idiosyncrasies"] (Biber et Al., 1998). Until recently, due to the absence of adequate software to analyse large series of data, this methodological problem, and therefore proper analysis, was impossible to elaborate on (Stubs, 2007). Tognini-Bonelli indicates that CL helps explore theories and hypotheses and according to the results it is possible to validate, refute or refine them (Tognini-Bonelli, 2001). Baker mentions that ["large corpora allow researchers to find evidence of rare or unusual cases of language, as well as shedding light on very frequent phenomena"] (Baker, 2010). The application of this approach and methodology is then particularly useful in the fields of political science and international relations, given that CL allows the implementation of a methodology that permits the use of a precise quantitative-qualitative tool to prove right or wrong certain assumptions that otherwise would be difficult to demonstrate.

Given that nowadays many of the available documents are available digitally, Kilgarrif and Grefenstette have coined the concept of web as a corpus (Kilgarrif and Grefenstette, 2003). Even though for this dissertation this concept does not entirely fit, the totality of corpus analysed have been downloaded from databases published on the Internet. This methodology has already been studied and tested by Mautner who described the use of web-based corpora in critical discourse analysis (Mautner, 2005).

## Critical Discourse Analysis (CDA)

Critical Discourse Analysis (CDA) has been widely used to study and understand the connections between discourse, power and society. As

Khan and Ghazali have highlighted, one of the most relevant characteristics of CDA ["is that it is more about what happens in society rather than what should or could have happened"] (Khan and Ghazali, 2011). In this sense it is important to note the socio-political dimension CDA entails. Fairclough, Mulderrig and Wodak have stressed that CDA is ["a problem-oriented interdisciplinary research movement, subsuming a variety of approaches, each with different theoretical models, research methods and agenda. What unites them is a shared interest in the semiotic dimensions of power, injustice, abuse and political-economic or cultural change in society"] (Fairclough, Mulderrig and Wodak, 2011).

The fact of accepting that CDA is a problem-oriented interdisciplinary approach welcoming and integrating different theoretical models and research methods, represents an important advantage for the purposes of this dissertation interested as it is in assessing how political entrepreneurs or brokers have dealt with issues such as power, injustice or political opportunism versus social benefit of socio-political sustainability.

Therefore, practically speaking, this approach reinforces the importance of collecting data from the real rather than the fictional world. This characteristic makes this method very appropriate to study and understand the connections within the short, medium and long run between society, political structures and the struggles for change – some of the most accessible kinds of data available are political speeches and statements (Van Dijk, 2011; Wodak, 2004; Locke, 2004).

Nevertheless, CDA has been traditionally used and approached by analysing either single texts or a small number of texts as a way of examining the usage of specific classes of words. However, the discourse is not limited to texts or classes of text, it is also ways of thinking about something. Therefore, considering the objectives of this dissertation, this approach explains the communication strategies political entrepreneurs and brokers have used to establish a new social thinking on sensitive issues in order to achieve pre-established political objectives.

## CL and CDA as Complementary Approaches

Since the mid-1990s some authors have attempted to integrate these complementary approaches (Hardt-Mautner, 1995). This has expressed itself in the growth of scholarly works on the area in the last twenty years (Koller, 2004). Most have focused on methodological issues. However, one of the first studies combining CL and CDA published in

2005 did deal with politics by providing an analysis of the discourses of refugees and asylum seekers in the UK press (Baker and MacEnery, 2005; Baker et Al., 2008).

Nevertheless, even though the aforementioned studies have been trying to harmonise both methodologies, their usage has been unbalanced and most have preferred CL over CDA, or vice-versa. Despite this trend it is important to align the use of both in order to attain more satisfactory results. Charles mentions that CDA ["prioritizes whole texts and their cultural context, identifying patterns that extend across sentences and paragraphs"] whereas ["CL tends to use techniques that decontextualize individual texts and focuses on recurrent patternings of small-scale items such as words and phrases"] (Charles, 2009).

For the purpose of this research, the contextualisation of public speech is fundamental. Otherwise it would be impossible to demonstrate how political entrepreneurs and brokers have been designing, defining, lobbying, changing and implementing their communication strategies over time by reading socio-economic and political needs and opportunities. Therefore, the combination of CL and CDA will be used simultaneously as a tool rather than a theoretical framework, to better explain the main objective of this text (Xiao and Tono, 2006; Flowerdaw, 2012).

## Contents

Chapter 1 discusses Spain's ambitions to become a member of the EEC as well as French opposition and fears. Such fears were well-founded as President Felipe Gonzalez was a key element in pushing Spain towards a new political and diplomatic dimension.

This international resurgence of Spain will be analysed by focusing on the period between 1985 and 1995. This was a decade of profound change in international politics. The bipolar balance collapsed, the consensus increasingly revolved around the acceptance of liberal democratic theories and migratory movements started to reach very high levels, similar to the rates experienced between the last two decades of the nineteenth century and World War I.

This chapter analyses the mechanisms and strategies Spain followed during, what at that time was defined as, "the great gallop". This was the period when Felipe Gonzalez invested huge efforts in diplomatic lobbying in order to gain political and diplomatic stature by identifying a number of political windows and opportunities.

Chapter 2 examines the Aznar period between 1996 and 2004. This presidency coincided with and drove attempts forward to develop and consolidate the Barcelona Process. Aznar's government was very conscious of the role Spain needed to play in the international arena. An obsession with projecting international power reached its peak when Aznar endorsed Washington's Iraq policy in 2002–2003 along with the United Kingdom and a handful of other countries.

While González's government developed good relations with Maghreb countries, especially Morocco, Spanish international politics changed dramatically with Aznar. He had no interest in strengthening links with this region and, because of some of his policies, the possibilities of interacting positively with the southern Mediterranean were seriously hampered. Parallel to this, migration-related issues gathered momentum and topped the government's domestic political agenda as migration increasingly came to be viewed in terms of criminality, terrorism and unemployment.

Chapter 3 analyses José Luis Rodriguez Zapatero's presidency from 2004 to 2012 and explores its implications and impact on Euro-Mediterranean politics. The chapter assesses how and why Zapatero wanted and needed to transform Spain's foreign policy in order to place Spain once again at the centre of EU decision-making processes. This chapter answers a number of key questions: To what extent was Zapatero able to return Spain as a key interlocutor between the Western and the Arab world? How was this political strategy defined? To what extent did the dialogue of civilizations initiative serve Spanish ambitions and objectives? How consistent was Zapatero's foreign policy with Spanish foreign policy over the medium and long term past? How did France react to these policies?

In continuing this evaluation of political entrepreneurs and brokers leading Euro-Mediterranean initiatives, Chapter 4 reviews the presidency of Nicolas Sarkozy in France between 2007 and 2012. For obvious reasons, this chapter starts before the presidential elections of 2007. Already in 2005 during the mandate of Dominique de Villepin as France's prime minister, Sarkozy, acting as Minister of Interior, exerted a zero tolerance policy to repress riots among second-generation immigrants in urban areas.

Many representatives from left-wing parties believed that Sarkozy destroyed his chances in the presidential elections as a result of this crackdown. They were wrong. The chapter analyses this reality and as well as Sarkozy's sponsorship of the Union for the Mediterranean (UfM) and its implications both for European – mostly in terms of the rivalry with Spain – and non-European stakeholders. This chapter also investigates France's initiatives to ban the burqa and the Muslim veil framing this example within the political entrepreneurship deployed by Sarkozy and his cabinet.

After considering Spain and France's foreign actions as political entrepreneurs and brokers and the way they shaped –or contributed to shape – Euro-Mediterranean relations and politics, it is relevant to discuss two of the most striking series of events that have shaken and challenged the international scene, multilateral policies and initiatives: the migratory issue in the Euro-Mediterranean region and; the Arab Spring. These two cases will help in understanding and better evaluating these multilateral efforts.

Chapter 5 inspects, by using a long-term comparative approach, the major role that migration related issues have played in influencing EU-Maghreb relations and stability in the Euro-Mediterranean region. Due to their geographical positions and regional standing France and Spain played a key role in this debate. The Euro-Mediterranean region progressively began to gain relevance in this context and, obviously, national and international interests oriented their sights on the Mediterranean basin. The migratory issue and the way politicians understood and managed it as well as its impacts on the European public opinion –and to a certain extent to North African countries – is crucial in order to evaluate the consistency and coherence of Euro-Mediterranean political and diplomatic initiatives. This double discourse between the establishment of win-win solutions and the de facto securitisation of the European fortress represents the cornerstone to understanding one of the most important causes that generated the failure of these initiatives.

Building on the aforementioned chapter, finally, Chapter 6 analyses the Arab uprisings considering that they are the product of a multilateral effort that has been cultivated over an extended period. These uprisings, their causes, their management as well as their escalation, spread and evolution test the solidity, coherence and consistency of the political and diplomatic efforts built over the last 15–20 years.

# 1 Spain and the Great Gallop: Strategies of a Political Entrepreneur

This chapter will explain how Spain transitioned – from the 1960s to mid-1980s – from a role of proto-entrepreneur to a role of political entrepreneur or broker. Spain's struggles and challenges to access the EEC were important. Strong European countries like France, Italy or Belgium among others, deployed intense political and communication campaigns to abort Spain's attempts to join the union. To what extent was France's dubious conviction regarding Spanish entry to the EEC justifiable? Did France think that Spain constituted a menace for French ambitions within European politics? Would Spain be able to maintain a durable socio-economic and political profile over the decades to come? What were the main difficulties and obstacles Spain must overcome in order to converge with its European partners? Given its socio-political, economic and institutional backlog and considering that Spain would attain international stature, what price must Spain pay to reach its goals? Finally, how could Spain manage old myths, prejudices and open wounds and set up a credible and consistent agenda for the years to come?

## 1.1 Spain's European Ambitions and the French Response

Spanish ambitions to enter the EEC date back to practically to establishment of the European Community as Spain started to have more contact with Europe. On the same day as the signing of the Treaty of Rome establishing the EEC, 25 March, the first group of Spanish migrant workers departed to Belgium (Oñate, 2005). The diplomatic offensive to gain EEC status started in the early 1960s at the time of the Economic Stabilization Plan, which followed a period when the Spanish economy started to emerge from the endemic crisis. Still a dictatorship, at this time EEC entry was not possible. Due to this reason, all member states staunchly opposed Spanish ambitions to become part of the EEC. As it is going to be explained later, France was the most reluctant and less supporting country to Spanish ambitions. This attitude was a political constant almost until 1985 when Spain accessed to the EEC.

By 1960, the Spanish government had initiated early diplomatic attempts to court the EEC. On the 9 December 1960, Spain's ambassador to Brussels, Count of Casa Miranda, presented his credentials to the president of the Commission of the EEC, Walter Hallstein. This act represented a declaration of intent. Two years later, on the 9 January 1962, Spain applied to become a member of the EEC in a letter addressed to the president of the EEC, Maurice Couve de Murville.

The original version of the letter was written by Fernando María Castiella, the Spanish minister of foreign affairs in Spanish rather than French, the diplomatic language of the time. The opening paragraph of the letter shows immediately the Spanish objective ["I have the pleasure of requesting, in the name of my Government, the opening of negotiations aiming at examining the possible engagement of my country with the EEC in the way most suitable to reciprocal interests"] (Arch. EEC and EAEC, 1970–851).

The Spanish minister justified his country's candidacy by enumerating a number of relevant elements ranging from historic and economic to the political (EEC-EAEC.1970–851). He stated that Spain was a country with a strong European vocation. A characteristic that has been demonstrated over the history and therefore, by joining the EEC, Spain could demonstrate its commitment towards the construction of Europe.

Paragraph four underlines one of the most important elements behind the French negative reaction against the Spanish request for accession to the EEC: The issue of agriculture. Even though this issue will be addressed subsequently, it is important to note here that the early mention of this issue highlighted major Spanish concerns regarding future negotiations (EEC-EAEC, 1970–851).

On the 7 March 1962, Couve de Murville acknowledged receipt of the letter, without indicating any kind of interest or encouragement regarding the Spanish proposal. Italy's *Corriere della Sera* soon after published an article warning that Spain's application to become a fully-fledged member of the EEC caused surprise, pleasure and perplexity in Brussels because member states did not expect such a proposal. For one, Belgium's highly regarded foreign minister Paul-Henri Spaak, a long-time critic of the Spanish dictatorship was appalled. He was also president-in-office of the EEC. Also in 1962, the *Courrier Socialiste Européen* was also commenting on Spain's proposal, defining it as something intolerable that might endanger the future and defence of democratic values because it was a fascist regime and ["le fascism est un crime"] (Wilhelums Burger, 1962).

After these episodes, in 1964 a second letter in French, Count of Casa Miranda, conveyed a message to the EEC emphasizing the fact that Spain had already started to liberalise its economy. Nevertheless, this argument ignored the dictatorship factor and therefore left the EEC unmoved. Pure economic reasoning was not enough to convince a reluctant EEC.

After four months, Spaak, responded to the request. His answer underlined the fact that the EEC might be willing to open contact with the Spanish government in order to analyse the economic problems that were affecting the Spanish economy. A somewhat deflating response for the Spanish considering that part of the objective had been to showcase the progress that Spain had made economically in preceding years.

Despite this general lack of appreciation, the Swiss press expressed their concerns with regards to these blockages coming mostly from France, Belgium and Italy, saying that in recognising this hesitation, the European integration should be considered a long-term process where the regimes might vanish, and the people would remain (Silve, 1964).

Over 1965, Spain carried on with its purposes of integration. Following a very similar rhetoric and political argumentation as the one exposed above, the Embassy of Spain to Paris elaborated a document justifying and explaining again the reasons why Spain should access the EEC. It was highlighted the new Europeanist fashion of Spain's foreign policy since Castiella took over the Spain's Ministry of Foreign Affairs in 1957. Within this letter it is important to stress how Spain started to show its ambitions to lead, somehow, international politics despite the international ostracism. The Spanish diplomacy mentioned their proposal to the United Nations Conference on Disarmament (UNCD) to organize a World conference for non-nuclear countries in order to contribute to the alleviation of the problems the world was facing at that time (Spanish Ministry of Foreign Affairs, 1965).

The document also mentioned that for the European project it would be important to have a partner with very good relations with Latin American republics and the Arab World. As it is going to be shown later, these two vectors –Latin America and the Arab World – were the two geographical and cultural elements that Spain would continue selling to the EU over the decades to come, in order to get more diplomatic stature and international weight. The democratic and civilising rhetoric deployed by these proto political entrepreneurs to convince the European public opinion focused on: The Spain-USA agreements signed in 1953 and renewed in 1963 as something that was defined ["by the World press as true alliance"]; The role of Spain would play in order to ["contribute to the defence of a free World"] and following its universal vocation devoted ["to the defence of Occident"] (EEC-.EAEC, 1970).

## 1.2 Trying to Build a New Image

In July 1969, Franco in preparation for the inevitable Spanish democratic transition named Juan Carlos of Bourbon, Prince of Spain. The international community greeted this, as well as other, move towards transition with suspicion. The Community did, however, sign a preferential trade agreement with Spain in the context of the accession of three northern European countries in 1973 –Denmark, United Kingdom and Ireland. This was followed by the signing of an additional protocol to that agreement (Oñate, 2005).

Just one month before Franco's death in 1975, EEC foreign ministers, along with Pope Paul VI, Olaf Palme of Sweden and the Mexican president Luis Echevarría, condemned the lack of respect for human rights displayed in the execution of one ETA (Euskadi ta' Askatasuna; Bask Country and Freedom) member, Angel Otaegui, and three FRAP (Frente Revolucionario Antifascista y Patriota; Revolutionary Front Anti-Fascist and Patriot) members, José Luis Sánchez, Ramón García and Humberto Baena (German Government, 1977; Jauregui, 1985).

Following Franco's death Spain faced a crossroads as the military, reactionary supporters of Franco, reformers and democrats all wondered what the future held. Juan Carlos I, was crowned on the 22 November 1975, just one day after Franco's death. The new King, had been chosen by Franco and during his coronation he paid tribute to the late leader. Despite the view of some authors such as Share (Share, 1986), Franco's legacy would remain, as McDonough, Barnes and Pina have shown, more polarizing that does the democratic system over coming decades and would prevail jeopardise the effective implementation of the democratic system (McDonough, Barnes and Pina, 1986).

In 1976 the Council of Europe via resolution 640 (1976) 1, guaranteed the support to the Spanish process of democratic transition on the grounds that Spain accept a multi-party system (Council of Europe, 1976).

On 5 December 1976, the 27th Congress of the PSOE (Partido Socialista Obrero Español; Spanish Socialist Workers' Party) was celebrated in Madrid. At that time the PSOE was not still recognised as a legal political organization. Two years before, in 1974, while still in exile, the PSOE at its 26$^{th}$ Congress, elected Felipe González as Secretary-General (Diez Cárcamo, 2006).

Two years on and celebrating the first meeting in Spain after the dictatorship, González and his party now had the support of the main European socialist politicians such as Willy Brandt and Olof Palme. González proposed a new political direction more in line with social democracy and away from traditional socialism and Marxism that characterized the past of the party. Within a year, the PSOE was already the official opposition force with the 29.2 percent of popular support.

The transition period to democracy was very vibrant. On 26 July 1977 Spanish president Adolfo Suarez wrote three different letters to the EEC applying to become a member of the ECSC (European Coal and Steel Community), the EAEC (European Atomic Energy Community) and the EEC (Central Historic Archives, Council of Europe, 1977). On the same day, probably as a political gesture to block Spanish intentions, the French government sent a memorandum to the EEC claiming urgent revisions of the Community regulations and policies regarding agricultural production (French Government, 1976).

Spain was not mentioned directly in the memorandum. But it was clear that France's fears regarding the entry of countries with the potential to be economic competitors. But the moderate tone of this letter was not shared by all. In very emotional language, the French communist party published an article in *L'Humanité* criticising and opposing stridently the EEC decision to start negotiations for the accession of Spain, Portugal and Greece (Lajoine, 1977).

On 28 July 1977 the Spanish minister of foreign affairs, Marcelino Oreja, submitted the official Spanish candidacy to the EEC. The responses were not immediate. The French preoccupation remained agriculture (Kergolay, 1977). As *La Libre Belgique* noted in December 1978 Spain was no longer simply a holiday destination. By some indicators (in this case those published by the OSCE) the tenth most industrialised country in the world (Anon. 1978).

The EEC responded officially to the Spanish request on 29 November 1978. The document was detailed and subdivided into six main categories: Industry, agriculture, fisheries, social issues, regional aspects and external relations. Point 53 expressed clearly the scale and complexity of the problems arising from Spain's accession (Spain's Application document, 1978). By the time negotiations began in early 1979, senior European officials from president of the Council, Jean François Poncet (Poncet, 1979) and Roy Jenkins, the president of the European Commission expressed satisfaction but emphasised the need for the move to democracy to continue (Anon, 1979).

## 1.3 French Reactions

As explained briefly above, France opposed Spain's accession to the EEC more than almost any other European party as far back as the 1960s. Fears of Spain making the economic situation worse in terms of continent-wide downturn as well as a concerns over an imbalance caused by an Iberian entry was summed to the fear that the membership could trigger a flood of migrant labour. In late July 1977, the French Communist Party expressed its most harsh opposition to the accession of Spain (as well as Greece and Portugal) (Souske, 1977).

This echoed somewhat the official French view. On 31 August 1977, Spanish president Adolfo Suarez visited the French Élysée Palace. His host, the French president Valéry Giscard d'Estaign –known for his lack of sympathies towards Spain-, was clear that his country would not sacrifice its position in Mediterranean agriculture (Anon, 1977). One month later, on 20 September 1977, Jean Taittinger, French secretary of state for foreign affairs, made a similar point at a meeting of the EEC Council of Ministers (Taittinger, 1977).

As mentioned above, Portugal and Greece were also negotiating their accession to the EEC at the time, but the Spanish issue was much more a preoccupation of France and the rest of the member states. It was, as *The Guardian*, noted ["the biggest competitive threat to the Mediterranean farmers of Italy and the South of France"] (Palmer, 1978). It was also the biggest country to be considered for membership since the UK in 1973, though unlike the UK it was a net recipient not provider of funds. France in her approach towards the Spanish potential accession was mixing political, economic and emotional concerns alike. As it has been mentioned in the precedent chapter, a long history plagued mostly by conflict and rivalry generated an aversion that used politico-economic excuses to defend national interests.

The Spanish reaction to European questions was one of concern. Between the 6 and 7 November 1979 a meeting in Madrid was convened in which the nine Spanish ambassadors to EEC countries discussed the issue. It was chaired by Foreign Minister Marcelino Oreja and President Adolfo Suarez. The goal of the meeting was to assess the political and economic relationship between Spain and the EEC countries. One month later Marcelino Oreja conceded an interview in *La Libre Belgique* that the meeting confirmed the fear that Spain had a number of difficulties to overcome across Europe.

During the first part of 1980 France took over the EEC Council Presidency and due to the French Communist's Party opposition against the Spanish accession there was some concern that this might be a setback for Spanish hopes. But overall, Oreja was of the opinion that the general political will in the EEC supported Spanish entry as the "preconditions" put forward by the French opposition ["seem to us unacceptable and do not, of course, reflect a truly European view of Community integration"] (Anon, 1979).

## 1.4 Amateur Government Paving the Road for the Next Steps

Following Franco's death institution and state building, communication systems, civil society, and external engagement had to be constructed from scratch. As one of the most authoritative political journalists in Spain, Fernando Jauregui, put it ["It was clearly an epoch of impressive activity. It was a moment of hectic activity where everybody had to learn"] (Interview with Fernando Jauregui, 2010).

This first period of accommodation lasted exactly two years after Franco's death from November 1975 to June 1977, the time of the first constituent elections. Notable as the first time Spaniards voted for the first new parliament after 40 years of dictatorship. Despite its democratic credentials, the first government was institutionally very weak. As Jauregui put it: ["That govern was mainly based on interpersonal relations. I remember when Suarez won the elections, there was a journalist –Pedro Calvo Hernando – who greeted the new President saying, *Bastard!* to which Suarez replied, *Pedro, I remind you that now I am the new President*"] (Jauregui, 2010).

In 1982, the socialist Felipe González won the elections and replaced Suárez. His government set a new standard for the way post-transition Spain was governed and there was a new focus on projecting external power. The role played by González in this was vital. As Jauregui explained in an interview with this author,

["Adolfo Suarez abroad represented a kind of the Spanish Evo Morales. Someone coming from Franco's ranks. Someone who did not speak foreign languages. Someone who never left Spain in his life. González was a guy coming from the Socialist International, substituting the mythical Yopis. González was legitimized by the history of socialism"] (Jauregui, 2010).

For instance, González looked to strengthen relations with Latin America, Spain's most natural partner. His foreign minister, Francisco Fernández Ordóñez, was a socialist who was successful in improving the Spanish image in Europe that.as Jauregui recalled, was still distrusted and looked down on across Europe.

This government had to deal with a very heavy past and with scarce political training and experience. This past was dragged by new enthusiastic politicians. As Jauregui said during the personal interview, when he was travelling across with the president Suarez ["we were despised people. Spain was a model for Latin America, but regarding Europe we were very badly considered"] (Jauregui, 2010).

However the negotiations to access the EEC were still very long, excessively long. West Germany was the key supporter for entry inside the EEC. In an interview with this author, Carlos Westendorp – who was a senior negotiator for Spanish accession to the EEC and Spain's Minister of Foreign Affairs between 1995 and 1996-, recognised that: ["The Germans were our main allies. Germany said that it was not possible that a Spanish soldier would defend us in the NATO whereas we deny the entrance of Spain to the EEC"] (Interview with Carlos Westerdorp, 2011). As Westendorp acknowledged during the personal interview, after all the efforts, it was the referendum for the NATO the element that unblocked all the process of accession.

The negotiations were finalised and signed in June 1985. At that time Spain had a voice, but no vote until full accession on 1 January 1986. The era of, as González put it the "Great Gallopade", was here. Spain could now define its identity, its role and its strategy in Europe and beyond. After achieving these complicated outcomes, Spain was ready to become a political entrepreneur or broker and therefore, it was vital to design a political and diplomatic strategy to gather greater European consensus –especially from the strongest member states like Germany – and pursue its ambitions: The baseline of this political and diplomatic strategy was the Latin America and the Mediterranean, the two traditional historical cards Spain could play.

## 1.5 A Political Entrepreneur Looking for a Strategy

From 1985 onward Spain deployed an important political and diplomatic strategy to gain influence in European politics in order to become a middle power. However, it is necessary to examine the extent that Spain was a political entrepreneur and to ask how Spain developed its entrepreneurial plan in the pursuit of its interests. Another relevant question is whether or not Spain encountered opposition from other southern Mediterranean countries – potential competitors or partners – such as France or Italy and how northern European countries viewed these developments.

Richard Gillespie has written that ["Spain has undoubtedly played a major role in persuading Europe that the problems of North Africa are European, and not merely southern European problems"] (Gillespie, 2005). Similarly, Soler i Lecha has pointed out that the Europeanization of Spain's foreign policy was the clear consequence of to the attempt to transfer its problems to the EU (Soler I Lecha, 2008). However, Soler i Lecha does agree with Gillespie that Spain looked to use the EU –in particular its economic and financial resources – in the service of its foreign policy needs, at the same time, making consistent diplomatic efforts to become the interpreter and the spokesperson of European's interests in the Southern Mediterranean (Torreblanca, 2001; Pereira, 2009).

Derisbourg goes further. The key of its influence ["has been (Spain's) ability to marry national interests with those of other partners, notably France, and to exchange policy support with major northern EU member states, especially Germany"] (Derisbourg, 1997).

As Gillespie has pointed out, Spain's prominence provoked within the short term, occasional rivalry with France, a traditional Mediterranean power. However this has been contested by some actors interviewed for this research as will be demonstrated later in Chapters 2, 3 and 4.

Nevertheless, this possible rivalry within the medium and long term transformed this competitive behaviour into a more cooperative attitude in order to work together to persuade Europe about the need of developing a consistent Mediterranean policy (Gillespie, 2007).

The leading role of Spain in developing a new Euro-Mediterranean policy in the context of Europe's evolving realist-security approach cannot be debated. In this Spain was able, as Bicchi incisively notes, to identify a Mediterranean political window. This began to be an issue of increasing interest in the earliest post-dictatorship period at a national level between 1982 and 1984, when Spain re-launched bilateral relations with southern Mediterranean countries. However, this was a foreign policy strategy that was inherited from the internationalist approach Spain tried to sell to Europe from 1957 onward as it has been mentioned above. Despite this political heritage that was mostly focusing on a national scale, Spain's activism shifted from the national sphere to the international arena between 1989 and 1992 (Bicchi, 2007).

## 1.6 The Spanish Gallopade: Looking for International Acknowledgement

Spain's accession to the EEC ended decades of isolation, though the country was still considered an underdeveloped country (Interview with Alberto Navarro 2011). Now Spain had the opportunity to demonstrate its potential to the rest of Europe, especially those countries that expressed scepticism that the new member would have an important role to play in the Community. The Spanish (and Portuguese) entry into the EEC in 1986 came at a moment of Euro-optimism.

As has been pointed out by Westendorp, ["Spain and Portugal promoted a new dynamic ... where Spain was always in the vanguard (of Europe) and were they brought with them special relations with Latin America, North Africa and the Southern Mediterranean"] (Westerdorp, 2011). As Ambassador Navarro, – who was the Spanish Ambassador to Morocco, he has worked on European issues occupying top positions in Brussels since 1985 and he was named Secretary of State to the European Union in 2004 – has explained over his interview for this research, Latin America did not exist for the EEC until Spanish entry. There was only one EEC outpost on the continent, in Santiago, Chile, that was moved to Caracas, Venezuela after 1973. Even by 1986 the EEC invested the same resources in Togo as it did in the whole Latin America, which had non-preferential status (Navarro, 2011). The potential contribution of Spain to the EEC was very clear: building up relations with Latin America. The role of Felipe González in leading this new political agenda, as well as in promoting Spain's new Mediterranean policy –and Latin America-, is widely accepted (Kausch, 2010; Del Arenal, 2011; Viñas, 1999; Powell, 2000).

González was central to Spain's growing standing inside Europe and inspired the new diplomatic team –a team that enjoy both ability and agency to propose policies – Spain sent to Brussels. Eneko Landaburu, former director general of foreign affairs of the European

Commission noted in an interview for this book that by 1986 many Europeans were saying, ["Look at these Spaniards! They are doing really well!"] (Anon, 2009). Landaburu continued that González always told him that ["We are not going there to beg, we are going there to work with the others, to build Europe"] (Interview with Eneko Landaburu, 2011).

González sent his most talented and trusted officials to Brussels: Abel Matutes, Anna Terrón, José Borrell, José María Gil Robles, Pedro Solbes, Loyola de Palacios or Javier Solana, among others (Navarro, 2011). People who left an important mark in Europe. They were tasked with building up Spanish influence. As Ambassador Landaburu recalled that González 'insisted' that Spain received the post of Direction General of Regional Policy, a key role in the development of the common market and the social and economic cohesion. González insisted very much to get the Direction General of Regional Policy. His close relationship with Commission President Jacques Delors aided in this task (Landaburu, 2011).

## 1.7 The Mediterranean Card

Carlos Westendorp has acknowledged that the Mediterranean was always a priority for Spain as it was believed very much that the region could contribute to the increase in Spain's relevance (Westendorp, 2011). Andreu Claret, Executive Director of the *Anna Lindh Foundation* –The Mediterranean platform integrating 43 states and embedded within the Euromed (Euro-Mediterranean Partnership)-has explained during a personal interview for this book, that the vision of Felipe Gonzalez's and his senior officials towards the Mediterranean was decisive for the evolving European approach to the region and was responsible for the attempt of the Community to transform risks in opportunities (Interview with Claret, 2011).

In other words, the importance that Spain attached to the Mediterranean was soon adopted by Europe primarily due to the entrepreneurial activity of the Spanish government. The actual Spanish role, in terms of the influence of regional politicians in this process, has not previously been addressed properly in the scholarly literature. On the list of Spanish politicians occupying relevant roles in the European Commission over the last two decades and a half, is interesting to note that many of them are from Catalonia. This is not a coincidence. Catalonia as a regional power within Spain played a very important role in pushing for developing intensively Euro-Mediterranean policies. A fact was later recognised in the launch of the Barcelona Process.

The former president of Catalonia, Jordi Pujol can be probably considered among the main political entrepreneurs of the Spain's Mediterranean political and diplomatic initiatives and policies. Andreu Claret has stated that it was Pujol's intervention that enabled Gonzalez to situate Spain at the centre of Europe's Mediterranean agenda (Claret, 2011). During an interview for this book Pujol –former president of the Catalonian government between explained that the commitment of the Government of Catalonia – *La Generalitat* – towards the Mediterranean was, due to historical, geographical, economic and political factors. Pujol reminded that Catalonia was the only region in Spain that belonged to the Carolingian empire and on top of that its permanent trade relations with the Mediterranean over the centuries have shaped this European and Mediterranean identity. Pujol continued: ["Hence, as Catalans and *Generalitat*, we firstly disseminated this message throughout European institutions and then lobbied the Spanish government to work for that"] (Interview with Pujol, 2012).

From 1987 onward, Pujol's objective was to make the Mediterranean an issue of importance for Europe's least inclined nations. He was a key figure in organising conferences in places like Stockholm that promoted the idea that the Mediterranean constituted ["potentially, a Euroregion"] (Pujol, 2006). The conference was held at the Grand Hôtel, Stockholm the 5 November 1987. After an historical introduction about the importance of the Mediterranean over the centuries, Pujol developed the central point of his conference by saying: ["The Mediterranean is not losing positions any longer, on the contrary, is recovered. It is not a passive area anymore. Today is a region full of initiative and creativity. It is an area that progresses, a lot"] (Pujol, 2012).

González, who was also convinced about the necessity of selling the Mediterranean to Europe found a very important and creative ally in Catalonia that combined to offer two complementary Europeanisms (Jauregui, 2011) – the Spanish and the Catalan. Evidence of the entrepreneurial action on these issues is seen in Pujol's explanation that: ["The Mediterranean policy of Felipe González, I think, it was his idea, however, what is true is that I went many times to speak with him to stress the fact that Spain should have a Mediterranean policy"] (Pujol, 2012).

It is important to stress that Spain was not alone in this Mediterranean adventure. Countries such as France, Morocco, Portugal and Algeria also demonstrated a commitment to this issue (Gillespie, 1997). Italy ably supported Spanish initiatives (Claret, 2011). As has been acknowledged by Claret the relationship between Spanish foreign minister Miguel Ángel Moratinos and his Italian counterpart Gianni De Michelis was very close during the presidency of Giulio Andreotti between July 1989 and June 1992 (Claret, 2011).

It was in these years that the first benefits of the earlier Spanish efforts to take a lead on Euro-Mediterranean policy, started to be seen (Gillespie, 1997). By this time the importance of the Mediterranean was being promoted by deploying a realist public discourse in the immediate post-Cold War era. New dangers and threats had to be publicised in order to attract international attention (Calleya, 2003). The Conference on Security and Co-operation in the Mediterranean (CSCM) was convened in this context. Philosophically this was inspired by the Conference on Security and Cooperation in Europe (CSCE) which opened in Helsinki on the 3 July 1973.

But its immediate roots can be traced back to the efforts of De Michelis in 1989 and the success of Spain in conceptualizing it in response to the weaknesses inherent in both the existing European Mediterranean Policy and the Renovated Mediterranean Policy (RMP) that had been developed by Abel Matutes during 1989–1990 as it has been explained in the introduction. Mediterranean politics so far –the existing political mechanisms and structures – as well as the European action towards Southern Mediterranean countries concentrated their attention mostly on trade related issues. The end of the 1980s, with a new global international dynamics, demanded a different political, economic, communicational and diplomatic approach, whether elements such as the understanding among cultures should be the key factor underpinning sustainable Euro-MENA relations.

In considering this initial period pre-Barcelona Process, Italy's diplomatic energy on this front lasted until 1992, when De Michelis concluded his time as a minister (Holmes, 1996). Until the end of the 1980s and at this stage, the continuous formulation of policies towards the Mediterranean based upon a "security-cooperative" formula to be applied in the Southern Mediterranean has been assessed by Calleja as a ["premature remedy for a region which now neither as a bridge nor it is a divide (…) It is simply a vacuum"] (Calleja, 1992).

Spain intended to fill this vacuum with an innovative discourse and a new political and diplomatic breath. There were four central elements to this vacuum filling (1) the European attitude towards the Mediterranean, (2) the need to develop a consistent communicative strategy that could justify further political actions, (3) the capacity to articulate the specific politic objectives within the short, medium and long term and (4) a consistent political discourse on bilateral and multilateral levels with regards to the implementation of policies.

In these terms the three pillars of Euro-Mediterranean relations from the time of the CSCM were: political-security, economic and sociocultural. These would subsequently form the basis of the three baskets of the Barcelona Process.

In this sense Felipe González had the intuition, identified the political window, lobbied with the strongest country, Germany, by deepening his friendship with Helmut Kohl and strengthening strategically his links with Jacques Delors, president of the European Commission at the time. Abel Matutes, – a member of the European Commission since 1986 and Spain's minister of foreign affairs between 1996 and 2000 during the government of José María Aznar – played a vital role in building ties to Delors. As Matutes explained during an interview with the author:

> ["The Mediterranean issue was very clear to Felipe González since the first day. I had the occasion of sharing all his ideas, and after my first mandate I asked him to help to me to convince Delors to give me the responsibility over the Mediterranean, Latin America, Asia and the relations North-South. He helped me with efficacy and honesty. At that time, we had the occasion of specifying a lot the contents of the policy that I wanted to develop in the Mediterranean and the role of González was crucial"] (Interview with Matutes, 2012).

In this context the reactions of other regional powers like France should not be forgotten. France opposed strongly Spanish entry into the EEC. It distrusted and opposed Spanish attempts to take the lead on a new Mediterranean policy, once it was inside the Community. However, there were subtleties to this dynamic. The CSCM was an ambitious Spanish diplomatic attempt to assert itself in the Mediterranean. It was, as noted above, a premature attempt that failed due to a number of factors: regional realities such as the ongoing failure to find Arab-Israeli peace and the ongoing tensions in the Persian Gulf; the opposition of some key partners such as the US, the UK and The Netherlands; Germany's reluctance to engage with the Mediterranean in a period of immense change in Eastern Europe and on its borders. For its part, France at that time France was developing a more modest diplomatic plan to cope with challenges and opportunities in the Western

Mediterranean. With this in mind, France expressed, what Valle Simón and Holmes have described as a non-negative attitude towards the CSCM (Valle, 1995).

## 1.8 The French Attitude

It was in the Western Mediterranean that both Spain and France had their most significant investment in the region. Jordi Pujol has gone so far as to argue that Spain should have limited its focus to this area and it is arguable that the failure to do so had dramatic and negative long term impacts on the failure of the Euro-Mediterranean Partnership. As Pujol put in:

> ["I always said that Spain should not get involved in the whole Mediterranean, only in the Western Mediterranean, from Malta to here. From Malta to here we are someone, from Malta towards the East we are nobody. Neither Italy nor France, even France is a nobody, that is for the north-Americans" (Pujol, 2012).

One conclusion from this is that this explains France's lack of interest in stamping is authority on Europe's Mediterranean policy from 1989 onwards. But in truth, as Pujol noted, though France distanced itself from a desire to take a lead in the Mediterranean at the end of the Cold War it did work behind the scenes to take any opportunity to extend and consolidate its power base in the region. For example, following the fall of the Berlin Wall, France pressed hard to take over the Mediterranean –Sixth Fleet – Command from the US.

It is in these terms that one should examine the French push in the Western Mediterranean at this time. President Mitterrand first proposed the idea of the 5+5 group in the early 1980s. This idea was re-launched by presidents Bettino Craxi and Felipe González during the second half of the 1980s involving five countries from the South-Western Mediterranean and five from the North-Western Mediterranean (Schumacher, 2004; Ureta, 2010). The 5+5 group meeting was held in Rome in 1990. Nevertheless, contextual political elements such as the Gulf War –from August 1990 to February 1991 – and the Lockerbie affair –from 1988 to 1992 and onward – impeded it smooth development and the dialogue among parts has been blocked due to these disputes. On one hand the First Gulf War generated new tensions between the Arab world and Western stakeholders in creating the basis of mutual distrust for future diplomatic developments. Following this aspect, Telhami has studied how the Arab public opinion reacted to this military intervention and therefore how this event conditioned future initiatives (Telhami, 1993).

On the other hand, the Lockerbie affair stopped the political and economic inclusion of Libya in times of strong economic crisis –and further political dialogue – due to the economic embargo issued in March 1992 by the Security Council of the UN –resolution 748 – in response to the Libyan attack to a Pan Am flight in 1988 (Sánchez Mateos, 2005). After this event Libya was defined as a terrorist state. As Mortimer has stressed, this politic and diplomatic issue not only affected Libyan-Western relations, but the stability of the entire Maghreb and existing partnerships like the Arab Maghreb Union (AMU) established in 1992 (Mortimer, 1993).

Disputes between Maghreb countries such as Algeria and Morocco, as well as rivalries between France and Spain for the leadership of this initiative also limited its effectiveness and survival. Ambassador Eneko Landaburu –EU Ambassador to Morocco and former Director General for External Relations of the EU, from 2003 to 2009 among other positions – responded to a question on this issue in the following terms: ["Tensions between France and Spain and Italy existed because France wanted more focus on the Western Mediterranean, and Spain and Italy [wanted] a broader approach"]) (Landaburu, 2012; Khader, 1995).

With regards to the apparent disinterest of France for leading the Mediterranean policy during the late 1980s and 1990s, it is possible to say, again in the spirit of that political pragmatism, that Mitterrand, especially between 1988 and 1995, was very much interested in blocking the potential German domination over France. Mitterrand was a leading driver of the Treaty on European Union in 1991, which contributed to establish a central European banking system along with a unified foreign policy and a shared currency partly at least to constrain German power. With this as a French priority the Mediterranean inevitably took second place (Baun, 1995).

## 1.9 Spain: Achieving Objectives

Spain's first attempts to promote a Mediterranean policy served as tests that confirmed that "political windows" can be opened and developed once the leading political entrepreneur enjoys the support of the largest number of partners or the economically strongest partners. These first attempts also saw Spain beginning to market the Mediterranean to Europe. The Madrid Conference on the Arab-Israeli peace process that commenced on 30 October 1991 acknowledged the potential role of Spain in Mediterranean politics, even though as has been noted by Gillespie, the Spanish role was reduced to that of mere organizer (Gillespie, 1997). Even leaving the side the symbolism of the Madrid venue had an important psychological importance, it is also true that Spain was more than a mere organizer at Madrid. Spain had earned the trust of Washington to organize, host and oversee this complex and historic meeting. As Carlos Westendorp recalls:

> ["The fact is that when [James] Baker –when George Bush was still president – asked Paco Fernández Ordóñez, Spain's minister of foreign affairs between 1985 to1992, to organize a conference in Madrid we were in Seville. I saw Paco holding the phone and with a very worried face he tells me: '*It was Baker, he is asking me to organize the conference in Madrid on Middle Eastern issues because he trusts us.*' And Paco Fernández Ordóñez who had a very strong sense of goal, accepted immediately and this was important. It brought more credibility with the US and with the world, because, first of all, it was not easy at all to convince Israelis and Syrians to come"] (Westendorp, 2012).

The role of Spain under Felipe González as a legitimate and influential interlocutor between the West and the Middle East started to be recognised. This resonates in the current era. Prior to the NATO intervention in Libya in 2011, González was asked to act as a negotiator with the Qaddafi's regime (Chicote, 2012). One reason the Libyan leader trusted González because in 1986 he had refused the US to use the Spanish airspace to attack Qaddafi (Marticorena, 2012).

Along with rising credibility in the early 1990s came another even more important development – German support for Spanish plans to develop its Mediterranean policy. As Westendorp points out, first of all Spain was rewarded by Germany for ["being a loyal partner in Europe"] (Westendorp, 2012). In particular, Germany was grateful for Spanish support over the re-unification of Germany.

## 1.10 Spain Sells the Mediterranean: A Threatening Political Discourse

By 1992 the political discourse regarding Euro-Maghreb relations started to be more present in the EC's agenda. This can be explained in significant part by the Spanish interest in attracting Community's attention to its southern border. As both Spanish Euro Commissioner Abel Matutes and Spanish Foreign Minister Francisco Fernández Ordóñez, stated in 1992: ("The Maghreb is truly a time bomb. The Community cannot remain indifferent") (Anon, 1992).

These statements were delivered during the European Council meeting in Lisbon, 26–27 June 1992. By using this emotional language, Spain was consciously trying to attract attention to the issue amongst its partners in Europe. All the more so when this was combined with diplomatic efforts to reduce the importance of the problems of Eastern Europe compared to those in North Africa, which was truly a vulnerable frontier.

The question that this raises, is the extent that Spain had enough symbolic power to drive home this message inside the Community? At that time, as has been suggested by Fontela, the EC was facing a choice between two hypothetical scenarios of action –variable geometry or co-development. The concept of variable geometry was considered at the Lisbon meeting. It refers to a method that promotes differentiated integration. This concept accepts that there exist sets of irreconcilable elements among partners that make permanent separation inevitable (Fontela, 1995; Grant, 2005). The more idealistic concept for a way forward is co-development. This idea postulates the view that relationships among partners are designed to overcome differences in order to seek for win-win solutions.

The main problem regarding the Maghreb is that in that area there are two contradictory streams: Westernization and Islamization. The former looks to steer Maghreb economies towards the open markets democratic values and respect for fundamental human rights. Fontela has argued that in these terms the Arab Maghreb Union (AMU) created on 7 February 1992 was a sign of westernization because they tried to follow the example of Western economic and trade integration. Others have disagreed with this assessment, due to the fact that, given that Maghreb economies are not complementary this integration would have opened the doors to both more regional competitiveness and economic and industrial efficiency and to the possible solutions of regional disputes and conflicts (Aghrout and Sutton, 1990; Mortimer, 1999).

Arguably, since the 1960s of all the initiatives regarding EEC-EU relations with southern Mediterranean countries, the Euro-Mediterranean Partnership (EMP) –or Barcelona Process – has been the most significant in terms of looking to increase co-operation among EU-MENA partners. Over this period of time, it is also true that four generations of commercial and trade agreements were signed between the EEC and southern Mediterranean countries since 1969 to 1996. Considering this timeframe, France was the strongest country projecting power in North Africa and due to this, it was reasonably to understand that also France was actively engaged in supporting Spanish or Italian proposals aiming at launching and establishing the EMP.

In order to see how the efforts mostly from Spain and Italy –and to a lesser extent France – impacted Europe's foreign policies and political plans in order to focus more on the Southern frontier, it is important to assess the texts emanated from the meetings of the European councils. In using the CL approach, it would have been desired to have access to the data since 1985. However the materials ready to be used start in 1993. Therefore the conclusions of the presidency of the European Council that are going to be used for this purpose start in 1993. The texts that have been analyzed belong to the councils of: Copenhagen and Brussels –1993-, Corfu and Essen – 1994-, Cannes and Madrid (extraordinary) 1995.

The variables that were used in order to understand how the penetration of certain concepts into the European public speech and political agenda have been evolving from 1993 to 1995 with the establishment of the Barcelona Process are the next ones: Mediterranean, migration, security, Arab/Muslim, Terrorism and Racism. The graphic number 1 shows this evolution.

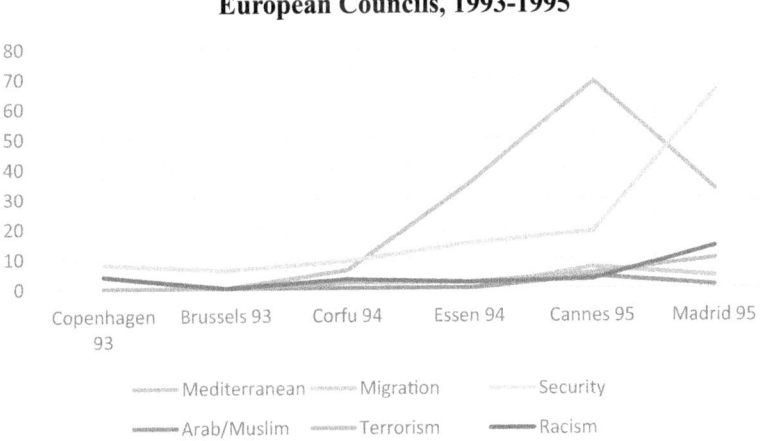

**Graphic 1.** European Councils, Conclusions of the Presidency.
Source: European Commission. Elaborated by the author.

As the graphic number 1 shows, the concept "Mediterranean" was not present until 1994 in the European Council celebrated in Corfu. Until then it is possible to say that the "entrepreneurial" activities developed by countries such as Spain or Italy were trying to lobby and to convince European stakeholders about the necessity of designing and developing a comprehensive Mediterranean policy. From then onward, this European interest towards the Mediterranean was publicly acknowledged, and therefore it is possible to appreciate the consistent growth as the Council was approaching the date of establishment of the Barcelona Process in 1995.

The drop between Cannes 1995 and Madrid 1995 is due to the fact that the council celebrated in Madrid was an extraordinary one, and therefore also the amount of pages of the document is shorter. Beyond this technical aspect, it is also interesting to note how the concept "Security" has been the constantly present –and before – since 1993 as European security at large is obviously the most relevant concern. Nevertheless, it is also interesting to see how since the concept Mediterranean started to be present in the political agenda, security related issues increased as well.

This correlation underpins the EU's hypothesis, affirmed during a personal interview with Abel Matutes–the aforementioned dilemma between the co-operation and variable geometry – that ensured that more co-operation and investment in Southern Mediterranean countries would reduce the incentives to migrate and therefore, by improving the general socio-economic conditions Europe would be safer.

Apart from the EU's political rhetoric that has been tried to sell the EMP as a win-win situation by deploying a liberal discourse, the real intentions behind the partnership is fully rooted in a neo-realist approach where the defense of European interests are fundamental as it is going to be demonstrated in Chapters 3,4 and 5. In observing this hypothesis it is possible to appreciate the differences between political entrepreneurs, political "brokers", and opportunists. Whereas, political entrepreneurs and brokers would define their strategies following a real and non-speculative win-win scenario, political opportunists would identify opportunities and design their *modus operandi* following unilateral benefits by speculating about their real intentions.

Completing this picture is also possible to appreciate how the variables "Racism", "Migration" and "Terrorism" increased also from 1995. This represents a growing political interest on these three variables considering the new environment of globalization which entails also transnational risks and uncertainties. These initial elements will constitute the most relevant political and diplomatic concerns and challenges the EU will have to face and deal with, especially from 11 September 2001 onward.

The use of the CL approach offers valuable insights to understand discover hidden aspects of the public speech that are important to better evaluate the outcomes of political proposals and initiatives. In considering the aforementioned corpora and in analyzing the list of most repeated words –out of 5.164 word types-, it is possible to see that within the top-15 results there are two verbs: Be (ranked 12 with 768 repetitions) and Will (ranked 15 with 630 repetitions). In searching for the concordance between these two verbs most of times the formula "will be" was used 174 times. The next verb represented in the world list is "is" ranked 21 with 431 hits. These elements clearly show that the usage of this political language is projected towards the future and it is mostly characterized by a declaration of intentions and political will and not necessarily driven by a clear sense of accomplishment. Assessing these political communication strategies and resources are relevant to understand whether these political initiatives and projects are mostly based on a "productive" –political entrepreneurs and brokers – approach or on a "speculative" one –political opportunists-.

Therefore, France, Italy and Spain were the main countries advocating a change of politics in the Euro-Mediterranean region. As it has been shown above, it was evident in 1994 during the Corfu and Essen European Council Summits (Lesser et Al., 1998). As the Bulletin of the European Community N°6/1994 summed up decisions made at the Council of Corfu that had been backed by Spain, France and Italy:

> ["In the field of external relations, the European Council confirmed its commitment to the development of existing links with the Mediterranean countries and to the peace process in the Middle East and stressed the importance of the European Agreements with the countries of Central and Eastern Europe (…) The European Council confirms the importance it attaches to the close links already existing with its Mediterranean partners and its wish to develop them still further so that the Mediterranean area may become an area of cooperation guaranteeing peace, security, stability and well-being"] (Bulletin of the EC, Corfu, 2010).

Here is possible to see the initial fruits of this diplomatic offensive to re-direct the EU's political efforts southwards. The same document noted that the importance of constructing the Algeria-Morocco-EU gas pipeline as a priority. Considering the importance of energy resources for the future of Europe, the Maghreb-Europe Gas pipeline (MEG) was originally proposed in 1963 by a consortium of French companies even though more structured proposals were developed during the 1970s following Spanish, Italian and Algerian interests (Hayes, 2006). Whereas the *Transmed* project began in 1983 to provide gas to Italy thanks to ENI the Italian ["strong and politically mobilized company"] (Hayes, 2006). Spain was not able to achieve its objectives for the creation of a national project until 1990s because both the government and its national gas company *Enagas* were not influential and strong enough (Prieto and Hall, 2013). The fact of highlighting the priority of developing the MEG –lately named Pedro Duran Farell pipeline – in this document reveals the positive outcomes achieved by Spain as a raising political actor from 1985 to 1995. The construction of the MEG began in 1996.

At Essen in December 1994 – Jacques Delors' last council as president of the Commission, – the Mediterranean issue was again raised as a priority. ["Ensuing the lasting peace and stability of the European continent and neighboring regions"] necessitated, the council meeting argued, ["preparing for the future accession of the associated countries of Central and Eastern Europe and developing *in parallel* the special relationship of the Union to *its other* neighbors particularly the Mediterranean countries"] (EU, Bulletin EC, Essen, 1994).

The emphasis on "parallel" and "other" in this statement reflects the still secondary interest in Southern Europe. The ongoing dominant view that eastern and central Europe was a natural part of the European project unlike those states in the Mediterranean who may never be fully incorporated into Europe, like Morocco. However in evaluating the consistency and coherency of potential win-win policies and diplomatic projects this heterogeneous aggregation should happen, otherwise, any integration project that does not consider this dimension is doomed to fail.

In an interview on Spanish television in 1984, King Hassan II of Morocco was asked to explain his recent declaration that ("Morocco was at least, as European as Greece and (….) should be fully-fledged member of the EEC") (RTVE, 1984).

For King Hassan II it appeared that membership of the EEC was primarily a matter of political will. According to him the entire Maghreb was entitled to become associated to the EEC because that region, without any doubt, ["is the base of the Mediterranean. It is the hinge between Europe and Africa toward the South of the Sahara. I believe that Europe should not let this occasion escape. But in any case, this proposal should not surprise to anyone. At an institutional level, at a constitutional level, at a geographical level is not an eyesore the fact of asking about being a fully-fledged member of the European Union"] (RTVE, 1984).

In the same interview, when asked about the role of Spain and whether Spanish accession was troubling to Morocco, Hassan II replied:

> ["First of all. Spain is a neighbor country. If its accession to the EEC is useful I wish that this accession should been done as soon as possible. Because it is a neighbor country, and a friend. But, if Spain shares the same feelings as Morocco at a bilateral level, I believe that Spain will do everything to avoid its accession affecting Morocco. I believe that this is a bilateral problem and not only a European problem"] (RTVE, 1984).

Spain's strategy to achieve greater diplomatic influence by playing the North African card was successful and overcame the resistances from Northern European countries that were more interested due to geo-strategic reasons in Eastern European countries. The establishment of the EMP or Barcelona Process was the material proof of such success. However, is it possible to consider Spain a political entrepreneur, a political broker or an opportunist? Despite Spain's interests in Morocco, it is possible to say that Spain was not really interested in defending the "mutual interests" expressed above by Hassan II. Spain had an instrumental interest in selling in southern Mediterranean problems as European problems as Gillespie has suggested.

After the efforts put in practice by Spain to develop its diplomatic and foreign action to become a leading European power, the following years would demonstrate that the Mediterranean would continue being central for Spain's foreign policy. The next chapter analyses Aznar's presidency and discusses the shifts that differentiated his views of the Mediterranean with the phase the allowed Spain to gain international credibility in Europe.

# 2 Lights and Shadows: The Assertion of Spanish Leadership in the International Arena during the Aznar Era, 1996–2004

Assessing José María Aznar's foreign policy in general, and in regard to the Mediterranean in particular, requires reflection on the origins and ethos of the Partido Popular (PP) (Baon, 2001). The PP was re-founded in 1989 out of the original Alianza Popular (AP), which was itself created in 1976 by a constellation of former Franquist ministers and headed by former minister of Information and Tourism (1962–1969) and vice-president (1975–1976) Manuel Fraga Iribarne. As such, it can be defined as a federation of 7 proto-parties intent on developing a conservative or right-wing political discourse in the context of the country's democratic transition. This required as a priority a re-constitution of Spanish identity. This meant that during the 1980s foreign policy did not top the AP's political agenda. Instead, the emphasis was on the domestic realm where politics was dominated by the Partido Socialista Obrero Español (PSOE).

As stated previously in Chapter 1, due to its socialist character the PSOE was very much influenced by the international dimension as socialism and internationalism can often be, and in this case were, two sides of the same coin. On the other hand, the PP which was re-founded as a unique party in 1989 to contest and counterbalance the majority of the PSOE, inherited the same philosophical approaches of AP with regards to engagement in the domestic and foreign spheres. The PSOE had engagement in the international arena in its blood. The AP and PP were the products of an introspective domestic and nationalistic political approach. As Jiménez Redondo has pointed out, the hegemony of the PSOE over three legislatures and the lack of a real political choice until the early 1990s limited the possibility of a valid and alternative foreign policy (Redondo, 2006).

## 2.1 Discussing the Paternity of Spain's Foreign Policy

It is possible to argue that the PP did not accept explicitly the PSOE's dominance of Spain's foreign policy after the transitional period between 1975 and 1978. As noted by Fernández, the PP regularly argued that the foundations of Spain's foreign policy was not conceived by the PSOE but by the previous Union of the Democratic Centre (UCD) (Fernandez Molina, 2007; Huneens and Nohlen, 1985). This was the very clear message published in the PP's government programme of 1993. The section devoted to foreign policy started with this statement: ["The greatest merit of the foreign policy of socialist governments have made was the adoption of approaches that were not originally theirs"] (Partido Poplular, 1993). This same point was made in 1996 during the PP's successful electoral campaign.

It is interesting to note, however, that in 1993 and through its government programme the PP revealed some key aspects of its foreign policy. It was mainly focused on Spain's relationship with NATO.

After that, came Latin America, the Maghreb and Equatorial Guinea. Though the first –Latin America – was classified as the priority, the Maghreb was also important as it was defined as an area of conflict with extraordinary potential. The goal was to establish preferential agreements with the region both through bilateral engagement and through the EEC. Bearing in mind this strategy of preferential agreements it is possible to appreciate the mercantilist and business-driven approach deployed by the PP's leaders.

This approach to foreign affairs corresponded with that of the PSOE. However, Aznar in 1992 also argued that the Maghreb raised the problems of ["massive emigration, economic and commercial dependence and unavoidable security concerns"] (Aznar,1992). At that time and since 1989 –after being the president of the Regional Government of Castile and León from 1987 to 1989 – José María Aznar was already the PP's leader and therefore he headed up the political opposition against the PSOE until he won the elections in 1996 (Magone, 2009).

These arguments were reinforced by the rise of the so-called "Islamic decade" between 1980 and 1990 following the victory of the Islamic Salvation Front (ISF) in municipal elections in Algeria in 1990 (Volpi, 2003). In response, some alarmist and arguably extreme comments emanated from analysts affiliated to the PP. For instance, Rafael L. Bardají, who since 1989 had headed up international affairs at the Grupo de Estudios Estratégicos (GEES) –he was also the former Executive Advisor of the Spain's Ministry of Defence during the PP governments, from 1994 to 2004 – wrote that since the end of the Cold War, the threats from Southern Mediterranean countries included nuclear proliferation, social instability due to a unstoppable demographic growth, underdevelopment and religious fundamentalism (Bardají, 1992).

This argument, coming as it did following the disintegration of the Soviet Union, led to a new strategy intended to identify new political windows by political entrepreneurs – or opportunists – willing to play a leading role in international politics.

However, by using a more moderate language and a more proactive and comprehensive approach, the architect of the new Renovated Mediterranean Policy, Abel Matutes attempted to promote an increase in living standards and the overall development in the South that transcended the alarmist discourse and potential threats. From 1988 to 1989 onwards, Matutes had attempted to propose and to implement the Renovated Mediterranean Policy. It was adopted by the European Union in 1990 precisely to avoid and to correct the inefficiencies of the old Mediterranean policy and it culminated in the work of Manuel Marin and the launch in the course Euro-Mediterranean Partnership in 1995 (Prat I Coll, 2004).

In this regard, Matutes commented during an interview for this book, that intercultural dialogue was considered as important as aid, as this allowed Spain to present itself as a valid interlocutor with the Southern Mediterranean countries and the Middle East:

("In speaking about the EU's Mediterranean Policy, I was in charge of redesigning, or designing to be more precise, the new Mediterranean Policy. On one hand it looked to improve financial protocols and support. On the other hand, it tried to help not only on financial level, but also to help them to create more wealth in their countries. I mean, develop more their potential. In order to do so, it was crucial to involve them in trade and provide them with commercial opportunities") (Matutes, 1992).

This declaration is certainly aligned with one of the two hypothesis explained in the precedent chapter of co-operating with southern Mediterranean countries *versus* developing asymmetric relations. However, as it has been demonstrated, within the long term this liberal public speech was a rhetoric resource that was useful to launch the basis of the EMP. Beyond this rhetoric baseline, existing strong geo-strategic and politico-economic interests prevailed and Northern Mediterranean countries focused on neo-realist approach where the strengthening of European security played the most fundamental role.

In any case this co-operative and comprehensive selling strategy played out well in the short and medium term. It was important to attract also the interest of Southern Mediterranean countries. Therefore, the new emphasis on Euro-Mediterranean political dialogue represented a fundamental element. Since 1986 onward, Spain's influence over Morocco increased notably despite the traditional political frictions such as Western Sahara open dispute, the question of Ceuta and Melilla or drug trafficking related issues among others (Ferrer-Gallardo, 2008).

Considering an economic point of view, Morocco over the 1980s was also more communicative both with Spain and Europe thanks to the establishment of an economic reform. Along with this economic reform and the Spanish increasing role as influential –neighbouring – stakeholder, there were signed bilateral agreements such as; the Framework Agreement on Economic and Financial Cooperation – 1988-; the Agreement on the Mutual Promotion and Protection of Investments – 1989-; the Treaty of Friendship, Good Neighbourhood and Cooperation – 1991-; and in 1996, just after the launch of the EMP, the Agreement on Economic and Financial Cooperation (Jordan Gandulf, 1997).

However, as it has been discussed before, these agreements and political will to increase bilateral co-operation –and the liberal and inclusive rhetoric strategy used during the selling process of the EMP – had to face the challenges imposed by the migratory issue, where it is possible to appreciate that economic integration processes and mechanisms cannot be implemented sustainably if further socio-political integration is not ensued as White has studied (White, 2007).

Nevertheless, highlighting the relevance and influence Spain exerted over Morocco over this process – and beyond bilateral episodes of understanding and misunderstanding – some Spanish politicians like Felipe González or Abel Matutes continued being influential even when they were not anymore part of the Spanish government. Matutes thinks that the dialogue that he had with Mohamed VI of Morocco during 2010–2011 played an important role in the evolution of the country's new constitution (Matutes, 2012). Matutes goes further and considers that this new constitution represented a clear benefit for Morocco and allowed the country to solve, or at least tackle, some of key problems that during the Arab Spring of 2011 destabilised both Egypt and Tunisia. This idea is shared by Dalacoura (Dalacoura, 2011).

In acknowledging these facts, Matutes can be considered the key figure in developing the PSOE's foreign policy with regards to the Euro-Mediterranean policy as well as the PP's foreign policy from 1996 onwards. That is why, in considering these elements during the early 1990s, it is practically impossible to find a difference between the PSOE's and the PP's views in the foreign policy sphere.

Leaving aside the paternity of Spain's foreign policy in the first years of the democratic era, the new PP, after being in the opposition for 7 years, won the elections in 1996 with a very tight margin. This victory followed the launch of the Barcelona Process. Prior to that, between 1982 and May 1996, under Felipe González Spain had looked to become a political entrepreneur in foreign policy but on a relatively modest level. An approach that was fitting for a newcomer who was required to demonstrate its value and political seriousness by northern European partners like Germany.

This modesty was expressed in a very telling and pragmatic phrase coined by Francisco Fernandez Ordoñez, Spanish foreign minister in the crucial years between 1985 and 1992: ("In European politics, our position is defined very clearly: we have to take the fifth") (Abian, 2010). Was this the key of the Spain's success in Europe between 1985 and 1995? Certainly, from 1982 to 1996 Spain successfully led on Euro-Mediterranean policy. In this sense Spain was the main political entrepreneur in selling the idea of the Mediterranean. This idea crystallized with the Barcelona Process, a political platform that raised doubts about its future almost since its inception due to the complex problems and ongoing conflicts present in the Mediterranean (Edis, 1998). The loss of momentum was a matter of fact and it became even more evident –and damaging for the future of the EMP – when Aznar, in the wake of the 9/11 terrorist attacks developed a foreign policy that prioritised relation with Washington, over the interests of the EU and the Mediterranean.

## 2.2 The Baseline of Spain's New Foreign Policy

Prior to its 1996 election victory the PP lacked of a clear profile in international affairs as stated above. Balfour states that the PP government followed a policy of continuity in relation to foreign policy (Balfour, 2005). They had no proper training in international affairs. However, as Valencia points out, there were cases where they had relevant experience. There was a major focus on economic related issues linked to the area of political economy aimed at reinforcing economic diplomacy (Valencia, 2000).

Nevertheless, this was not fully evident during the early stages of the first PP government. From an operational point of view, the nomination of Miguel Ángel Moratinos (PSOE) as the EU's representative for the

Arab-Israeli peace process from 1996 to 2003, placed Spain in a strong position to play a role in that key foreign policy issues (Gillespie, 2000). It is evident that the EU focused its attention on Moratinos, due to his regional knowledge and contribution to the development of PSOE's foreign policy towards the Mediterranean.

This mandate confirmed Spain's role in lobbying and working for a comprehensive Euro-Mediterranean policy. As Aoun stresses, over the 1990s the EU has not played an influential role in managing the recurrent crises presented by the Arab-Israeli conflict (Aoun, 2003). However as Alpher has mentioned, Moratinos, already during the first year of his activity filled ["the vacuum created by the stalemate in the process and the reduced activity of US mediator Deniss Ross"] (Alpher, 2008). On the other hand, Moratinos' nomination coincided as well with Jacques Chirac's announcement of the new French foreign policy towards the Arab World aiming at ["reversing France's marginalization as a political player"] in the region in order to become more influential (Wood, 2008).

Beyond these initial considerations, it is important, however, to describe, how, at a philosophical level the new government faced the challenge of developing Spain's foreign policy. As Aznar's personal advisor, Alberto Carnero has stated during a personal interview for this book:

["If I should explain the PP's foreign policy I would start by explaining the idea of Spain that had the President. Aznar said, *we have the ambition of making out of Spain one of the best democracies in the world*. I would frame this phrase to describe both his foreign and domestic policies. I am politician and diplomat and after many years I would say that those dimensions should not be differentiated. And I quote again the President when he says that *there is no best foreign policy separate from a domestic policy*"] (Interview Carnero, 2012).

This same idea is defended by Abel Matutes who, in speaking to this author, stated that both Felipe González and José María Aznar shared this outlook:

["In foreign policy this is very clear. This was said always by Felipe and Aznar and I believe that generally speaking they practiced that. It is a state policy, of permanent interests that need being constant and permanent. If you go from one band to another by making a party policy you cannot achieve anything and at the end of the day that is the end of your foreign policy"] (Matutes, 2012).

This political framework and conceptualization expresses the main lines of Aznar's visions for Spain's foreign policy. This argument can be used to justify the PP's lack of international projection in historic terms. That said, Aznar's visions of international affairs were founded upon two principles. First, the consolidation of Spain as a respected medium sized power. Second, the intertwining of his foreign and domestic policies, because as it was expressed above, for Aznar the best foreign policy had to be and had to concur with a strong domestic policy, where permanent interests should not change.

## 2.3 Aznar and the Mediterranean: The First Step

These two principles are a good starting point for analysing Aznar's foreign policy. First, there were a number of continuities in Spain's foreign policy during Aznar – Europe, Latin America, United States and the Mediterranean (Carnero, 2012).

Focusing on the Mediterranean, the 1996 PP electoral programme followed the spirit of the Barcelona declaration and was more liberal and cooperative compared to the outlook between 1988 and 1992 that defined the relationship in terms of potential threats. This new electoral programme focused instead on economic prosperity and stability; a new immigration policy adapted to the exigencies of the Schengen agreement –despite the challenges posed by an increasing migration flow – (Bazo, 1998); the promotion of human rights and fundamental liberties and the processes of political reform, attention to rising Islamic fundamentalism and the resolution of the Western Sahara conflict. In all of these areas one constant consideration was migration.

There was a strong economic and realist approach behind this agenda. Like Barcelona, it was conceived in terms of a belief that the liberalization of the economy would accelerate regional development, reduce migration and mitigate potential risks derived from deep socio-economic cleavages, thus improving regional security.

As discussed in the precedent chapter this hypothesis proved wrong and represented the biggest obstacle to developing Euro-Mediterranean relations. However, initially and theoretically speaking, the acceptance of this hypothesis by policy makers was a driving force as Matutes explains:

> ["It is true that the financial protocols could have been larger, that the trade could have been more intense, and that a more integrative policy may have

been wanted, of course, but beyond that, this ideas represented a big advancement, because those countries had a much lower life standard in the past"] (Matutes, 2012).

In these terms, Aznar, from the start of his government, was very interested in developing bilateral relations between Spain and Morocco. That explains why Aznar decided to visit Rabat on his first official visit on 27 May 1996 following his 3 March 1996 election victory. He had a meeting with King Hassan II and first Minister Abdellatif Filali. They discussed, among other issues, illegal immigration, fishing agreements, drugs trafficking, the Western Sahara question and the sovereignty of Ceuta and Melilla.

As Andreu Claret explained during an interview:

["During the first mandate, Aznar governs in coalition, and that pact made possible a more moderate foreign policy. I spoke a lot with him (Aznar) on Mediterranean issues. When he was elected President he did what had to be done – visit Morocco. The first official trip has to be to Morocco. He saw immediately that the Mediterranean was very important. When politicians go to the Council each one speaks about what he or she has. So, Aznar, since the beginning sold and promoted the Mediterranean policy"] (Claret, 2012).

In terms of strengthening collaboration and improving bilateral political relations with the Maghreb, the PP government concentrated its attention on three countries. The first was Morocco where the relations were consolidated with Mohammed VI after his accession to the throne in 1999 (Cembrero, 2006). As the level of internal violence in Algeria started to diminish at the end of 1990s, Spain started also to look for increasing contacts (Stora, 2001; Bustos, 2003). Third, as soon as Libya started to be integrated by the international community, Aznar's government showed full political support for the process, support that was openly noticeable from September 2003 onwards. In fact, Aznar was the first western leader to visit Qadaffi once the UN ended the sanctions against Libya on 12 September 2003. Five days later, on 17 September 2003, Aznar visited Tripoli together with 28 Spanish entrepreneurs and businessmen (Cembrero, 2011). The making up of this delegation alone highlights the business focus of the Aznar government, especially during its second term (Feliù, 2005).

Despite the recognition of the strategic importance of the Maghreb and the Mediterranean during Aznar's first term, scholars like Núñez Villaverde considered Spanish leadership on the Euro-Mediterranean level decreasing or even entering into a ¨("hibernation period") following the Barcelona Process (Núñez Villaverde, 2001). Certainly the PP was unable to maintain the same diplomatic rhythm as the Gonzalez's governments developed, because due to its political philosophy and practice the PSOE had a much greater internationalist approach whereas the PP historically speaking has been more rooted into domestic politics.

In order to analyse and to understand if the aforementioned "hibernation" of Euro-Mediterranean related issues and diplomatic activity is correct, it is important to analyse EU's political priorities. The CL approach is again used to examine the conclusions of the presidency of the Council of Europe. The studied period correspond to the first four years of Aznar's government, 1996–2000. The same method and the same variables used in the case exposed in the precedent chapter have been considered for consistency. This evolution is demonstrated in graphic number 2.

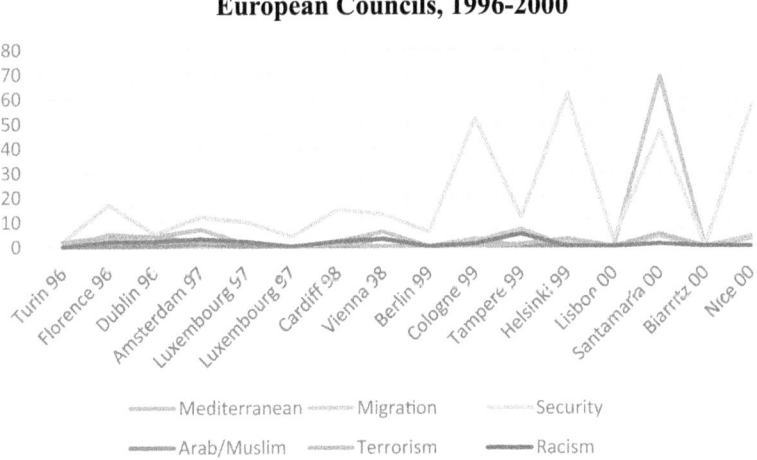

**Graphic 2.** European Councils, Conclusions of the Presidency.
**Source:** European Council. Elaborated by the author.

Quantitatively speaking and focusing on Mediterranean issues, the 1996–2000 period is very different to the 1993–1995. The graphic above shows that from 1996 to 2000 –Lisbon council – the vibrant atmosphere experienced before the launch of the Barcelona process decreased notably. Per the variables migration, Arab/Muslim, terrorism or racism, they have also curved. However, within this apparent lack of activity in 1997, during the Amsterdam Council, three important Mediterranean ideas/projects were raised: the establishment of a common Euro-Mediterranean area of peace, prosperity and stability; the project of creating a Euro-Mediterranean Free Trade Area; the positive attitude towards the signing of a Euro-Mediterranean Interim Association Agreement with the PLO (European Council, 1997).

These three elements represent by themselves the three most relevant objectives and obstacles any EU's Euro-Mediterranean project has to face: without economic and politic stability in Southern –Maghreb – Mediterranean countries, security for EU members is very limited; the economic interests based on the creation of a Mediterranean Free Trade Area were decisive for EU's politico, economic and geo-strategic objectives; any Euro-Mediterranean project –its success or failure – will be determined by the evolution of the Israeli-Palestinian conflict and how Western stakeholders mediate and deal with it.

Over the examined years these three elements have constituted the permanent baseline of the European foreign policy towards the Mediterranean. Migration flows have been also a contextual variable that have determined the evolution of the EMP as well as its consistency and coherence within the long term. Already in the council celebrated in Vienna in 1998, it was discussed the necessity of developing a European migration strategy (European Council, 1998). In this council it was also approved the creation of the Area of Freedom, Security and Justice. As it is possible to see in the graphic, the variable security is the most relevant one, and all the policies and projects proposed by the European Council are designed to increase European security in order to control and reduce actual or potential threats.

The Cologne council of 1999 represented a peak with regards to security issues. During this council it was mentioned the evolution of the tasks assigned to Moratinos as the special envoy to the Middle East. But most importantly it was intensively discussed the need of developing a Common Foreign and Security Policy following the agreements of the Council celebrated in Vienna (European Council, 1999). Following the same trend, the Council celebrated in Helsinki in 1999 highlighted the importance of developing a common strategy for the Mediterranean, Eastern Europe and Western Balkans.

Bearing in mind Mediterranean issues is possible to confirm that 1996–1999 was in fact a period of low-middle intensity, where the accent was focused on discussing and implementing the mechanisms to create a common European security and defence policy. It is also possible to say that despite the interest of Northern European countries to support the European expansion towards the East, Mediterranean issues remained more important in the European agenda. In considering all the councils celebrated between 1996 and 2000 the variable Mediterranean was mentioned 101 times whereas Eastern-Europe was mentioned 35 times.

Nevertheless this period of relative "hibernation" should be better defined as a period of "realisation". The 1996–2000 window represented the medium term where politicians and diplomats realised the real problems and difficulties to achieve the pre-defined –certainly ambiguous – objectives described by the declaration of Barcelona. This realisation somehow paralysed the initial optimism deployed in 1995.

As the previous graphic shows, 2000 represented a clear landmark with regards to Euro-Mediterranean issues. During the celebration of the Council of Santa María, it was expressed that the problems in the Middle East determine the entire Mediterranean project and therefore it would be necessary to adopt a Euro-Mediterranean Charter for Peace and Stability (European Council, 2000). After five years, the European Council stressed that ["the EU will together with its Mediterranean partners undertake a comprehensive review of the Barcelona Process with the aim of reinvigorating the process and making it more action-oriented and results-driven"] (European Council, 2000).

This important statement reveals that so far, the EMP was not producing results beyond the political will expressed over the EMP's conferences and therefore, not relevant outcomes had been achieved. During this conference it was also stressed the EU will in strengthening political and security related dialogue with Mediterranean partners, increasing co-operation with the AMU in order to stimulate south-south trade, as well as collaborating with Southern Mediterranean countries on the management of migration flows. These three elements reveal again the interest of the EU in security and trade. The 2000s deepened these trends and challenges as it is going to be explained in the next epigraphs.

## 2.4 Aznar's New Foreign Policy: Changing Methodology

Aznar's victory in the March 2000 elections by an overwhelming majority allowed him to govern the country without relying on the support of nationalist groups. In his second start he began to adopt a more presidential approach to foreign policy which required Spain taking a stand on key international issues and no longer remaining silent or deferring to larger EU partners. Therefore, as Woodworth has mentioned Aznar thought that those who were not aligned with him were against democracy (Woodworth, 2004). This attitude was defined by Cebrián as "Democratic fundamentalism" and he interprets it as a "disease which the Spanish right suffers in an extreme form" (Cebrián, 2011). However, as the personal political advisor of Aznar –Alberto Carnero – says:

> ["The position of Spain was very comfortable, in the middle, trying to not disturb anyone. Aznar wanted to change this aspect very consciously. And to change that it was necessary to change the foreign policy.... I think that if one analyses those years, clearly, the political objective that provoked the change as that Aznar developed a foreign policy that had an impact on the domestic sphere. (...) Having said that, this denoted this ambition of becoming one of the best democracies in the world. Having an idea of Europe. Moving forward. To follow with the policies of the past. But with a different intensity and with ambition"] (Carnero, 2012).

This necessitated Aznar to design a more active and engaged public discourse that strategically speaking was aligned to the dominant western power, the US, even at the expense of the position of the EU. These presidential ambitions led to the creation of the Consejo de Política Exterior (Council of Foreign Policy, CPE). Within this context, a new and fundamental change of status was experienced, designed and implemented through the Plan Estratégico de Acción Exterior (Strategic Plan of Foreign Action, PEAE) (Jiménez Redondo, 2006). This was the instrument that changed Spain's foreign policy. The PEAE was directed by Josep Piqué, foreign minister between 2000 and 2002. It was conceived as the tool for Spain to use to gain political influence, international stature and global prestige.

Most of the interviewees –putting aside political inclinations or personal problems with Aznar – are in agreement that Aznar's ambitions and the foreign policy approaches in which they were embodied and expressed damaged greatly the Euro-Mediterranean policy developed by González. As Jordi Pujol put it:

> ["First, I don't know how he did it (Aznar), but he ruined totally relations with Morocco, both during the first and the second term. Second, he was not interested in Europe. He was interested in Europe for the cohesion funds. He doesn't feel sympathy, neither for France nor for Germany. For France feels great antipathy. He despises Italy and then, he focuses on the United States and the United Kingdom because they go together and the Atlantic. Hence, the policy initiated by Felipe González was interrupted"] (Pujol, 2012).

As stated previously, implementing his ambitious policy required a regional and philosophical shift embodied in Aznar's Atlanticist policy. Aznar's political advisor, Alberto Carnero, justified this Atlantic policy on the grounds that the Aznar government was very much conscious of the importance of the Mediterranean and that this was a motivation for deeper collaboration with the US during the late 1990s:

> ["The first time that Spain and Aznar supported to the US was with Bill Clinton, when Saddam Hussein expelled UN observers. That was the first time, but what I would like to say is that, since the first moment, there was a very clear vision of making Spain a privileged partner of the US. And this strategy came from the transition, from the 1953 agreements, ratified with all the turbulences that we already know. (…) That was very important, also for the Mediterranean, because at the end of the day, if there exists a Mediterranean power, it is the US"] (Carnero, 1992).

Why the US is undoubtedly the major power in the eastern Mediterranean this is somewhat less obvious in the western part of the region where Washington's capacity to influence the region by drawing on commercial, cultural, economic interests and a legitimate moral authority were less developed than in Israel and the Arab world. It is arguable that Aznar miscalculated on this point when engaging the US for the interests of projecting Spanish influence in North Africa.

One can even argue that Aznar's approach to foreign policy, especially during his second term, was a significant contribution to the failure of the Barcelona Process as Spain lost the previously acquired credibility as a main negotiator and as a recognised interlocutor between western countries and the Arab world. It is also possible to argue that this Atlantic shift contributed to increase miscommunication and misunderstanding between European and Arab stakeholders. However, as it is going to be demonstrated later in this chapter, beyond any criticism against Aznar's detachment from the Europe, the EU developed a very similar political agenda and public speech.

## 2.5 Mutating Axes: The Atlantic-Mediterranean Approach

Good relations between Spain and the US did not happen as a direct consequence of the 9/11. The first official visit George W. Bush paid to Europe was to Spain in July 2001. One reason for this choice of destination was the US interest in increasing the NATO presence in Spain as well as boosting economic ties and consolidating their cooperation on

Latin America (Tremlet, 2001). During this visit Bush declared that it was important to work together in order to ["prevent or solve regional conflicts, to eliminate barriers to free trade, to extend Europe's zone of peace and stability (...) to meet new challenges to our security"] (Anon, 2001). Bush decided to go first to Spain because as Carnero, has ruminated on this point:

> ["Spain was a growing country. Spain enjoyed prestige, a dynamic economy, assumed more responsibilities with regards to some international questions. It started to participate to the NATO's structural budget in 1997 and bit by bit, it was evident the ....US started to see Spain as a privileged ally"] (Carnero, 2012).

Having said that, the Mediterranean element would become a crucial factor in the bilateral relationship just few months later, after 9/11. Aznar became something of a link to the region. One of the key activities in this context was the Foro Formentor (Formentor, Majorca, Spain). It represented a parallel initiative to the Barcelona Process. The Forum Formentor is very important in understanding Aznar's vision of the Mediterranean and his view of the role Spain should play within this political and diplomatic environment, otherwise it would have not been necessary to create alternative platforms to an existing process. It also illuminates the "Mediterranean-Atlantic shift", whereby Spain used its standing in the Mediterranean and the leverage that brought in the security sphere to make itself more attractive to the US.

It seems plausible that this Forum – especially after the 9/11 – served strategically to re-launch Spain's political influence not only in Europe, but on a global scale. In other words, the Mediterranean was once more the political opportunity for Spain to show its relevance and crucial role as political stakeholder and entrepreneur.

The Formentor Forum, was funded by Foundation Repsol YPF, the Spanish largest oil and gas multinational company. It started in 1999 and ended in 2006. Those who attended over its six years life included Tayip Erdogan, Hosni Mubarak, Simon Peres, Driss Yetú, Jorge Sampaio and Yasser Arafat (Pérez Maura, 2005). On one occasion during the third meeting 2001 – 2˙3 November– Aznar and Mubarak met Arafat and Peres in the attempt of boosting the peace process in the Middle East (Guerrero, 2001).

The third meeting of the Formentor Forum was the moment when José María Aznar announced his clear intention to re-launch the Barcelona Process and hence, to become again a policy entrepreneur by marketing and selling the Euro-Mediterranean issue. Aznar took advantage of President Bush's first visit to Spain in July 2011 and the events of the 9/11 to develop this new Spanish strategy and foreign policy. His speech at the third Formentor Forum underlines this. He began by highlighting the deadlock in Israeli-Palestinian peace talks. It was in this context, he argued, that it was ["very important what happened here in Formentor. Because, evidently in my opinion, I think that this can be the beginning of a recovery of trust between the Palestinian National Authority (PNA) and the Israeli government"] (Aznar, 2000).

It is important to note how Aznar started this speech by stressing the importance of this Forum, and its location, by addressing the most sensitive political in the Mediterranean. Immediately after this introduction he spoke about the role of the Spain within the Euro-Mediterranean politics, which, after 9/11 became global politics.

["The second point I would like to make is that we want reinforce and relaunch in a very clear and decisive manner the Barcelona Process. I think, (…) that the Barcelona Process in all its aspects, intercultural dialogue among civilizations, the economic aspect and its political aspect, it is worth re-launching toward the future"] (Aznar, 2000).

Here Aznar is arguing that Barcelona needs to be reconceived in the context of 9/11, which required that the security pillar play the crucial role. As he subsequently argued:

["From a political point of view, we have to increase, evidently our dialogue and to work clearly on the issues related to security, to arms, to the fight against terror for everybody. We have to create new financing instruments, because it has been demonstrated that the current mechanisms are not enough. And, we have to demonstrate, with our political dialogue, that we are not currently facing a clash among cultures, but we are in front of an operation, among very clear operations to end the terror in the world"].

His discourse and political purposes in adopting this approach were very much aligned and influenced by the tense political and diplomatic environment post 9/11 and by the rhetoric deployed by the Bush's administration. To understand better Aznar's intentions regarding the exploitation of this political window one should note that subsequently he described the: Barcelona Process and the Euro-Mediterranean Dialogue as one of the key aspects of their action and their presidency.

The political and entrepreneurial strategy here seems to be clear – to build a "Mediterranean-Atlantic" approach to address key security issues emanating from the Mediterranean. As Carnero has explained to this author in an interview: ["All the Arab world saw Spain as a guide and a channel to send the messages to the US. And this does not happen only in the Mediterranean, it happened also with Iran"] (Carnero, 2012).

Despite these political initiatives, justifications and declarations of intentions, Aznar's relations with crucial strategic countries such as Morocco were not as strong as he desired. His presidential approach to foreign policy in his second term resulted in a quite nationalistic way of understanding foreign relations. This led to a worsening of relations with Spain's most important southern neighbour, Morocco.

Aznar did attempt to offer a welcome approach to Morocco. He visited the country in May 2000, were he spoke positively in favour of better cooperation between the two countries. However following Mohammed VI's accession to power in 1999 relations deteriorated as tensions escalated. In April 2001, for example, there was a deep crisis between Rabat and Madrid over fishing negotiations with the EU (Vaquer i Fanes, 2003). According to Andreu Claret, Aznar overreacted in his dealings with Morocco once relations started to worsen, a move that impacted negatively on perceptions of the Spanish leader, especially as there had always been difficulties with Morocco." (Claret, 2012).

Tense bilateral relations between Spain and Morocco did not, however, stop Spain's interest in developing and fostering a multilateral engagement with regards to Euro-Mediterranean issues. As Barbé, Mestre and Soler i Lecha point out, both during the PP and the PSOE mandates there were two events that reconfirmed the interest and the engagement of the Spanish government and its diplomacy in the Barcelona Process. In fact, in 2002, during the Spanish Presidency of the Council of Europe the international community assisted
Spanish attempt to reactivate the Barcelona agenda (Montobbio, 2002).

The first event coincided with the Euro-Mediterranean Conference held in Valencia in April of 2002 (Barbè et Al., 2007). The success of this conference was compromised by the escalation in violence between Israel and the Palestinians since the start of the al-Aqsa intifada in 2000 as well as by the evolving US plans to invade Iraq. However as Claret recognised during a personal interview, this ministerial meeting was successful in establishing the Action Plan for the creation of a Euro-Mediterranean Parliamentary Assembly (EMPA) and the Euro-Mediterranean Foundation for the Dialogue Between Cultures and Civilizations. The latter idea was the Anna Lindh Foundation.

According to Claret, vice-president of this organisation, this was a key proposal that contradicts in some ways Aznar's subsequent approach to foreign policy:

> ["Various ministerial meetings were important, but the one held in Valencia was essential for the creation of the Anna Lindh Foundation. And this is interesting because this is a Foundation to promote intercultural dialogue. It was finally created in 2004 in Valencia as well, and it was the moderate reaction to the 9/11 events. I mean, it was a reaction that said, *let's avoid the combat*. Let's look for the way of dialoguing, of understanding"] (Claret, 2012).

It is possible to argue, as Soler i Lecha and Weltner-Puig have done, that the Spain's image as a leading Mediterranean power was reinforced by the decisions taken at this meeting (Soler i Lecha and Weltner Puig, 2002). Nevertheless, the presidential approach would ultimately be a cause of reduced Spanish political effectiveness in regard to the Barcelona process. Indeed, one can argue that the decline of Spain in the political sphere, as one of the leading political entrepreneurs of Euro-Mediterranean policy, brought about the wider decline in the Barcelona process. This situation was compounded from 2004 onwards by the implementation of the European Neighbourhood Policy (ENP) that promoted bilateral relations and shifted away from a multilateral and multidimensional approach.

The events of 9/11 marked a point of no return in Aznar's foreign policy and ruled out any attempt to reformulate Euro-Mediterranean dialogue or politics. The last two years of his second term were decisive on this front. Tensions between Spain and Morocco that started in 1999 and led to the retirement of the Moroccan ambassador to Madrid in 2001 and clashes over the ratification of the fisheries agreements, culminated with the incident on Perejil island between 11-20 July 2002. The Moroccan government set up base on the disputed island explaining that the presence there was needed to better control illegal immigration. However the tension with the Spanish government started straight away.

This happened three months after the Valencia meeting and the response of the international community was illuminating. This is crucial to understanding how the dynamics between Spain and the EU had started to shift. The Spanish response to that event was massive and disproportionate and clear evidence of a new level of power projection. Both Commission president Romano Prodi and the Danish EU presidency urged Rabat to leave the island. Gillespie has considered that this avoidable conflict evidenced another failure of the CFSP and the lack of commitment both from the Spanish and Moroccan side to remain committed to the exigencies of the EMP (Gillespie, 2003).

This event can also be analysed from a different perspective that views Aznar's political strategy, as driven by personal ambition, which in turned generated a negative political response from European partners such as France and Germany. The consequences were negative. As Fernando Jaúregui explains:

> ["They generate arrogance. Aznar thought that in a given moment Spain could dominate and lead Europe and he allied with the wrong people, against those countries that are Europe's engine: France and Germany. And obviously, both France and Germany did not forget this movement"] (Jauregui, 2011).

In effect, the Perejil affair highlighted the lack of support from the big European powers for Spain. It also highlighted, as it has been said above, the weaknesses in the Common Foreign and Security Policy mechanism. Ultimately the US, in the form of secretary of state Colin Powell, had to intervene to mediate the clash. This in turn marked a clear point when Aznar and his senior officials chose to move away from the European political sphere and establish a stronger alliance with the US. The relationship between France and Spain became more difficult and Aznar later accused Jacques Chirac of causing problems for Spain during the crisis.

However, according to Barreñada, Martín and Sanahuja and Iglesias Cavicchioli, the most relevant event that changed definitely the Aznar's conception of foreign policy was 9/11 (Barreñada, Martín and Sanahuja, 2004). Aznar's political discourse started to be strongly influenced by the fight against terrorism a new political window, to be used to propel Spain to a leading global role.

Strategically speaking the post 9/11 context was favourable to this approach. As Sistiaga has pointed out, from 2001 to 2002 the fight against the terrorism constituted the main pillar, of both Spain's domestic and foreign policies (Sistiaga, 2003). This reminds us of and reinforces the point made above that for Aznar the best foreign policy was one that was also at the heart of domestic policy.

It is arguable that Aznar's own personal experience as a victim of a terrorist attack in 1995, influenced this approach. Certainly the centrality of terrorism in his political discourse and diplomatic action was a constant from 2001 to 2004.

In January 2002 during a speech setting out Spain's EU presidency programme in Strasbourg, Aznar proposed to work to develop three main priorities: To design a response against the terrorism; to create an area of greater economic prosperity to safeguard the European social model; to work towards the consolidation of the foundations required for an enlarged Union.

From this perspective, his approach found a staunch supporter in US president George W. Bush who saw in Aznar ["a firm combatant in the fight against terrorism"] (Aznar, 2003). Both leaders believed that the future of the global peace depended upon the disarmament of Iraq and Bush claimed that Aznar was championing the battle against the post 9/11 threats at the UN, the EU and inside NATO.

Aznar's decision to develop an increasingly presidential foreign policy, the alignment with Washington and the preoccupation with terrorism had negative effects in the medium term. Most importantly, it pushed Spain away from its past role as a valued interlocutor with the Arab world and from its tendency to see its foreign policy in terms of the interests of the EU's common foreign policy. As Fernández Molina stated, if since the Spain's accession to the EU, the socialist governments consolidated the relationship between the European dimensions and the Mediterranean, Aznar, oversaw the separation. In effect the triangular Spanish-EU-Mediterranean relationship was substituted by a Spanish-US-Mediterranean relationship.

## 2.6 Aznar *versus* the EU? A Converging Attitude, Different Approaches

From 2001 to 2002 onwards, after 9/11 Aznar's rhetoric integrated more the elements Islam and Arab world. However his most important rhetoric resource, his most important "product" as political broker, was terrorism. The graphic below shows the number of articles where the selected variables are represented and they correspond to his entire political life. Beyond the most representative geographical variables, it is possible to see how terrorism and global occupy both third and fourth position, whereas Arab/Islam are underrepresented.

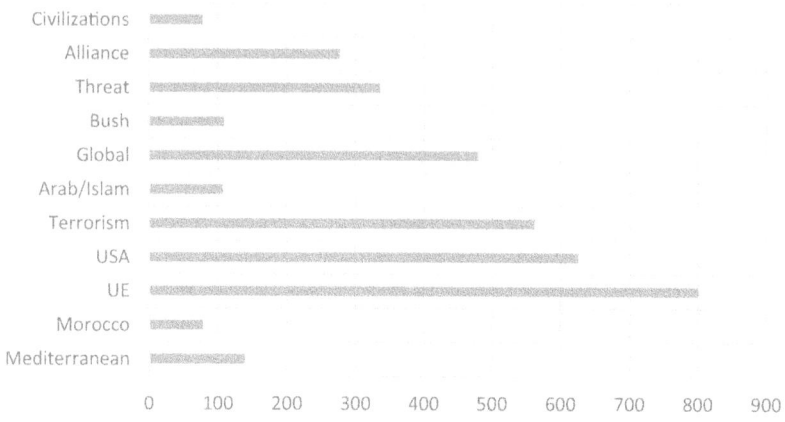

Graphic 3. José María Aznar, Discours 1983–2013.
Source: www.jmaznar.es Elaborated by the author.

Aznar was convinced that his foreign policy would make Spain an international power of the first rank. Over his second mandate his speech towards Islam and the Arab world was moderated. During his first visit to Egypt in 2000 he mentioned that the Arab, Islamic and Jewish heritage that is present in Spain's history gives the opportunity to Spain to become a mediator with the Arab world (Nafie, 2000). During his official trip to Iran in 2000 he even said that ["Hezbollah is a movement, a Lebanese stream (...) that it is fighting for the country's freedom, with a lot of sacrifices and, in reality, it is the symbol of the Lebanese resistance against their occupants"] (Aznar, 2000).

After 9/11 his discourse immediately started to be aligned towards the theses –fight on global terror – defended by the Bush administration. This context represented the best opportunity for Aznar as a political broker to launch his foreign policy despite the lack of consensus from most of European countries, including Spain. In October 2001, he explained to the Congress of Deputies that Spain decided to join the US in Afghanistan because after 9/11 ["it has been created a new alliance of countries, sharing a consensus without precedents in contemporary history: active consensus against the terrorism"] (Aznar, 2001). He also stated that the ["Islam practiced by those fanatics, is an historic invention (...) and this battle is not against Islam"] (Aznar, 2001). Therefore it is clear that Aznar splits up and does not generalise –at least rhetorically speaking – over the concepts of terrorism and Islam. This idea was repeated in Madrid during Mubarak's official visit to Spain one month later when he said that ["Spain was not in conflict neither with Islam nor with among cultures"] (Aznar, 2001). However, it is clear how he tries to convince the deputies by arguing that the new diplomatic alliance has not precedent in the contemporary history, what places Aznar –he wants to place himself – in a central position within this new historical moment.

As Bush's foreign policy started to be more focused on the weapons of mass destruction (WMD) owned by Saddam Hussein, Aznar was more convince about his support to the US and his support was the strongest in history as Iglesias-Cavicchioli has stated (Iglesias Cavicchioli, 2007). One of the most relevant events of this period was represented by the Azores Summit where Bush, Blair and Aznar –and Portuguese President José Manuel Durao Barroso – launched an ultimatum to Iraq quoting UN resolutions 1441, 1483 and 1511. This summit can be also assessed as an ultimatum to Iraq but also to the UN. Within this context, Aznar expressed that ["this transatlantic link, this Atlantic solidarity has been always, it is, and it has to continue being, to my mind, a great European commitment"] (Aznar, 2003). Aznar places Europe at the centre of this statement complaining for the lack of support to his foreign policy.

Spain's president was aware of both this lack of European and Spanish support. In the same intervention he mentioned that they knew that the international public opinion was very worried about these developments, however ["we also know very well our responsibilities and our obligations"] (Aznar, 2003). It is clear that Aznar was defying the international public opinion. In line with this example during a personal interview with Fernando Jaúregui he said:

> ["During a lunch with him – Aznar – I asked: *The 85 percent of the Spanish public opinion is against the intervention in Iraq. How do you dare to maintain that policy?* Aznar replied: *It is characteristic of the statesman to defy the public opinion when is convenient*"] (Jaúregui, 2011).

In questioning this challenging and provocative attitude towards both the international and the Spanish public opinion, some months later – after the killing of seven Spanish soldiers in Iraq – Aznar had to explain to the Spanish Deputies Congress – 2 December 2003 – his political stances and manipulative political communication strategies, especially once it was also demonstrated that WMD did not exist (Kull,

2003). In defending his postures, he stated that we ["are defending the international peace and the international security and also combating a network of international terrorist. They are threatening our lives and liberties. The withdrawal cannot be an option to terrorism"] (Aznar, 2003).

Analyses on this speech have been also conducted by van Dijk, Pujante and Morales López. (Van Dijk, 2005). According to the last two authors Aznar developed his speech following three ideological meanings. First, terrorism represents a global threat and within this global threat is possible to place ETA as well. Second, Spanish support to the US is embedded in a universal mission. Third, ["the PP government has the clearest insight into our destiny as a nation"] –the nationalistic vision – (Pujante and Morales, 2008). In fact, Aznar was very much interested in defending his posture because he focused mostly on internal security matters –due to his nationalistic approach – and the fight against ETA. That is why Aznar was very interested in getting the US support and acknowledgement of ETA as an international terrorist organization.

Aznar's foreign policy strategy was characterized by a number of inconsistencies and contradictions, as well as political opportunism and incoherence. While in office he repeatedly argued that his policies challenged such failings. In a speech in Washington in 2003, for example, he said: ["I think that the political action, the coherence and maybe, or surely, responsibility, do not always trigger applause; but they are, at the end of the day, the elements that create trust within the citizens to whom is commended the task of governing and adopting decisions"] (Aznar, 2003). Aznar was convinced that over his eight years in office he was able to create an economically strong country and a respected medium size power within the international realm, although this does not mean that Spain became a leading international player.

The Mediterranean and North Africa occupied fourth place on Aznar's list of foreign policy priorities going into the 2004 elections behind Europe, Latin America and the US and transatlantic relations. Officials working in the Mediterranean at the time were not impressed (Partido Popular, 2003). As EU Ambassador to Morocco Eneko Landaburu explained in an interview with the author:

> ["For me Aznar's policy was very negative for Spain's interests. Aznar and his people were not committed to Europe. They are Spanish nationalists, and they believe that, all of a sudden, when the things change economically and they go

well, they think that they can play a new role alone within the international community being a privileged ally of the US. And of course, at the end of the day they consider Europe as simply a source of structural funds to ensure the development"] (Landaburu, 2011).

Ambassador Landaburu added that in Europe, Spain under Aznar was increasingly not considered as a partner. It was, at least by some, viewed as nationalistic, anti-French and not truly European. Another interpretation is that under Aznar, Spain, or at least the Spanish right wing, regained its own ideology, history and identity. This however, may well be the Spain that fears other Europeans, refused to trust liberal ideas and placed its interests alongside those of the US under George W. Bush. For all these reasons, Ambassador Landaburu argues, Spain lost significant influence (Landaburu, 2011).

Consistent and coherent public discourse and political actions and policies constitute the fundamental pillars of international dialogue, especially a dialogue maintained between stakeholders separated by cultural, religious, demographic, economic and political factors. The strategy developed by Aznar deepened the initial inconsistencies that existed in the past. He did so by accentuating a type of political entrepreneurship focused on the fight against terrorism and building up ties with a US administration deeply distrusted in Europe, the Arab world and North Africa.

However, it results also necessary to explain and understand if this European disagreement towards Aznar's foreign policy is completely justified. To be justified the EU would have to follow a different and more integrative approach with regards to its foreign policy especially focusing on Mediterranean issues. Following the CL approach and searching for the same variables as in the precedent case the next graphic has been produced. This graphic considers Aznar's second mandate and covers the period 2001–2004.

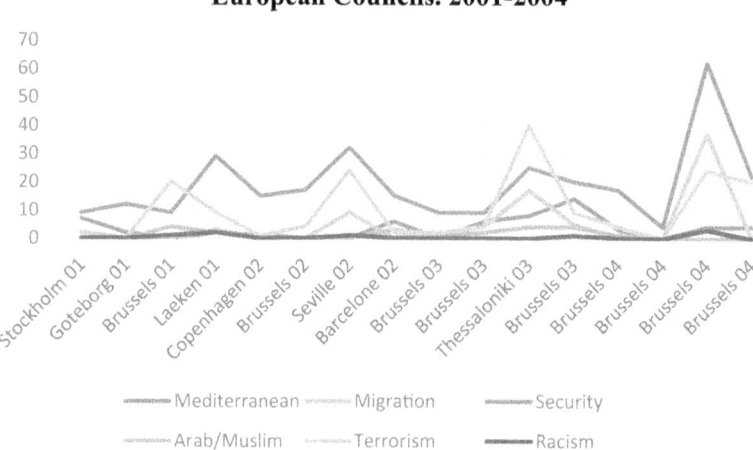

**Graphic 4.** European Council, Conclusions of the Presidency
Source: European Council. Elaborated by the Author.

As the graphic number shows, over this period beyond the security issue that remains the most important concern, there are also two variables that were not especially relevant during the last period 1996–2000: terrorism and migration. The aftermaths of the 9/11 provoked these reactions. During the council of Laeken in 2001, it was already commented the necessity to start managing migration flows in order to control illegal migration and crime as well as the need of strengthening the Area of Freedom, Security and Justice in a context in which "religious fanaticism, ethnic nationalism, racism and terrorism are on increase, and regional conflicts, poverty and underdevelopment still provide a constant seedbed for them" (European Council, Laeken, 2001). This statement marked the trend to follow in the successive years.

During the Council celebrated in Seville in 2002, it was said that terrorism was a ["real challenge for Europe and the world and poses a threat on our security and our stability"] (European Council, Seville, 2002). Therefore it was highlighted the importance of strengthening the contribution of the CFSP and the ESDP in order to fight against this European and global threat.

Variables like Muslims, Islam or Arabs were not present over the last period of study. However over this period these variables were raised several times, linking them to security, migration or terrorism beyond the traditional Israeli-Palestinian conflict. Already during the extraordinary European Council celebrated in Brussels in 2001 it was mentioned that the European Council ["needs to combat any nationalistic, racist or xenophobic drift, just as it rejects any terrorism with the Arab and Muslim world"] (European Council, Brussels, 2001).

The linkage between Muslims/Arabs and terrorism/security was integrated then within the European public discourse of this period. In 2002 during the second meeting celebrated in Brussels, Iran and its nuclear plan was related to terrorism and its relations with the rest of the Middle East (European Council, Brussels, 2003). In order to face and to deal with this problem from 2003 to 2004 it was stressed the importance of ["deepen the dialogue and collaboration in all fields with the Arab and Islamic worlds"] (European Council, Brussels, 2003).

The lack of tangible results provided by the EMP since its inception in 1995 urged the EU to invent new and parallel mechanisms to deal with these challenges. Within this context in 2003 it was proposed the Wider Europe New Neighbourhood Initiative –afterwards ENP – that originally was supposed to reinforce the activities developed by the EMP.

Migration represents the other relevant variable given that the migratory flows from Southern Mediterranean countries skyrocketed within this context of increasing "securitization" as it will be explained in Chapter 5. In spite of the successful Euro-Mediterranean conferences of Naples, Palermo, Venice and Rome – 2003 – during the third Council celebrated in 2003 in Brussels, it was raised the question of the adoption of ["the mechanisms for monitoring and evaluating third countries against illegal migration"] following the principles implemented by the European Security Strategy and taking into account the existing policies and programmes of the EMP and the ENP.

Over 2004, as it is possible to see in the graphic, migration, terrorism and security related issues were the correlated variables that topped European Council's agenda. Within this context during the 1st Council celebrated in Brussels that year, it was raised the question of the necessity of implementing a strategic partnership with the Mediterranean and the Middle East (European Council, Brussels, 2004). During the 3rd Council celebrated in 2004 the correlation between security and migration was definitely evident. It was proposed to intensify the cooperation and dialogue on migration and asylum with Mediterranean countries together with terrorism and border control.

As it is possible to say the variables used and correlated by Aznar and his foreign policy and EU's public speech and approaches did not differ strongly. Both kept the same tone and approach towards Southern Mediterranean countries and linked security problems. Therefore, it is true that Aznar tried to follow his own political strategy beyond the European circles, however, both the objectives and the philosophy was almost the same.

## 2.7 Aznar's Strong Political Stances and the End of His Mandate

Gustavo de Arístegui, a Spanish diplomat affiliated to the PP has made the point that it was important to increase the international cooperation and promote stability, prosperity and freedom in the Islamic world in general and especially in neighbouring countries. And the way to do so should be through cooperation and dialogue (Aristegui, 2000). Aznar as a political broker was also interested in using the Centrist Democrat International (CDI) –evolution of the Christian Democrat International (CDI) – as a platform to increase this dialogue and to overcome the idea of war of civilizations or religions. During the CDI international conference celebrated in June 2003 Aznar said: ["Is it possible to say that we have already overcame the threat the Islamic world posed to the Western world?"] (Aznar, 2003).

However, it is not possible to increase cooperation and dialogue if the basis of such communication is bound up with the securitization and criminalization of the migration issue. The consequence was a notable isolation of Spain from the EU's political objectives and policies and the weakening of the mechanisms that allowed in the past a more fluent communication with the Arab world, specially after supporting the invasion of Iraq and after being aligned with the US. However, Aznar tried to defend several times that his foreign policy did not isolated Spain.

In fact, in 2003 he stated that he was proud that Spain was not living isolated because the real isolation would come through ["some socialist and communist proposals that bring straight away to an international isolation and straight away towards the confrontation against our allies in the international world"] (Aznar, 2003).

As Fernando Jaúregui said during a personal interview with regards to the foreign policy towards North Africa and the Middle East: (Aznar) ["destroyed everything that was built in the past"] (Jaúregui, 2011).

This view is also shared by Keating (Keating, 2010). Aznar's attitudes and foreign policy defined him as a political broker. As a politician who speculated deploying a political communication strategy defined to achieve his objectives rather than constructing an environment of co-operation and social peace.

The Madrid bombings of 11 March 2004 confirmed that Aznar's foreign policy provoked reactions from the radical Islamist rim (Reinares, 2010). Soon after the PP lost the elections because Aznar kept on confirming stubbornly that ETA was responsible for the attack. The US immediately rejected this hypothesis (Lara, 2010). Despite these episodes Aznar during a seminar held in Siena in July 2004 –four months after the elections – said: ["I believed in the role of Spain as an active and constructive nation within the international realm and I did whatever I could over the eight years of government to achieve that. And I think that in part I achieved it. I equally believed that the transatlantic link was the backbone of our security and prosperity and I did as much as I could to reinforce it"] (Aznar, 2004).

After his mandate Aznar became more outspoken with regards to the Arab and Muslim world. In 2006 he spoke at the Hudson Institute in Washington. In assessing Pope Benedict XVI's latest considerations on violence and Islam, he said that ["Muslims should apologize for occupying Spain for 800 years and an UN-backed programme to encourage dialogue between them and West is stupid. (…) it is them or it is us. There is no middle ground"] (Aznar, 2006). This confirmed his real nationalistic and catholic-rooted stances towards Islam.

Jose Luis Rodriguez Zapatero replaced him as Spanish leader. One of his primary tasks was reactivating the previous Spanish role as a bridge between Europe and Southern Mediterranean countries.

# 3 Zapatero's Attempt to Reposition Spain in the Mediterraean

Following the 2004 Spanish elections, the PSOE after 8 years in opposition, was now back in power. The new government critiqued the PP for breaking the "Política de Estado" in the realm of foreign affairs while in office. During his inaugural speech Zapatero, talked about re-developing a foreign policy where all major political forces would share the same objectives and approach (Del Arenal, 2004). Even though he recognised that Spain's new time could not start from scratch but taking advantage of a shared political experience that has evolved over different phases (Zapatero, 2004). However Catalan party Convergència i Unió (CiU) in September 2004 criticized Zapatero's political stances by saying that it seemed that he wanted to establish a ["new transition"] (Fied, 2009). A second transition that, as Woodworth has mentioned, he seemed to be unaware ["of the legacy of the first transition"] (Woodworth, 2005).

It was now a priority for Spain to return to its central role in European affairs. In fact PSOE's five political axes were represented by: a renewed public life; a foreign policy characterized by a European and Europeanist vision; economic development supported by education, research and innovation; new social policies and; development and expansion of civil and political rights and equality. Aznar may have attacked González for begging from Europe in 1992 but was Spain's support for German reunification that won his government the support of Germany in its foreign policy approach and in its effort to become one of the biggest beneficiaries of the EU cohesion fund (Marks, 1996).

The bombings in Madrid represented the extremist response to a foreign policy that increasingly developed a more public speech slanted to US's foreign policy theses. In his inaugural speech, Zapatero stressed the fact that Aznar's decisions in foreign policy were wrong in issues that affected Spain's coexistence and progress. In analysing Zapatero's discourse it is important to note that his speech started mentioning the Madrid bombings and the victims. Beyond the contextual importance of this event, the bombings represented the material evidence of Aznar's mistakes and the issue of terrorism topped again Spain's political agenda. In his discourse, Zapatero mentioned 18 times the variable terrorism whereas another important issue such as democracy was mentioned 4 times. Now, following his accession to power in March 2004, Zapatero looked to return to the mandate of Felipe González following a legacy of ["dialogue, respect, pluralism, tolerance and transparency"].

As Gillespie and Youngs have noted, by the early 1990s Spanish foreign policy interests were channelled and pursued overwhelmingly through Europe (Gillespie and Youngs, 2007). The success of this depended on Spain's ability to sell its particular geographic interests. As has been stressed by Viñas and Pollack and Hunter, North Africa and by extension, the Mediterranean represented an essential part of that tradition (Pollack and Hunter, 1987; Viñas, 1999).

But following the Aznar era, the environment was especially challenging with regards to the reactivation of the Spain's role in the Mediterranean. The new socialist government had to face a very peculiar political, social, cultural and economic context. An unknown leader lacking charisma, José Luis Rodriguez Zapatero faced a tough task in re-asserting Spain's position as global political entrepreneur.

## 3.1 Back to the Mediterranean. Back to the Roots

In 2004, Spain's new foreign minister, Miguel Ángel Moratinos, an expert on Middle East and Mediterranean issues looked to develop a new foreign policy to rebuild the consensual role that he believed Spain had lost during the Aznar era (Moratinos, 2004). In considering the Aznar era Moratinos stressed that:

> ["Spain during the last 25 years, knew how to develop [a genuine State policy] through a integrative spirit, understanding that all decisions in the foreign policy ambit are rooted on internal reasons, and, by adopting them, revert to the ambit of domestic policy. A responsible government should know what it wants and what is in the interests of its country; only on this basis is it possible to develop a coherent foreign policy, solid and ambitious"] (Moratinos, 2004).

Though some argued that Moratinos was not a strong supporter of the EU, the first step towards this was the rapprochement with the EU (the informant prefers not to be quoted). Without this initial movement it would not be possible to propose and legitimize complex policies and mechanisms. Moreover, it was required to achieve both political consensus and support and the financial means to develop new policies focused on Spain's diplomatic and politic interests. This was the same strategy Felipe González followed from 1986 onward. First Europe. Second, the identification of a political window that would benefit national interests. Third, an action of political lobbying in order to get political and diplomatic support and financial means to increase diplomatic power and presence.

Strategically speaking, following this return to Europe, so to speak, was the need to identify a political window that would benefit national interests. This included a new relationship with the US based on the principle of sovereign equality, as set out in the 1988 Cooperation Agreement. However, Zapatero's distant approach towards the US marked one of his most important U-turns with regards to Aznar's foreign policy. As Cavicchioli has mentioned, Zapatero was the first Spanish prime minister in the thirty years of democracy that has not had any summit with an American president over the first years of mandate (Cavicchioli, 2007). As Woodworth pointed out Zapatero was very interested in taking Spain out from ["that photograph in the Azores"] (Woodworth, 2004). In April 2004 Zapatero ordered Spain's Minister of Defence José Bono to withdraw Spanish troops from Afghanistan as soon as possible. Nevertheless, Zapatero had to pay the price of placing Spain away from the US. US government, press and public opinion ignored Zapatero in numerous times (González, 2010).

Moratinos also elaborated on relations with Latin America and the Middle East and the Mediterranean. Moratinos appointment as foreign minister had confirmed Spanish intentions with regards to the Arab-Israeli conflict, the Western Sahara conflict, and Iraq. His approach, like that of his prime minister, was based on dialogue, negotiation, cooperation. On the other hand, the new Spanish foreign policy with the US changed its views as far as Jauregui pointed out, Moratinos has been a diplomat concentrated on the Palestinian side, not on the Israeli one (Jaúrequi, 2011).

In Zapatero's inaugural address in office he noted his desire to place dialogue, understanding and respect to other's opinions at the centre of his foreign policy.["I am willing to make this the legislature of dialogue, understanding and, the meeting (…) In the Mediterranean we have to recover the objective of the dialogue, the understanding and cooperation present in the declaration of Barcelona"] (Zapatero, 2004). In considering his priorities, Zapatero explained in an interview for this book that:

> ["Improving relations with Morocco was an important objective that I established for our foreign policy towards the Mediterranean. Since then, relations with Rabat have been acquiring greater specific weight, covering all the fields

and permeating all the sectors integrating a strategic relation of neighbourhood. This spans from tight cooperation on issues such as the fight against the illegal immigration or the terrorism, to economic relations and Euro-Mediterranean co-operation"] (Personal interview Zapatero, 2011).

Here it is possible to see that the conception and political postures with regards to the Maghreb as a whole and to Morocco in particular, marked the most evident difference between the PP and the PSOE. Actually approaches to the Western Sahara issue were probably where the strongest differences between the PP and the PSOE lay. In effect, as Fernández Molina recognises, the accession of the PSOE to power coincided with a moment where Morocco addressed the proposals of former US secretary of state James Baker –Plan Baker II-, which had been approved by the UN Security Council on 31 July 2003 (Fernández Molina, 2003).

The PSOE supported new plans put forward by Rabat. These plans would guarantee the independence of the Western Sahara territory under Moroccan sovereignty. While the proposal covered socio-cultural aspects that were common to past Spanish approaches to the problem, the Spanish embrace was viewed in some quarters as evidence of the abandonment of the traditional Spanish position on this sensitive issue. Ruiz Miguel, for example, argued that it would be prejudicial to Spain's national interests as it would be the legitimisation of independence for the Western Sahara (Ruiz Miguel, 2006).

As mentioned previously according to Bardají and Portero, who were clearly criticising the new PSOE government's Moroccan policy (Bardají and Portero, 2007), the PP was more interested in developing commercial relations with Algeria. This policy unbalanced regional dynamics and created more complex situations and misunderstandings between Madrid and Rabat.

Zapatero came to power at the same time as the Barcelona Process reached its tenth anniversary. As President Zapatero stated during a personal interview:

["When I acceded to the Presidency, I felt a very wide support from Europe, and in general from the whole international sphere. We were conscious of the weight and influence of Spain, and I perceived that it would be possible to reinforce Spain's role as global actor (…) The European policy towards the Mediterranean shows Spanish efforts to establish the bases in order to create a space of peace, security and prosperity between both rims. This approach was defined in 1995 with the signature of the Barcelona Declaration, that illuminated the Euro-Mediterranean Association. Spain was central in this process and continued being crucial for the construction of the institutional architecture of the Euro-Mediterranean Association until the creation of the Union for the Mediterranean in 2008"] (Zapatero, 2011).

There are few politicians or diplomats who would openly criticise the Barcelona process. Ambassador Navarro described it as a multidimensional political programme that deserves praise on a number of levels, notably as the "only place" where Israel and Syria sat together (Navarro, 2012). Ambassador Landaburu, speaking more pragmatically acknowledged that:

["We made many mistakes, very big mistakes. One of these mistakes was that we believed that we could develop a dialogue with these Arab countries, from region to region without taking into consideration the internal fractures that exist in these countries. Another mistake is that we did not took into consideration the radical influence in the conflict between Israel and Palestine"] (Landaburu, 2011).

As has been already mentioned, the Barcelona process was based on the conviction that a neo-liberal economic and trade model would trigger off long-term socio-political and cultural transformations to the benefit of Euro-Mediterranean relations. However, as Bassols pointed out, the key point of the Barcelona process was the creation of the Mediterranean free trade area by 2010 was the only exact date that was present in the Barcelona declaration. This target date was very important for the EC because, as Bassols has highlighted, Europe had very strong commercial policy but ["today if we would have proposed the same, Southern Mediterranean partners would not have accepted"] (Bassols, 2012).

While this objective –the economic one – was partly the reason for the weakness of the process, it is debatable whether Aznar's political shift towards the Atlantic during his second term deserves the majority blame for this. According to Ambassador Eneko Landaburu: ["I don't think so. I mean, the strength we had was not important enough to leave a gap in case of disappearing"] (Landaburu, 2011). On top of this Spain's priorities did not cause the divisions within the Mediterranean countries that made progress on the Barcelona front so difficult.

On the other hand and putting aside the technical difficulties of the Barcelona Process, the ENP was conceptualized between 2002 and 2004 but it was implemented in 2007, and highlighted some contradictions in the Euro-Mediterranean Policy's philosophical and practical pillars. Nevertheless as Ambassador Landaburu stressed, ["we luckily had the capacity of launching and developing the ENP. Because at least that has allowed us to maintain certain contact with southern Mediterranean partners"] (Landaburu, 2011). As Barbé, Mestres and Soler have stressed, within this period of time both the PP and the PSOE had two splendid opportunities to re-launch Spain as a Mediterranean power by hosting two important conferences (Barbè et Al., 2007).

As mentioned in the preceding chapter, Aznar had a very good opportunity during the Valencia conference in 2002 to showcase Spanish diplomatic power (Gillespie, 2003). In Barcelona in 2005 the PSOE hosted a celebration of the Euro-Mediterranean Summit that reflected its goal to ["re-launch the Barcelona Process with strength and determination"] (PSOE, 2004). The PSOE also wanted to build a new defence and security policy, and develop transatlantic relations, Latin America and the Mediterranean.

Zapatero also wanted to use the Euro-Mediterranean Summit to show Europe, and his PP critics, that he had a vision for Spain and a vision for Spain in the international arena. In fact what the PP criticised more of Zapatero's foreign policy was his vision of Spain. As Carnero has stated, Zapatero did not have a clear idea of which kind of Spain he wanted to defend and without that clear idea it was difficult to defend and develop a coherent foreign policy (Carnero, 2007).

These initial diplomatic efforts began to be rewarded during the Euro-Mediterranean Ministerial meeting held in The Hague in 2004. During this conference, 2005 was chosen as the Year of the Mediterranean. The Barcelona meeting the following year, attended by leading figures from of almost all the EU members, was the main event celebrating this. However the majority of the Southern Mediterranean members did not send top level representatives. However, the 2005 Barcelona conference was intended first and foremost, from a Spanish perspective, to gain support from the UK, who held the EU presidency between June and December. This came at a time of major crisis inside the Community with the Dutch and French 'No' votes on the EU Constitutional Treaty (Whitman, 2006).

The UK wanted initially to preside over a low key presidency. However, Prime Minister Blair, in June 2005, ultimately presented himself as the saviour of the EU in its time of crisis. This was important for Zapatero's purposes. Blair's public support for an early Turkish accession into the EU and his wider approach to the Mediterranean was very much in line with Zapatero's approach. The British leader declared that the accession of Turkey to the EU would be clear proof that ["Europe is committed not just in word but indeed to a Europe of diverse races, cultures and religions, all bound together by common rules and a sense of human solidarity and mutual respect"] (Kubicek, 2005). This request represents the cornerstone of any Euro-Mediterranean policy or mechanism. If rhetoric is not ensued by concrete facts – measurable facts within the sort, medium and long term that involve and empower southern Mediterranean countries beyond European interests – these policies and projects are doomed to fail.

This UK leadership was important for Zapatero's purposes. The Turkish accession was actually very much criticised long time ago by France. As Leparmentier and Zecchini remind, Valerie Giscard D'Estaing, manifested that the Turkish accession to the EU would mean the end of the EU (Leparmentier and Zecchini, 2002). France, on the contrary did not share the same vision. Chirac did not follow the extremist vision of D'Estaing and reluctantly said that the French population should be call to decide upon referendum (Mathieson, 2005). Zapatero also considered that an earlier accession of Turkey to the EU would contribute to the creation of a space of security and prosperity.

Zapatero started to develop his foreign policy from where Felipe González decided to act: the Mediterranean. At this time it was suggested that Spain should be leading Mediterranean politics as Germany was leading Eastern politics (Claret, 2005). Once the Mediterranean political window was definitely re-identified as the opportunity to increase Spain's diplomatic stature, it was necessary to formalise this ambition with a concrete mechanism.

## 3.2 The Alliance of Civilizations: Building on the Sand

Contextual elements such as increasing influx of migrants from Southern Mediterranean countries or the threat of terrorism of Islamic matrix among others provided Zapatero a good starting point to design and justify Spain's own entrepreneurial proposal. Diplomatically speaking a number of initiatives started to develop in the aftermaths of the 9/11. On one hand, the UN defined 2001 as the Year of Dialogue among Civilizations. As Dallmayr has put it, these initiatives somehow tried to raise awareness on the consequences of an unstoppable globalization process and related consequences on global social justice and inequality (Dallmayr, 2002). In November 2001 the UN General Assembly adopted a resolution aiming at developing the Global Agenda for

Dialogue among Civilizations. Article 6 of 56/6 resolution highlighted that ["governments shall promote, encourage and facilitate dialogue among civilizations"] (UN Resolution, 2001).
This article opened the path for political entrepreneurs willing to fill that gap. However within the short run there was not an immediate response from any particular western government aiming at covering this political opportunity. In February 2002 it was held in Istanbul the Organization of Islamic Countries (OIC)-EU joint initiative. Despite the nature of the meeting –designed to enhance intercultural dialogue – governmental representatives from Iraq, Syria, Iran, Kuwait and Lebanon openly criticized the US for their unilateral efforts in defending homeland interests and its hegemony and Israel for the Palestinian question (Ministry of Foreign Affairs, 2001). These manifestations are the evidence of the challenges any initiative aiming at fostering intercultural communication and dialogue has to face.

This initiative celebrated in Turkey opened the path for a new phase of Turkish foreign policy. As Balci and Mis have highlighted from 2002 onward, new Turkish government administered by Justice and Development Party (JDP) and headed up by Prime Minister Tayyip Erdogan, was interested in accelerating Turkish presence in the world. This new attitude represented a major turning point for Turkey's both domestic and foreign policy (Balci and Mis, 2008). The JDP's ["non-confrontational and consensus-seeking"] approach was relevant for the domestic realm and for international politics alike. This approach was publicised and spread by Erdogan since the beginning of his mandate. Erdogan's approach to become one of the fulcrums of intercultural dialogue summarizes a political strategy that would have facilitated and justified a process of integration to Europe. Process that should have started by 2004 (Erdogan, 2007).

The post 9/11 international context, the interest of Turkey in getting greater international integration by bridging the existing cultural and political gap and the interest of Spain for developing its Mediterranean card announced and justified a Spanish-Turkish joint initiative.

One of his first Zapatero's initiatives a political entrepreneur was his proposal of a project to the UN General Assembly – 24 September 2004 – named Alliance of Civilizations. As it has been noted by Balci, Zapatero's concept of ["alliance" evolved from the concept of "dialogue" that was the central idea from 9/11 onwards. Conversely it was according to Barreñada, an initiative that, though sharing the same theoretical background, challenged Samuel Huntington's "Clash of Civilizations"] thesis (Barreñada, 2006).

However as Balci mentions, the idea of "alliance" entails the acceptance of "clash" and the potential survival of such an initiative would depend on the continuation of such a "clash" of civilizations, otherwise it would not make sense. As Zank has suggested the concept cooperation of civilizations would have entailed a more proactive and less belligerent approach (Zank, 2009). Nevertheless the idea of clash –more sellable politically speaking – was shared both by Zapatero and Erdogan (Balci, 2009). As a matter of fact, Zapatero very timely announced this concept of "alliance of civilizations" right after the Madrid bombings as a way to combat terrorism.

This means that Zapatero reacted like an opportunist and used the concept "alliance" ambivalently: as a means to fight terrorism at a domestic level and to reach international audience as well. This rhetoric strategy using terrorism as a variable to get political and diplomatic consensus, recognition and influence was also used by Aznar as we demonstrated in the precedent chapter. Therefore it is possible to say that Zapatero despite his interest in detaching his foreign policy from Aznar recurred to very similar strategies as a political broker.

Technically speaking, Zapatero's speech at the United Nations followed a very understandable rhetoric. Before presenting his proposal he focused his attention on the threat posed by international and national terrorism. He mentioned 11 times the variable terrorism within his discourse. After that he linked the variables terrorism-security with an alliance between the western and the Arab-Muslim world. Therefore he was narrowing the idea of alliance of civilizations and targeting Western societies versus Islam. None other religion or civilization was mentioned. Hence the concept of "alliance of civilizations" was not appropriate from a philosophical and practical point of view. On 13 June 2005, Turkish Prime Minister Tayyip Erdogan agreed to co-sponsor this initiative with Spain and it was finally adopted in 2007 (Kausch and Barreñada, 2005).

As shown above, French disenchantment towards the EU allowed Spain to identify a new political window by re-launching its EU and global leadership via Mediterranean-related issues. In these terms the Alliance of Civilizations can be considered one of Spain's most successful foreign policy projects within the short and medium term.

In promoting this, Spain was attempting once again to play the role of political broker. However from an organizational point of view, this initiative was neither carefully planned nor strategically developed. The PSOE's electoral programme did not mention it for instance and it has been suggested that this initiative was originally formulated during a flight over the Atlantic a few hours before the UN meeting in New York.

If it was improvised this would reveal one of the most relevant features of Zapatero's government and both policy making and decision-making processes. This improvisation has been harshly criticized by members of FAES, the PP's think-tank. Borrowing the expression coined by Spanish journalist Miguez attacked Zapatero's diplomacy as the "diplomacy of the smile" (Portero, 2005).

So, the argument went, the PSOE's foreign policy would align national interests to the EU's global objectives; would go beyond the defence of national sovereignty and the national dignity; reject the expansion of the liberal democracy because its principles were not universal; the "democratic fundamentalism" incarnated by the US model would represent the main triggering factor of terrorism around the world. Abstraction and relativism seem to be the main ingredients of such diplomacy.

After presenting the idea very abstractly, The Alliance of Civilizations would operate on three main pillars: Anti-terror cooperation, addressing economic inequalities and cultural dialogue. These priorities were set out in a more structured way in 2006 when they were published in a report written by a high level group established under the AoC.

The whole document skirts around the idea of the emergence of Islamic extremism (Anon, 2006). All the other pillars such as cultural dialogue, or the measures to improve socio-economic cleavages were justified as a means to fight against the potential threat of Islamist terrorism. The Spanish newspaper *El País* reported on how the Spanish government in 2004, following the Madrid bombings, had wanted also to propose the renovation of the national pact on international terrorism including cooperation with Muslim countries (Aizpeolea, 2004). The interesting element of this document is that it stressed the necessity of eliminating the link between Islam and terrorism. This trend ensued over the coming years and by 2009 Spanish Ministry of Defence published a document titled: ["From the Clash of Cultures to the Alliance of Civilizations: New Contributions for the Security in the Mediterranean"] (Sanz Roldán, 2009).

All these aspects shaped and determined the impreciseness and blandness of the Alliance of Civilizations. Interestingly, Zapatero's proposal was not far away from Franco's approach with regards to the Arab world. In fact, during the dictatorship, Franco was very much trying to establish diplomatic relations with the Arab world by claiming a sort of shared lineage and history (Kamen, 2004). In fact, during the years of the international isolation Franco developed a sort of cultural diplomacy through the ["Hispano-Arab brotherhood"] (González González, 2007). Regardless these historical reminiscences and similitudes it is important now to assess the consistency and political seriousness of Zapatero and his government as political brokers in presenting and managing this proposal.

## 3.3 A Political Broker Managing an Abstract Political Opportunity

Henry Kamen dissects the Alliance proposal by analysing three important vectors. They are vital to understanding how a political entrepreneur or broker should identify a political window and opportunity and, after that, determine a conceptual and material strategy to achieve objectives within the short, medium and long term. The questions Kamen ask are with whom and with what is the Alliance constituted? Who should finance this project and how? And ending by interrogating on the conceptual, historical and ideological flaws and inconsistencies of the proposal.

On the first point, Zapatero was not interested in – either conceptually or practically – exporting to the Southern Mediterranean and the Middle East "obsolete" concepts such as women rights, freedom of speech, liberal democracy or religious freedom. This cultural relativist approach looked to avoid the imposition of certain values and norms that are constituent features of Western democracies as a way of fostering dialogue.

The opposite would block any potential dialogue according to Zapatero's approach. However, to what extent this hypothesis would work? Is it possible to say that this approach was naïf? Probably it would be more dangerous and would have entailed more risks and failures than benefits. Actually in the aforementioned working paper published by the Spanish Ministry of Defence, Sánz Roldán by quoting scholar Pedro Martínez Montávez, concurred with an idea that is anchored to the dependency theory. He considered that the origin of the problems with the Islamic-Arab contemporary world today is the European colonialist expansion that entered in those geographic spaces without understanding what existed there over the centuries. That generated strong traumas, some of them not solved, like for instance the deep division among Arab people and the great tragedy of the loss of Palestine (Sánz Roldán, 2009).

However, it is practically impossible to ensure a solid alliance between partners through dialogue and mutual understanding alone unless essential political, philosophical and ideological elements are shared. The events of the Arab uprising have demonstrated that Zapatero's hypothesis was wrong. Ambassador Eneko Landaburu addressed this point during a personal interview:

> ["It was tacitly accepted in Europe that these southern countries were going directly towards a political and religious radicalism. What we had to do was maintaining and supporting stabilization policies and that explains the EU's help to Ben Ali, Mubarak and others' regimes. We supported dictators because they ensured us a certain security, because they controlled migration flows and terrorism. And, of course, we did not check closely what they were doing with their citizens. This is the *realpolitik*"] (Landaburu, 2011).

In Strasburg, on 27 January 2011, the Parliamentary Assembly of the Council of Europe (PACE) acknowledged this failing: ["Europe also has its share of responsibility since it failed to condemn the nature of the regimes, preferring to take advantage of its apparent stability to carry out its business"] (Anon, 2011). These two episodes confirm the conceptual, organizational and strategic failure of initiatives such as the Alliance for Civilizations.

Funding requirements were also key for the success of the Alliance of Civilizations. For this, it is essential to map potential stakeholders and "investors" who eventually are going to fund the proposal. But money alone, while it can help to establish and maintain short-term stability in an area, does not necessarily bring substantial or sustained change.

This second aspect is intrinsically related to the first element discussed above. Elaborating a congruent concept and project is crucial before starting mapping potential stakeholders and "investors" who eventually are going to fund the proposal. Initially, the first country to adhere to Zapatero's proposal was Mongolia – 5 % Muslim population-, country that was clearly interested in attracting the attention from the West.

There are some other alliances or associations that are well funded, such as the Arab League, which existence depends greatly on US funds. Since 9/11 the US has been strengthening financial collaboration with Middle Eastern governments aiming at exporting democratic values and norms. As Dalacoura mentions, the USAID increased aid to this region from 2001 and by 2002. Colin Powell launched the Middle

East Partnership (MEPI) – 2002 – in order to support this approach (Cranner, 2006). Within this same context also the US planned to create a free trade area in the region by assuming that an economic liberalization would allow a better implementation of democratic values and practices (Dalacoura, 2005). These alliances can work within the short term normally, thanks to political will, funds, and someone promising to follow and respect certain common principles and values and a set of protocols. However it has been demonstrated how –i.e. Arab spring, African ODA (Riddel, 2007; Moyo and Ferguson, 2010) – even with millionaire figures, socio-economic and political changes are very often doomed to fail. The money can help to establish and maintain –"buy" – stability in an area, but not necessarily provoking neither substantial nor sustained and enduring changes.

Kamen was not sure about how Zapatero could ensure enough financial resources to bolster his initiative. However as is going to be shown Zapatero was able to do so. Nevertheless, probably a better question then would be; once the diplomatic and financial support has been achieved, how is going to be used those resources? According to that it is fundamental to set the precise criterions that should be guaranteeing the efficiency and sustainability of the project. These aspects are related to the capacity or incapacity of managing a complex programme by achieving short, medium and long run objectives. This is going to be discussed later. However a question that could be asked is: to what extent Zapatero and his supporters were interested in effectively solving the existing problems and threats –Islamist terrorism – through the hypothesis of increasing dialogue and mutual understanding? Or, was it enough to try buying the aforementioned stability and the obedience from Southern countries? These questions are answered in the following epigraph.

## 3.4 Lack of Clarity and a Fainted Strategy: Missed Opportunities?

Zapatero was able to gain enough funds to support his initiative. The question then was how were those resources going to be used? The organizational model of any project should be defined by a clear strategy. This is only possible if the political entrepreneur leading the project has identified clearly the political window or opportunity. On top of that it is important that the political broker leading the proposal remains being interested in developing the mechanism forward within the medium and long term. However, from its initial inception the Alliance proposal lacked this coherence and consistency. Linked to this, Zapatero, as Balci has mentioned, lost his motivation in the alliance over the three years after the bombings because ["the lesser the clash threatens to spread in his country, the lesser Spain needs the Alliance"] (Balci, 2009).

This comment would reinforce the idea role of political broker. However the PSOE's 2008–2011 electoral programme showed a different approach. The second section of the program was dedicated to foreign affairs under the title ["A stronger Spain within a fairer world"] (PSOE, 2008). The sequence of priorities –the top five ones – presented by the PSOE was as follows: Alliance of Civilizations for peace and protection of human rights; co-operation and development; Latin America; transatlantic relations; promotion of peace, democracy and development in the Mediterranean. This means that the flagship of Zapatero's foreign policy remained the AoC.

Using CL to analyse relevant variables of the proposed program it is possible to appreciate that policy development at different levels, cooperation and security were the some of the most representative variables and this is shown in graphic 16. That expresses the priorities and approach the PSOE wanted to communicate to the voters. A second layer would be integrated by issues such as migration, human rights, future and terrorism whereas AoC was mentioned more times than the word crisis –element that is almost as quoted as radical Islam-. This is meaningful especially considering that from 2008 onward Spain started to suffer the consequences of a rampant –global and national – economic and financial crisis. This crisis was initially accepted in July 2008 and communicated to the congress in September 2008 (Navas and García, 2008).

## Variables

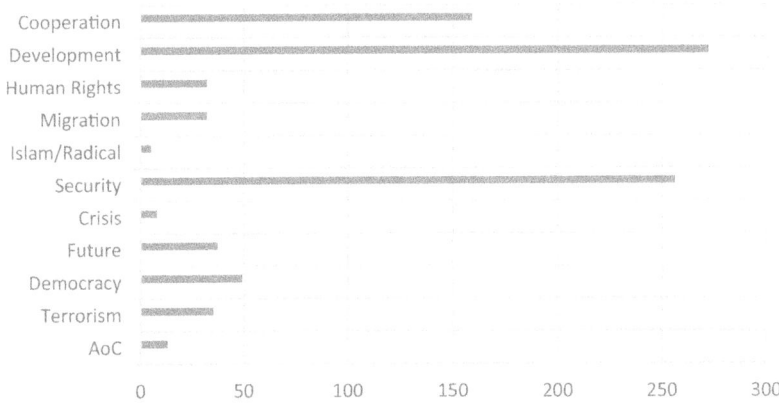

Graphic 5. PSOE 2008–2011 Electoral Program
Source: PSOE Electoral Program. Elaborated by the Author.

Considering this renewed interest in the AoC as the main diplomatic mechanism to propel Spain's role in international politics, it is important to assess how the initiative was managed from 2008 onward. Zapatero's second mandate would have been important for the consolidation of the AoC.

The first AoC Global Forum was celebrated in Madrid in January 2008 (UNAOC, 2008). In April 2009 a second forum was held in Istanbul (UNAOC, 2009). In analysing the reports produced after these two summits it is possible to say, that according to what it was said before, the AoC was an initiative that bipolarised –since the beginning and over its consolidation phase – the concept of "civilizations". The tension Western/Islam worlds is evident. As the graphic number 17 shows, among the selected variables "religion" represents the most quoted concept. The variables "muslim", "Islam" and "arab" are also relevant and superior when compared with some other potential competitors such as "indus" "jews" "protestants" or "catholics". It is also relevant to appreciate how geographical factors place the initiative very close to Europe, whereas the US plays a marginal role in contributing to the AoC. Therefore it is possible to define the AoC as a Eurocentric initiative that has assumed and incorporated the concept of clash of civilizations.

## Variables

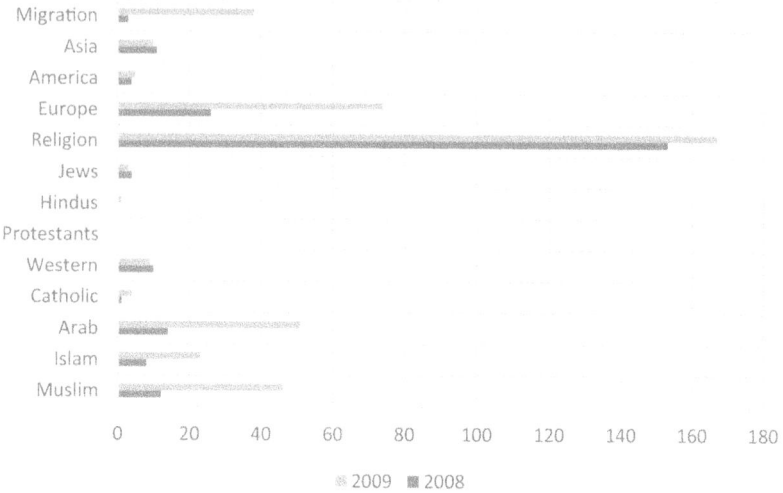

Graphic 6. AoC Madrid 2008–Istambul 2009.
Source: UNAOC Reports, Madrid and Istanbul. Elaborated by the Author.

As the precedent comments and graphic number 17 suggest, the AoC was not conceived neither as global alliance nor as an inclusive mechanism. This biased and asymmetric approach –especially over the period of consolidation – endangered the sustainability of the proposal. As Lachmann has stressed, the ["universalistic outlook of such efforts is challenged by the essential place of states, the singling out of tensions between the 'West' and the 'Muslim world' which points to exclusionary tendencies, and the reliance on security references to favour stakeholdership by international actors in the community-building attempt"] (Lachmann, 2011).

In assuming these institutional and organisational limitations, the selection process of new members and supporters can deepen existing unbalances especially if they contribute to potentially increase this asymmetry. Over 2008 and 2009 Spanish diplomacy played a very important role in attracting political and diplomatic supporters. These efforts contributed to the creation of the AoC group of friends (UN, 2011). This group grew up to 136 members by 2013 (MAEC, 2013). Within this strategic effort of project building Spain and involved partners worked to achieve a greater recognisance. In November 2009 the UN approved resolution 64/14 supporting the activities of the alliance (UN, 2009). Another important partner, the US joined AoC's Group of Friends by May 2010 under Obama's administration. This association accompanied Obama's first steps in foreign policy focused on the rapprochement between Western and Muslim Worlds. His political and diplomatic stances towards the achievement of this objective were expressed during his speech ["A new beginning"]in Cairo on 4 June 2009 (Obama, 2009).

As it has been said above, within AoC's phase of consolidation choosing controversial partners might entail miscommunication consequences and therefore potential failures. For instance, some Israeli media players considered that Obama was joining a "pro-Muslim" association (Levi Julian, 2010). However, considering the ethos of the Alliance and its peculiarities the most controversial partner was NATO.

In April 2009, Zapatero offered NATO Secretary General Anders Fogh Rasmussen, the AoC as a platform to help reduce conflict and strengthen coexistence. This offer did not take into account the impact such a NATO role would have in damaging the possibility of strengthening dialogue between "different" civilizations (Sjursen, 2004).

The NATO had both interests and experiences in the Mediterranean. In 1994 NATO established its Mediterranean Dialogue. This originally included Jordan, Mauritania, Morocco, Israel, Tunisia, Algeria and Egypt. This initiative was a clear example of the organisation's attempt to find a political role after the end of the Cold War. Continuing with the focus on the Mediterranean, in 2001 –after 9/11 – the NATO activated the Operation Active Endeavour to fight against terrorism (Mayer, 2011). Following this trend of institutional innovation and identity renovation on 2009 – organization's Sixtieth anniversary – during the NATO summit held in Strassburg/Khel, the heads of state and government adopted the new Declaration on Alliance Security.

Strategically speaking it is possible to say that Zapatero's invitation to NATO would help to damage any existing pillar or possibility to strengthen dialogue between "different" civilizations. Seems to be certain that the NATO over the last years has been trying to find a new identity or a justification to exist. As has been arguing authors like Williams and NewmannNATO has been trying to become a security community (Williamans and Neumann, 2000). This opinion is also shared by Gheciu. She expresses serious doubts, however, about the NATO's real possibilities to become an agent of socialization (Gheciu, 2005).

However, this reorientation, this seek of a new identity, cannot eliminate its history. As Sjursen has argued, the attempt to define NATO as an association or community of liberal democratic values and norms is problematic. Within the first decade of the twenty-first century, these historical and institutional contradictions have become increasingly evident. As has been acknowledged by Razoux, despite NATO's increasing activity in the Mediterranean, its institutional and organizational image remains negative (Razoux, 2008).

Zapatero's belief that NATO was a legitimate partner in the Alliance project shows that he failed to identify a proper political stakeholder to support his agenda in the Mediterranean. This damaged Zapatero's credibility in the Mediterranean as a leader and interlocutor between the Arab and the western worlds. As a direct consequence, the Alliance of Civilizations suffered from this lack of leadership.

By 2009 Spain had to face a contradictory and worrying scenario. On one hand, when the global economic crisis started to hit, Zapatero failed to fully acknowledge the dimensions and scope of the economic crisis (Zapatero, 2008). But at the same time Spain was a participant at the G20 meeting in London, the NATO summit, the EU-US meeting held in Prague and the second meeting of the AoC celebrated in Istanbul where it served as co-president (Moratinos, 2009). As former foreign minister Moratinos acknowledged, the country had re-established its standing and this ["represents a historic moment in the role of Spain's international relations, without precedent in our contemporary history"] (Moratinos, 2009).

From 2004 to 2008, according to Moratinos, Spain's foreign policy and strategy was the removed the unilateralism that characterized Aznar's style of governing. Moratinos believed that Zapatero understood that the new international order of the twenty first century required multilateralism and a global approach to the most pressing issues.

This culminated in the AoC, a multilateral formula that placed Spain at the heart of the international system. However both Spain's and Zapatero's image and reputation as international players were delicate. On one hand new migration dynamics and the way Spain started to manage them, rapidly demonstrated the inconsistency between Zapatero's international speech and more pressing national demands. The increasing securitization of migration related issues promoted a fiscal and punishing image within Southern Mediterranean countries (Lavenex, 2006; Leonard, 2010; Balch, 2010). This hostile image was spread throughout the EU as well as long as countries such as France, the Netherlands, UK and Germany failed their integration processes and started to experience xenophobic sentiments against migrants as Zapata Barrero and Witte have studied (Zapata and De Wite, 2007). These facts were especially salient since the beginning of the global economic crisis (Furlong, 2010).

Therefore both the economic crisis –with the sharp and intense deterioration of the labour market – and new migration policies started darkening Spain's immediate future as a successful Euro-Mediterranean leader (Royo, 2009). In considering this context Spain started to face a very delicate situation. On one hand Spain in behaving as an entrepreneur and broker used migration related issues as one of the most important leverages to get support from the EU and attain greater diplomatic influence. Spain achieved success within the short and medium term. But on the other hand, once Spain had to implement restrictive migration policies from 2006 onward –and therefore abandon an inclusive and progressive rhetoric – Spain started to be targeted by Southern Mediterranean countries as a hostile government. This diminished Spain's negotiation power and diplomatic ability.

This loss of credibility – from a Southern point of view – was also replicated at a European level once Spain demonstrated its incapacity to manage the financial crisis. On one hand as Guillen has demonstrated it is true that Spain over its economic and industrial growth period – from 1995 to 2005 – gained also international stature (Guillen, 2005). On the other hand, and despite good economic and financial contexts, Spain had always to fight against a historical and enduring image problem. As Guillen stresses that the "remarkable economic progress of the 1990s and early 2000s has not yet fully erased the perception of decadence, relative backwardness and exoticism" (Guillen, 2005).

Within this context and diplomatic environment, in 2010, Spain acceded to the EU presidency. During this period the intention remained constant – using an international diplomatic role to increase prestige by engaging with global priorities in the service of national interests and priorities. In other words, the role of the political entrepreneur and broker in promoting self-interest needs to do so by embracing multilateral concerns. This is arguably the very root of the failure of multilateral diplomacy and mechanisms.

Spain's intentions for becoming a regional leader is clear and all national efforts to lead euro-Mediterranean politics where in a way threatened by the initiative launched by Sarkozy, the UfM. As it was said before, when Sarkozy presented the proposal Spain started to be nationally and internationally weakened. However the Spanish official discourse insisted in situating the UfM inside the broader framework of the Barcelona process. This is a rhetoric attempt of fortifying Spain's dominance within the Euro-Mediterranean politics:

> ["With regards to the Mediterranean, Spain will lead a needed and urgent debate to consolidate a Euro-Mediterranean area as a space of peace, prosperity and progress throughout the development of the Barcelona process that frames the proposal Barcelona Process: Union for the Mediterranean"] (Moratinos, 2009).

This paragraph insists in the factor of Spanish leadership within a process that should be designed to delineate the areas of cooperation. How possible is cooperation when a particular or individual government or group of governments design their diplomatic strategy in order to reinforce their international dominance? Leadership and cooperation are two vectors that can work together when national interests are put aside. When this condition is not respected the future of diplomatic strategies and multilateral mechanisms and policies may be doomed to fail in the medium and short term. The communicational component that is present in this model tends to be vertical, excluding and restricted to specific priority elements the dominant player wants to develop according to the agenda. This model does not enhance cooperation but aims at creating or reinforcing –even unconsciously – systems of dependence.

## 3.5 European Reactions

In applying the CL approach and in selecting the same variables studied in precedent chapters it is important to see how the European Council has been translating the worries and the political priorities of EU member states and how political brokers and entrepreneurs have been impacting and shaping European politics and decision-making processes. The graphic below shows the period of Zapatero's first mandate.

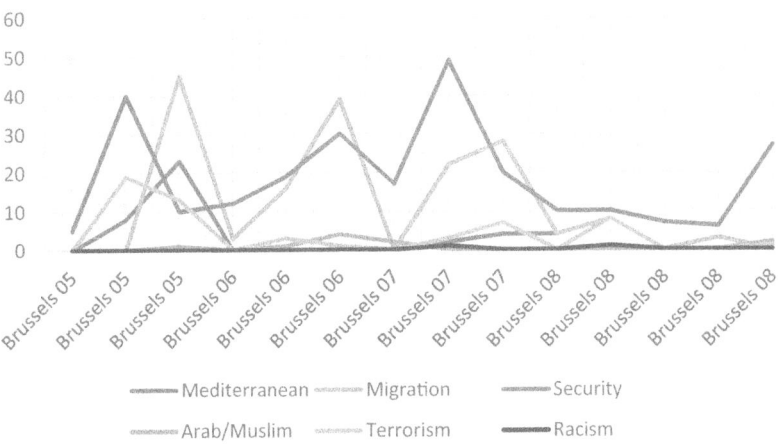

Graphic 7. European Councils, Conclusions of the Presidency.
Source: European Council. Elaborated by the Author.

This graphic shows that for the studied period of time there are three main variables that stick out from the other ones: security, migration and Mediterranean. In considering this period, it is clear that terrorism, even though, it remains an important topic over 2005, its presence within the official texts curbs. However it is important to note how migration related issues remain the second relevant political issue for European countries. This trend confirms the evolution of this variable over the period of time studied in precedence, 2001–2004. Therefore, this trend reinforces this dissertation's hypothesis which has considered that migration related issues represent the most important political and diplomatic factor that allows understanding the challenges and failures of both EU public speech and diplomatic communication strategies.

As it has been stated above, 2005 represented the tenth anniversary of the Barcelona Process. Within the framework of this review, the EU approved the report on the implementation of the Strategic Partnership between the EU and the Mediterranean Region and the Middle East (European Council, 2005). In considering the strategic importance of the Mediterranean and the Middle East for the interests of the EU this partnership –based on the interim report of 2004 that was mentioned earlier – aimed at strengthening all the mechanisms and policies supported by the Barcelona Process and the ENP. At a rhetorical level there are a number of interesting elements that have to be analysed. This partnership insists in the idea of designing policies and mechanisms reinforcing the principles of joint ownership and partnership.

Technically speaking, joint ownership is the fundamental aspect that might guarantee win-win scenarios. However it would also entail the existence of control and accountability systems to allow a reciprocal evaluation. In any case, due to the strong institutional development of European partners and the opposite structure in southern Mediterranean countries, this symmetric approach cannot be possible. Therefore the achievement of these win-win or co-operative scenarios is doomed to fail. This stronger political consensus and diplomatic structure in the EU, allowed at least the discussion – during the $7^{th}$ Euro-Mediterranean Ministerial Conference in 2005 – on joint conclusions to be adopted for the first time, on the need to promote political and social reforms in the partners countries. In the conclusions published after this conference it was said that ["its vast potential is far from being exhausted and sets the objectives for many years to come"] (EMP, 2005). Although the potential of these policies remained very vague from an operational-managerial point of view considering that the only exact –and measurable date – was 2010 when it was supposed to create the Euro-Mediterranean Free Trade Area.

On the other hand, in the same conclusions, this concept of "joint conclusions" was restricted to a paper presented by southern Mediterranean countries where they were exposing their diplomatic stances and desires. After the problems and challenges posed by an increasing southern migration towards Europe or by the Middle East peace process among others, the mentioned phase of "realisation" advised diplomats to consider dialogue among partners as the baseline of the futures Euro-Mediterranean project. The following graphic shows that at a rhetorical level, the European Council placed dialogue before economic, trading or security objectives.

**Variables**

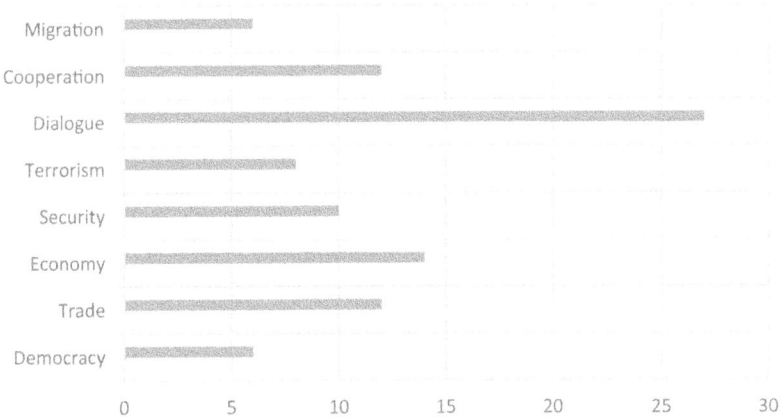

**Graphic 8.** Strategic Partnership between the EU and the Mediterranean and the Middle East
**Source:** Strategic Partnership EU-Med-ME. Elaborated by the Author.

Despite this apparent –rhetoric – convincement to strengthen dialogue among partners, the migratory issue remains very sensitive as it will be deeply explained in Chapter 5. Especially when according to the graphic and the contents of these European councils the variables migration and security –European security – are imbricated. This element represents the basic failure of the symmetric proposal based on the reinforcement of the feeling of co-ownership.

During the third 2005 Council it was also adopted the five year work programme and a code of conduct on countering-terrorism. This programme established the medium term objectives in the fields of political and security partnership –first priority-; sustainable economic growth and reform; education and socio-cultural exchanges; migration, social integration; justice and security. It was also highlighted the need of developing a consistent global approach to migration and it was planned that for 2006 it was necessary to hold the Euro-Mediterranean ministerial meeting focusing on migration issues.

Following the same line –and clashing with the rhetoric betting for a Euro-Mediterranean dialogue – it was also discussed the Mediterranean Coastal Patrol Network –the Mediterranean Surveillance System – named FRONTEX. During the second Council celebrated in 2006, it was linked ["organised crime, corruption, illegal migration and terrorism"] (European Council, 2006). It was also stressed that cooperation on migration it was an important part of EU's Neighbourhood Policy. During the third 2006 council it was highlighted that migration represented challenges and opportunities and that it represented one of the major priorities of the EU at the start of the 21$^{st}$ Century.

During the third council of 2007 it was expressed that the "council calls for better coordination between migration and integration policies. In the context of the 2008 year of Intercultural Dialogue" (European Council, 2007). This statement is contradictory and clashes against the increasing securitization and criminalization of migratory issues. Integration policies cannot be fully developed within an environment of restriction and securitization, because as it has been demonstrated in Chapter 4, public opinion reacts negatively against migrants –and therefore it blocks potential integration processes – when political communication strategies use migration as a political opportunity.

After showing how Spain during Zapatero's mandates tried to continue working along the same lines to remain a relevant international player, both national and international dynamics challenged the hypotheses and policies defended by Spain as a political entrepreneur and broker. Spain identified this moment of weakness and Sarkozy was ready to take over the Euro-Mediterranean leadership. The next chapter explores how Sarkozy developed his Mediterranean project and assesses how Spain, in losing part of the diplomatic capacity weakened by strategic and managerial errors had to accommodate and re-think a diplomatic strategy aiming at ensuring a certain leadership.

# 4 The Presidency of Nicolas Sarkozy and the Mediterranean Frustrated Ambitions, Failed Leadership

## 4.1 Jacques Chirac's Foreign Policy and the Arab World

Analysing Sarkozy's political and diplomatic engagement in the Mediterranean requires a brief review of President Jacques Chirac's political initiative with regards to French and Euro-Mediterranean relations. During his period as France's Prime Minister – 1974–1976 – he demonstrated a clear enthusiasm to promote the *Politique Arab de France* (PAF) (Taheri, 2003). Chirac's presidency – 1995–2007 – covered important years for the development of a communitarian Mediterranean policy. As Guitta points out, Chirac inherited a strong pro-Arab foreign policy (Guitta, 2005). A policy that was consistent with the Gaullist tradition established in 1967 onward (Behr, 2009).

Even though as Gerecht and Schmitt have demonstrated, Chirac during his second mandate –from 2002 to 2007 – differed from De Gaulle is showing a more proactive attitude towards the US (Gerecht and Schmitt, 2006). Putting aside this comment, Chirac immediately after taking office aimed at boosting further French-Arab relations by implementing a new *politique arabe*. Chirac wanted to reverse François Mitterrand's partial lack of engagement within the Mediterranean and the Arab World (Moisi, 1982). In fact during Mitterrand's mandate France's foreign policy developed more its European side and marginalised the relations with the Arab World. On one hand, that attitude provoked the obsolescence France's foreign policy towards the Middle East –especially during his second mandate from 1988 to 1995-and did not allow France's full engagement in the design of the new Euro-Mediterranean project (Kodmani-Darwish, 1995; El Moustaoui, 2011).

As soon as Chirac announced his intentions to further develop French-Arab relations, Arab leaders welcomed his decision. This announcement was pronounced at the University of Cairo in April 1996 during an official trip to Lebanon and Egypt. Chirac mentioned that a new French-Arab policy should be developed because at that time in France there were already four million Muslims. On the other hand, Chirac, taking advantage of the developments promoted by the Barcelona Process assured that France's engagement in the region should be shared also with EU institutions, mechanisms and political actors (Chirac, 1996). This attitude revealed France's interest in repositioning the country as a Euro-Mediterranean political and diplomatic leader after the socialist hiatus.

However beyond these rhetoric aspects, the question that remained was: how did Chirac plan to re-launch France's *politique arab*? Strategically speaking, as Wood has noted, it is clear that Chirac wanted to reverse France's marginalization. As a part of this strategy, Chirac also wanted to play an important and leading role in contributing to the solution of the Middle East peace process (Hollis, 1997). But the fulfilment of his goals depended upon US's interests in the area, so the best possible alliance had to be developed together with the EU (Wood, 1998). This position between powers was already tested and experienced by France between 1970 and 1974 within the context of the oil crisis (Gfeller, 2011). However even though Chirac supported EU's initiatives towards the Mediterranean, he wanted to take advantage of the previous economic and cultural influence within the region. The Élysée deployed a strategy that could be defined as entrepreneurial and industrial diplomacy. This is not the same as being political or diplomatic entrepreneur.

By entrepreneurial and industrial diplomacy the author means the inner-national impulse – bilateral – one given single country works out in order to achieve greater regional influence through economic and trade relations. This attitude does not seek photo-opportunities. This attitude is not guided by visual effects but by a productive and tangible approach that aims at developing long-term collaborations.

During Chirac's first mandate – from 1995 to 2002 – France reached the top three among trade partners within the Arab World. This position has been consolidated over the next decade. By 2012-2013 France was number one trade partner – imports – in Morocco, Tunisia; second trade partner in Morocco – exports-, Algeria – imports-, Libya – exports-. That demonstrates French economic influence in North Africa. Nevertheless, this intense entrepreneurial and industrial diplomacy was not articulated or architected to increase France's leadership in boosting EU's Mediterranean policy. It basically remained as a national effort addressing French national interests.

As Telhani has studied through a survey, among Arab countries President Chirac was one of the most admired leaders (Telhani, 2003).

Within the same survey references to Spain or any Spanish President were inexistent. However, beyond a charming attitude and a sporadic activism, Aeschiman and Boltanski have defined Chirac as a leader who has understood very well on-going transformations within the Arab World. But at the same time, he has been showing incapacity to overcome a diplomatic inefficiency that has generated immobility and lack of concrete results (Aeschiman and Boltanski, 2007). These two authors concurred with the fact that at the end, beyond the PAF's potential, Chirac's *politique arabe*, has been reduced to a particular "vendetta" against Syrian president Bashar al-Assad. This tense relation with Damascus impeded a fluid integration of Syria within the Euro-Mediterranean process. Therefore, this fact added complications to a process that was already damaged by these complicated regional and international relations. Nevertheless, if France wanted to play a more active and leading role within the Euro-Mediterranean process relations with Syria had to be solved. The next France's president –Nicolas Sarkozy – had to change strategy and include Syria within his agenda if he wanted to gain leadership (Zisser, 2009).

Against this background France had a chance to recover its Mediterranean diplomatic ambitions within a context of institutional weakness. Weakness shared by the limited results provided by Chirac's foreign policy towards the Middle East, on one hand, and by the quasi-failure of the Barcelona Process on the other hand. All this framed by increasing migration flows from Southern Mediterranean countries and the beginning of the global financial crisis.

The 2007 French presidential campaign seemed very much to focus on domestic problems rather than foreign policy. But as the Spanish case has shown there is often a fine line between how issues – such as migration or terrorism – are located in the domestic and foreign spheres.

France, for example, with the highest number of immigrants of Muslim origin in Europe – 7 million, from 1995 to 2007 this number increased of three million – knows this better than most. So did Nicolas Sarkozy. When Chirac was elected as President in 1995 he defended the new PAF considering also French – Muslim population. However, the acceleration of migration flows experienced by Europe since the 2000s, started to challenge this pro-migrant rhetoric. As Minister of Interior – under Chirac's presidency – Sarkozy demonstrated a zero-tolerance policy in tackling riots by second and third generations of immigrants in Rouen, Aubervilliers, Sein-S. Denis, Rennes, Dijon, Nice and Marseille.

Many on the left of the political spectrum believed that his actions during this period destroyed his chances in the 2007 election. Others such as US diplomats based in Paris thought foreign policy would not matter in the election. In a cable from the US Embassy in Paris back to Washington it was noted that "foreign policy has not and probably will not play a prominent role in the French presidential election campaign, and neither Nicolas Sarkozy nor Segolene Royal has enunciated a fleshed out foreign policy vision" (US Government, 2010). They were wrong. He won and in doing so highlighted that France's domestic problems are often also its foreign policy problems.

During their campaigns both Sarkozy and his socialist opponent Royal engaged in political discourse very similar to that of de Gaulle's. Both emphasized human rights and democratization as a way of restoring France to its proper international standing and underlined its "universal mission" on a global stage. Despite the rhetoric, it needs to be assessed just how much, following his victory was Sarkozy genuinely interested in these issues and especially in how they related to the Mediterranean?

## 4.2 Sarkozy and the Mediterranean Window: Launching the Mediterranean Union

The relationship between Sarkozy and the Mediterranean became evident during 2005 when in a speech in Morocco he commented on the possibility of creating a Mediterranean Union (Schmid, 2008). However, it was not until two years later when Sarkozy was elected president that he launched his Mediterranean program. As Romain Nadal, an adviser to the French president, noted during an interview with the author, while Sarkozy was interior minister he worked closely with Spanish officials and leaders in the area of counter-terrorism (Interview with Romain Nadal, 2012). Whether this continued once Sarkozy came up with his personal Mediterranean project is an interesting issue examined below.

During his presidential campaign, in Toulon in February 2007, Sarkozy announced his intention to launch a "Mediterranean Union". He raised this objective in the context of ending the "lack of hope" in contemporary France, where there is no certainty about itself, its "identity, its role, its future" (Sarkozy, 2007). Indeed, within nine sentences Sarkozy used the word "hope" six times. As Balfour has mentioned there was also a strong post-colonial component to Sarkozy's words (Balfour,

2009). ["In Toulon, I came to tell the French that their future is here, in the Mediterranean. Here where everything has began (...)"] (Sarkozy, 2007). In using the CL approach it is possible to appreciate in the following graphic, that Sarkozy was – quantitatively speaking considering both ranking and frequency – articulating his speech in a very precise way: first putting first himself as the agent of change; second mentioning "we" including and involving French citizens within this new process: third, incorporating within the process the "Mediterranean" as the chosen element to boost this change being; four "France" the country to be responsible for it; five, placing "Europe" in a secondary position.

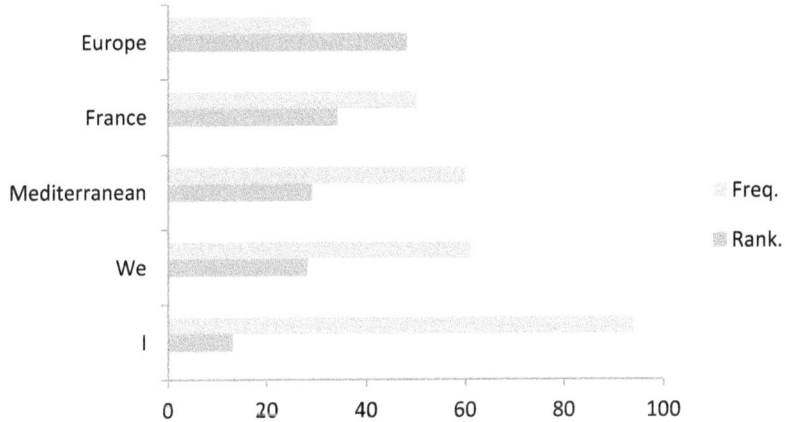

**Graphic 9.** Sarkozy, Discourse Toulon. 2007.
Source: Sarkozy's complete discourse, Toulon, 2007.

Undoubtedly, this rhetoric was mainly an electoral strategy directed to address some French problems. As Gillespie has noted there were also a number of economic and commercial interests behind Sarkozy's proposal (Guillespie, 2008). In three interviews for this book, with Monica Frassoni, co-spoke person of the Green Party in Brussels and Paolo Bergamaschi and Michelle Rieu, Green party foreign policy advisors, it was noted that Sarkozy's interest was in part making France into the main supplier and provider of nuclear energy technology and infrastructure in the Southern Mediterranean in general and in Libya in particular (Interviews with Frassoni, 2011 and with Bergamaschi and Rieu, 2012).

In fact during June 2007, one month after being elected as president, Sarkozy visited Tripoli on an official visit to meet with Colonel Qaddafi. Sarkozy described this as an attempt to help Libya to come back to the international order (Le Figaro, 25 June 2007). However the trip also had strong political, strategic and economic connotations. As *Le Figaro* noted, it was during this trip that French foreign minister Bernard Kouchner and his Libyan counterpart, Abderrahmane Chalgham, signed a Memorandum of Understanding on Cooperation in the Field of Civilian Nuclear Applications, and a number of parallel agreements on defense and security. Subsequently commercial agreements were signed to develop civilian nuclear energy (Girard, 2011).

This relationship with Libya was representative of Sarkozy's development as a political entrepreneur in the Mediterranean by providing a "brilliant and aggressive foreign policy to satisfy the French and pull them out of depression" (Torreblanca, 2008). Some argued his plans for the Mediterranean would be a duplication of the EU (Schmid, 2008). If this proposal intended, as Jamet hypothesized, to be a more regional "Union" from a conceptual point of view, any envisaged process of regional integration would have been much more difficult than a union among European partners (Jamet, 2008).

This explains the badly planned diplomatic and political strategy Sarkozy deployed. This chapter intends to demonstrate that this proposal from its inception to its partial implementation was an unnecessary political initiative. First, it showed a lack of understanding with regards to the socio-economic needs and obstacles of the broader Southern Mediterranean. Second, those who wanted to lead this project, like Spain, Italy and France demonstrated a lack of willingness to develop a flexible approach to the development of the project. Third, the willingness of some EU Member States to provide EU-taxpayer funds on a poorly thought out project. Fourth, the lack of political responsibility in negotiating with dictatorial regimes in the Mediterranean countries.

These issues raise an important question as to what exactly was the strategic objective of Sarkozy's Mediterranean project? As Nadal put it in an interview:

> ["I think that he did it very *à la* Sarkozy. With egocentrism (…) The main difficulty at the Elysèe at that time is that the one who brings up and pushes this project is Henry Guaino, who conceptualized it with Jean-Louis Guigou. Henry Guaino is very anti-European, and he considers this project

as an alternative project to the Barcelona Process, not as an occasion to modernise it. Because of this approach there was a very strong fight at the Elysèe between Guaino and Jean Davide Levitte, diplomatic advisor"] (Nadal, 2012).

According to this view there was a divide between Sarkozy's senior advisors and according to Nadal, these tensions impacted negatively on this project from the beginning. According to Guigou – founder and general delegate of the Institute de Prospective Économique du Monde Mediterranéen (IPEMED)-, also in an interview for this book, there was not a particular ideology driving Sarkozy's actions: ["Sarkozy did not prepare anything. It was a bomb.... He scared, he was strong and he was malignant"] (Interview with Guigou, 2012). Guigou's strong statement against Guaino's and Sarkozy's proposal was justified by the strong work developed by Guigou and the IPEMED within the Mediterranean world since 2006. It is possible to say that many of the ideas taken by Guaino and Sarkozy were rooted in Guigou's Mediterranean thought.

Sarkozy launched his proposal without taking into consideration any other potential partners. As Balfour and Schmid noted, ["Paris has (...) begun seeking consensus *ex post* on an idea that it did not discuss in advance with potential partners but now cannot afford to either drop or pursue in isolation"] (Balfour and Schmid, 2008). This lack of strategy clashed with the EU's interests in the area and challenged those countries like Spain and Italy playing an important role in leading the EMP. As Schumacher has also stated, Sarkozy underestimated the internal dynamics ["that a bloated framework of 43 members which such different political, economic and socio-cultural backgrounds would generate"] (Schumacher, 2009).

As some political commentators have stated, it seemed that Sarkozy was trying to consolidate his political credentials on a global level by acting as the diplomatic bridge between the North and the South of the Mediterranean (Simons, 2008). In doing this Sarkozy forgot or ignored the fact that the Mediterranean was a zone of common interest. As Daoud has stated, during his five years of leadership, part of the reason Sarkozy failed to ["leverage appropriately and responsibly his country's global leadership position as a major economic and military power"], was because he looked to take the lead in the Mediterranean alone (Daoud, 2012). The EU did not wait to react against this manoeuvre.

## 4.3 European Reactions

Sarkozy decision to engage unilaterally in the Mediterranean provoked severe responses from his EU partners and fuelled existing rivalries –economic and political – that did not help to develop a coordinated Euro-Mediterranean process (Guigou, 2012). It is important to bear in mind that economically speaking, as Guigou has mentioned, among European countries there is pure rivalry and therefore, spurring those geo-strategic and economic tensions would contribute to annihilate or weaken any socio-political initiative.

Initially Sarkozy's political discourse designed by Guaino was based both on emotion and nationalism. In strategic terms his first rhetorical approach was aimed at three specific objectives: 1) Criticizing any existing policy, 2) offering a new alternative and 3) opening a new frame of multilateral relations in parallel to the EU but led by France.

In retrospect it is possible to say that the first objective was successful. Sarkozy actively criticised and disqualified the Barcelona Process during his official visit to Tunisia in April 2008 (Marti Font, 2008). However, Spain's Secretary of State for the EU, Diego González Garrido reacted immediately and defended the Barcelona Process (González, 2008).

As the director of the European Institute of the Mediterranean (IEMeD), Andreu Bassols has noted the second one –proposing an alternative – offered the possibility of achieving certain consensus. However: ["…this alternative did not work out with the Turkish who immediately received that discourse with great scepticism, and even with certain hostility. And I know that because few weeks after the discourse I was in Ankara and the message we got from the Ministry was very clear"] (Interview with Bassols, 2011).

The third objective did not succeed. That is why, according to Bassols, there was a desire to call it the Mediterranean Union from the start. However, this was a very ambitious name for a very underdeveloped organization. As such, the name chosen was the Union for the Mediterranean.

European stakeholders did not welcome this specifically nationalistic proposal launched independently by Sarkozy. As ambassador Landaburu has stressed, Sarkozy's proposal was unexpected in Spanish political and diplomatic circles (Landaburu, 2011). Former president of Catalonia Jordi Pujol also expressed this view: ["Sarkozy had a political campaign where he never spoke about the Mediterranean. (…) I was amazed when during his first discourse after winning the elections he said that they would create a Mediterranean Union that would integrate

North African countries and Europe"] (Pujol, 2012). Spanish diplomats found very difficult to accept the proposal.

Sarkozy lobbied hard across Europe and as ambassador Landaburu highlights: ["They did not dare to oppose against Sarkozy. And there, there was also a pact of Southern countries against the Eurocrats and Germany, a pact that France wanted to avoid"] (Balfour and Schmid, 2008). Having said that Spain did not react due to two reasons, first it had no other alternative proposals and second they were also happy to let Sarkozy ["burn himself in the Mediterranean"] (Landaburu, 2011). On the other hand it is also true that this political and diplomatic storm helped to reposition the Mediterranean within the European agenda.

However, Sarkozy was willing to cooperate because he wanted the initiative to succeed. In particular, he wanted the support of the larger northern European EU powers Germany and the UK ["German Chancellor Angela Merkel, openly accused France of excluding non-Mediterranean countries in an attempt to sideline existing EU policies and hijack European funds to support French foreign policy initiatives"]. The UK said that it ["would not spend an extra penny on the project"] (Balfour and Schmid, 2008).

Smaller member states such as Portugal and Slovenia, both of whom held EU presidencies during this time were suspicious of the proposal as contradicting the EU's own plans for the Mediterranean during their presidencies. The important Mediterranean stakeholders of Italy and Spain were also suspicious. In June 2007, Sarkozy had a meeting with Romano Prodi in the Elysèe in order to try to get Italian support. But the proposal as it was presented was rejected immediately.

The context was very difficult as Echeverría states. This new ambiguous proposal should have to solve the problems that were not solved over the last twelve years. It seemed to be more a question of political will, idealism and illusion rather than political efficiency and realism. Summarizing, apart from internal opposition, Sarkozy's proposal had to contend with deadlock in the Middle East peace process, differences over the potential accession of Turkey to the EU and the European Neighbourhood Policy (ENP) (Echeverria, 2007). According to Turkey's Ambassador to the UN Oguz Demiralp who was interviewed for this book, Turkey viewed Sarkozy's proposal as ["a trap designed only for Turkey"] so Turkey could be told ["you have the Mediterranean Union, a virtual or fictitious entity, so, don't try to come to the European Union. But at the end he had to change"] (Interview with Demiralp, 2012).

With these challenges Sarkozy realised that without the Spanish and the Italian support the proposal would sink. The French president organised a dinner with Zapatero in Rome in order to explain the proposal. Spanish foreign minister Moratinos supported the proposal because he believed that it was in Spain's interests to back the initiative in terms of Spain's role within the overall Mediterranean process (Bassols, 2012). These strategic actions demonstrate how the French diplomacy had to react very actively in order to get the proposal afloat.

As Bassols pointed out during the interview, Spain's minister of Foreign Affairs, Miguel Ángel Moratinos went on board quickly as understood that it was in Spain's interest to support this initiative in order to promote the advancement of the process, even though, probably, Moratinos not being a very convinced Europeanist, was mostly thinking about Spain's role within the overall Mediterranean process. Nevertheless at a diplomatic level, the interest in pushing the proposal towards Europe was probably the most pragmatic option to gain some time in order to re-channel the initial project and to have more chances to gain some political influence.

From Moratinos' perspective, Sarkozy's proposal was an instrumental tool to overcome the problems the Barcelona Process faced in its attempt to construct a real Euro-Mediterranean geopolitical space (Moratinos, 2007). In other words, its support was an attempt to transform and translate French moves into a specific action that should benefit all the stakeholders involved in the Euro-Mediterranean process.

On top of that it would not be prudent forgetting the global economic crisis that started to be widely recognised from 2008 onwards. This factor, has been contributing to deepen the difficulties of such a complex multilateral project on a number of vectors: a global economic crisis summed to a less Mediterranean approach makes more difficult the allocation of limited financial resources to develop required political projects; the bilateralism proposed by the ENP would also block a multilateral approach; as a consequence, the diminishing interest in the Mediterranean linked to the difficult global economic situation would constitute one of the most difficult obstacles to overcome by the project, beyond any kind of political willing or particular/national geopolitical or geostrategic interest.

## 4.4 Europeanizing the Project: Rebuilding Trust

On the 5 December 2007 a summit met to discuss Mediterranean issues. Both Prodi and Zapatero offered political support to Sarkozy if the new proposal was integrated into existing EU mechanisms and objectives and if it complemented the existing EMP. Later that month,

on the 20 December 2007, the presidents of Italy, France and Spain met in Rome. They released a statement –*L'Appel de Rome* – in support of the UfM describing it as a mechanism that would be at the heart of Euro-Mediterranean cooperation in the region. It also made the point that the Union ["should be established over the principle of cooperation but not over the principle of integration"] (French Ministry of Foreign Affairs, 2007).

Through this statement they also called for the first UfM meeting to be celebrated by 2008. Nevertheless, this summit was also important given that it worked out as an event where Sarkozy, Prodi and Zapatero tried to rebuild the trust among them. As former French diplomat Denis Bauchard has stated, the potential success of this initiative was linked to three fundamental factors: trust among southern Mediterranean partners; trust among EU partners, and; a clear and specific method to implement the new mechanisms (Bauchard, 2008).

With this, Sarkozy's proposal was being Europeanized. Nevertheless, Germany was still not entirely convinced that these changes were substantial enough. Merkel's harsh criticism in 2008 was focused on her belief that the project was not compatible with existing EU mechanisms, objectives and policies.

This Franco-German tension made the role played by Spain and Italy more important but the key remained Franco-German agreement. That came during the European Council on 13 March 2008 and this was the moment when the proposal was finally Europeanized in full.

This decision guaranteed, at least in principle, a sort of continuation between the Barcelona Process and the new concept related to a Union for the Mediterranean, which explains why it was re-baptised as the "Barcelona Process: Union for the Mediterranean" as Guillespie has pointed out.

Linking this new project to Barcelona made sense, as abandoning it would have given credence to those who believed that the whole Euro-Med process was a failure. Barcelona also provided the institutional framework and experience for the EU to deal with the Mediterranean and despite internal differences within the EU, there was still a very big political, economic and strategic need to find a way of dealing with the region.

In fact, this institutional and diplomatic interest can be justified at least for three main factors. First, despite existing contradictory versions with regards to the failure or the success of the Barcelona process, a "re-shaped" project would give the idea –to the public opinion mainly – that the new concept would polish and re-launch a worthy common project. Second, from a theoretical and accountable point of view, if it would be possible to say that the Barcelona Process failed since its conceptualization and inception, it had to be justified that all the financial and economic resources that were wasted underpinning all mechanisms launched by the Barcelona Process could not be simply stopped. Abandoning and closing the "Barcelona Process" chapter would have supported the ideas of those who thought that the overall experience failed.

Considering this scenario, the EU would have been vulnerable and a serious evaluation should have been launched in order to look for responsibilities. Third, probably, considering the strategic needs of the EU with regards to Southern Mediterranean countries, the new project, at both rhetorical and practical levels would be very much needed to exert political, economic and diplomatic influence over the Southern Mediterranean rim.

All three aspects are reflected in the European Parliament resolution issued of 5 June 2008 (European Parliament, 2008). Specifically interesting are the points where the resolution expresses its strategic concerns and its reflection upon the partial failure of the Barcelona Process: (A) ["Whereas the Mediterranean region and the Middle East are of strategic importance to the EU and whereas there is a need for a Mediterranean policy based on solidarity, dialogue, cooperation and exchange, with a view to meeting common challenges and achieving the aim of creating an area of peace, stability and shared prosperity"] and (D1). ["Whereas the overall assessment of the Barcelona Process is that despite its insufficient achievements, compared to the initial objectives, it has potential which should be optimised.... Welcomes the above-mentioned Communication from the Commission entitled 'the Barcelona Process: Union for the Mediterranean', and shares the aim of this new initiative to give fresh political and practical impetus to the multilateral relations of the EU with its Mediterranean partners by upgrading the political level of relations, through greater co-ownership and enhanced sharing of responsibilities, as well as by developing regional projects responding to the needs of citizens in the region"] (European Parliament, 2008).

The Euro-Mediterranean summit held in Paris on 13 July 2008 may well have been, in the words of Turkey's Ambassador Demiralp, a ["good photo opportunity"] (Demiralp, 2012). But it also revealed also some challenges that the new process faced. The first was the Mediterranean partners Sarkozy had to deal with – Mubarak, Ben Ali, Assad. As Claret asked rhetorically in his interview, ["you had to wonder how you could build a future with these people. I understand the *Realpolitik* but we should say the things very clearly"] (Claret, 2012).

It is true that since the Barcelona Process there was a principle of conditionality. However practically speaking, this principle was segregated to few declarations and the way of working was mainly bilateral. As Claret highlights, with the UfM it was introduced the issue of the positive conditionality, which seems to be more relevant. To his mind, this principle had to be applied much earlier, and, in addition to this, much more support to those organisations advocating for human rights would have been to be supported more intensively and consistently.

Nevertheless, considering the partners involved in the project it was very difficult to ensure a neither continuity nor any substantial novelty with regards to a new process involving new objectives and mechanisms. Reflecting upon the possibilities of succeeding, as Gillespie states, a strong and honest analysis of the main failures of the Barcelona Process was not conducted. Therefore without any kind of evaluation or systematization of good or bad practices, the UfM was launched. But the problem was not simply the capacity or commitment of external partners. It is arguable that there has not been a real euro-Mediterranean leader –neither Spain nor France – able to identify regional priorities, goals and mechanisms beyond particular national interests.

As Balfour and Schmid have pointed out the Quai d'Orsay explored a number of options over the summer 2008 in order to define the geography of the new project. They examined whether it should be a Western Mediterranean approach or cover the whole Mediterranean including the Balkans or an enlarged option involving all EU member states and all other countries with interests in the Mediterranean, including the states of the Persian Gulf (Balfour and Schmid, 2008).

The first option was the most realistic as it did not have to address the Arab-Israeli conflict. It would also have allowed for the creation of an intermediate platform to negotiate – prior to a wider Mediterranean approach. As Jordi Pujol noted, the Western Mediterranean also had the advantage of not being a space dominated mostly by the US (Pujol, 2011). The second and the third options were more ambitious, but past experience had underscored their propensity for failure (Cornet, 2007).

The ministerial meeting in Marseille between the 3 and 4 November 2008, organised under the EU French presidency and attended by foreign ministers was a key step in the process during which the Union idea broke its links from the Barcelona framework.

The Union now committed itself to the creation and the reinforcement of a common area of ["peace, stability, security and shared prosperity, as well as full respect of democratic principles, human rights and fundamental freedoms and promotion of understanding between cultures and civilizations in the Euro-Mediterranean region"] (European Union, 2008).

Present in this statement, as expected, is the classic EU rhetoric regarding the noble intentions and objectives of such a partnership. However, at the very same time, EU member states were operating in the opposite way in the pursuit of national interests and domestic agendas in the face of the global economic crisis and the Arab uprisings of 2011 (known as the Arab Spring). Within the declaration of Marseille as the following graphic shows, there is continuity with the main driving elements that characterized the Barcelona Process. Both "dialogue" and "cooperation" represent the operational elements that act as common denominators, whereas the most important aspects are related to "trade", "security", "migration" and "economic" related issues, whereas "human rights" occupy a marginal position. This consistent trend shows that the same theoretical mistakes that provoked the partial failure of the EMP were repeated by the UfM.

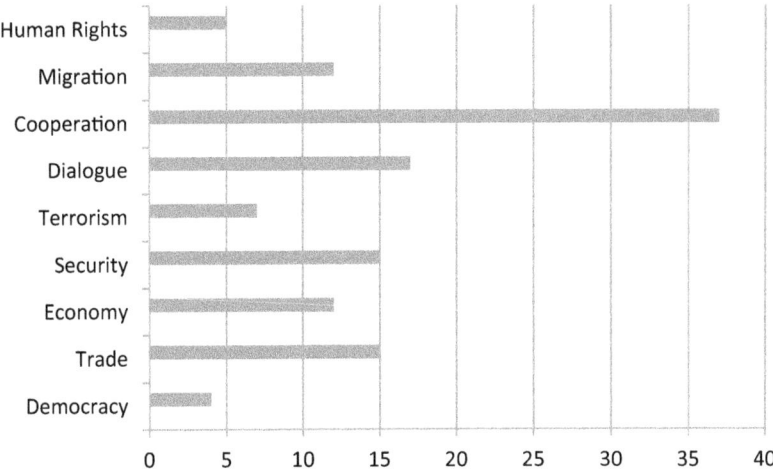

Graphic 10. Declaration of Marseille. Variables.
Source: Declaration of Marseille. European Council. Elaborated by the Author.

Leaving these considerations aside for the moment, it is worth noting that the Marseille document continued by setting out the main areas that the UfM should develop: ["De-pollution of the Mediterranean, Maritime and Land Highways, Civil Protection, Alternative Energies: Mediterranean Solar Plan, Higher Education and Research, Euro-Mediterranean University and the Mediterranean Business Development Initiative"] (EU, 2008).

It also noted the main obstacles the UfM faced in achieving this. Most were diplomatic and related to inter-Arab and Arab-Israeli tension and the relationship of Balkan countries and transnational entities like the League of Arab States in the process.

The declaration also addressed technical issues such as the operational mechanisms and the role of the co-presidency, senior officials, the joint permanent committee and the secretariat. The secretariat would have a technical role and political matters would be tackled by foreign ministers and senior civil servants.

## 4.5 Initial Reactions from the South

Any project-building process such as the one set out in the UfM has to integrate all stakeholders from the start. The communicational process is crucial in order to ensure a sense of ownership. The UfM, firstly a French-centric project and secondly a Euro-centric proposal, did not take this properly into account. Southern Mediterranean countries were informed direclty, or followed the events from a certain distance, but were not directly involved in discussions despite the lesson of Barcelona, where Arab countries became further removed from the process as it developed (Kausch and Young, 2009).

In specifically analysing the process of discussion and implementation of the UfM it is possible to say that Southern Mediterranean countries were not considered in the negotiation process. In fact, given that the process had to be Europeanized in order for it to be accepted by Sarkozy's EU partners, the initial priority was to include EU member states and stakeholders in early discussions. For their part, non-EU countries were informed about how the project was progressing but were not consulted fully until the process had already become a European affair.

On top of this were all the traditional challenges to engaging the South in a viable way. The EU was very institutionalized, whereas southern states were very fragmented. Ongoing regional tensions between Morocco and Algeria for instance were an obstacle to progress. Notably, the proposal to appoint a Moroccan to a senior post in the process was strongly opposed by Algeria.

## 4.6 Spain Becomes Home to the UfM

From a strategic point of view, establishing the UfM's headquarters in Barcelona would give the impression of continuity with the Barcelona process and would reassure Spain of its importance in the making of Euro-Mediterranean policy. However, as Anna Terron declared during an interview –former Spain's Secretary of State and Spanish politician who was part of Moratinos' team that negotiated this – Spain still had to ["work a lot to get the secretariat"] (Terron, 2011).

These efforts were facilitated by French interests and desires. As Terron noted, though many felt that Marseille might be a candidate for the headquarters, ["France is Paris. And something that is important for France cannot be based in Marseille. A French diplomat would consider that establishing something in Marseille is downgrading the project"] (Terron, 2011).

However according to confidential sources France had reasons, other than geography, for supporting Barcelona as a location. France wanted was the UfM's secretary to be based in Tunis with a French secretary-general. This approach would have given to France total control over the project. However, as Bassols acknowledged during an interview, EU partners would not have accepted a French secretary based in an Arab country (Bassols, 2012). It had major political implications, all the more so in the context of Israel's invasion of Gaza in December 2008. This happened few months after the celebration of the summit held in Paris.

When this idea fell through and with Marseille ruled out the two alternatives for France were Malta and Spain. As the more powerful candidate Spain won out because France, in the words of Bassols ["wanted to avoid, in any case, the failure of this initiative. I think that the French diplomacy was behind this proposal with all the power and they demonstrated an important political will"] (Bassols, 2012).

Speaking from a French perspective Nadal believes that it was good that Spain won this battle because a base in Tunisia would have collapsed during the Arab Spring that followed (Nadal, 2012). Classified information expresses that in the beginning before the designation of a Moroccan secretary, Algeria opposed to that hypothesis.

The start of the Barcelona-based secretariat was difficult. Its efforts were paralysed the Israel-Hamas conflict in Gaza. In June 2009, when discussions restarted there were further complications and planning was hampered further by the lack of poor objectives and poor coordination. Extra complications and disagreements delayed the start of the Secretary that at the end initiated during March 2010. All these institutional efforts to re-develop and revamp a Euro-Mediterranean policy were marked by lack of objectives, poor coordination, and it may seem that the entire proposal followed a hectic calendar that would represent a new total or partial failure.

## 4.7 The Benefits of the Union for the Mediterranean or for the South?

The success or the failure of such a complex project as the UfM depends on the relationship between stakeholders involved. In this case there was a very asymmetric relationship –culturally, economically, politically, socially, financially and institutionally. In these terms was the UfM presented as an opportunity for Southern Mediterranean countries?

As the communication from the European Commission to the European Parliament and the Council noted in 2008 its main objective was to ["enhance multilateral relations, increase co-ownership of the process and make it more visible to citizens. Now is time to inject more momentum into the Barcelona Process"] (European Commission, 2008).

The question of ownership or co-ownership is the most relevant and decisive aspect a complex project like the UfM should face. It is also the key element that can support or destroy the possibilities of a real partnership. By using very open and idealistic language, it was hoped that this partnership would ensure that all dimensions of the process will be open to all participants on an equal footing. But, what was meant by co-ownership? As Balfour has noted ["the equality between states also depends on the distribution of political and economic power, which is by and large tilted in the EU's favour, though the energy exporting countries of the South can exercise a great deal of leverage"] (Balfour, 2009).

Beyond the difficulties caused by traditional conflicts in the region (such as the Arab-Israeli conflict), it is almost impossible to set a regional agenda, prioritize objectives, define the mechanisms to achieve goals and design common strategies when strong political barriers exist. On top of this there are also economic, politic, social and demographic differences that pose major problems. As Bocquillon, Confavreux and Voionmaa have explained, the Mediterranean, in all these ways, is not comparable with other regions in the world (Bocquillon, Confavreux and Voionmaa, 2009).

There has been little scholarly research examining how the southern Mediterranean states have perceived the methodological and rhetorical aspects of the UfM. Most of the analyses have come from European or western scholars. Gillespie tried to consider and discuss, partly, these southern responses but his analysis was brief (Gillespie, 2008). Gillespie –following a similar rationale to that used by Kamen to assess the launch of the AoC – stated that financial resources both from private and public sources would be one of the most evident obstacles the new proposal should face. However Khatib has produced interesting findings, albeit in a different context (Khatib, 2010). For southern actors, Khatib argued, financial constraints were not the key issues. Political aspects, most notably, the Arab-Israeli conflict, were the main concerns.

In these terms it is not surprising that the first Euro-Mediterranean Summit, planned for May 2010 had to be postponed to November and put off once more then until further notice due to the Arab-Israeli conflict.

The conflict blocked or modified as well the UfM's launch of initiatives (Fernández Noguera, 2010a). The organisation's first secretary-general, Jordan's Ahmed Masa'deh, explained during an interview that

UfM's main objectives should be more economic and social rather than political (Fernández Noguera, 2010b). During a meeting in Brussels in November 2010, the UfM's budget was reduced by a more than 60 percent for 2011, to €6.2 million, of which €3 million was to be disbursed by the European Commission and the rest of funds via other mechanisms. The refusal as major EU players –Germany, the UK, to invest heavily in this process ["this reflects the willingness and the orientation that the countries have"], as former UfM secretary-general Masa'deh stated (Fernández Noguera, 2010b). As Fernández points out, this lack of political was also reflected in the fact that many ministerial meetings did not take place as planned and many of those that did made little progress.

Water was one of the issues that from a practical point of view was vital to all southern partners to the UfM. This issue was meant to be discussed during the first ministerial meeting – 2008 – but it was postponed twice due to the tensions produced by the Arab-Israeli conflict (UfM, 2008). Political reasons blocked one of the most representative social programmes in the region. NGOs and environmental groups like the World Wide Fund (WWF) expressed frustration over the repeated cancellation of the ministerial summit on the grounds that the UfM "represents a unique opportunity to face all the hottest environmental problems, like water management or the climate change.

This opportunity should not be lost and for that reason the WWF asks to the UfM's member states to progress and achieve results (WWF, 2011). The political pressure the Arab-Israeli conflict exerts on any kind of Euro-Mediterranean initiative is huge. For instance in 2012, the Palestinian Contractors Union menaced UNICEF –the organization in charge of building the desalinization plant in the Gaza strip funded by the EU – to boycott the process because it was supposed that two Israeli companies – *Odis Filtering* and *Nirosoft* – would take part in the works.

In operational terms, the lack of political will to overcome regional obstacles was evident from the beginning in terms of allocation of personnel. Six months after its establishment only 25 officials were in post (a quarter of the agreed total). Officials were even briefing the press that the organisation was ["something completely conceptual, nothing has passed to a practical level"] (Colombo, 2011). On January 2011, after less than one year into the job, the first secretary-general resigned (Fernández Noguera, 2011).

When the author visited the UfM headquarters in Barcelona for meetings with the Deputy Directors Ambassador Attard-Pirotta and Rafik Husseini on 24 January 2012, the building was quite empty and was hidden and isolated from the vibrant streets of Barcelona. This detail evidences the lack of integration of the UfM headquarters within the vibrant and vivid atmosphere of Barcelona. As Mr. Masa'deh highlighted, if Member States don't send their experts ["who is going to do the job?"]. On January 2011, after less than one year of sterile hope, the first Secretary General resigned. According to an interview to AFP a UfM's officer acknowledged that the organization ["is something completely conceptual, nothing has passed to a practical level"] (Colombo, 2012).

Aliboni and Ammor have asked, ["What does the UfM really want to achieve: a more political, or a more developmental oriented agenda?"] (Aliboni and Ammor, 2009). This fundamental question was also posed, though somewhat differently, in relation to the Barcelona Process. On both occasions, and in practical terms, the most satisfactory answer is that the political vision, shared both by EU and non-EU partners, is to maintain a status-quo by adopting a neo-realist approach.

As Khatib has noted, one of his interviewees, from Tunisia, argued that ["there are too many projects and too many speeches, sources for funding are rare and projects are the weakest link (…) there is a lot of rhetoric and much weakness on the citizens/people dimension. At the end of the day there is little new in the UfM"] (Khatib, 2010).

This negative perception amongst Mediterranean partners encapsulates the common tendency of southern officials attack the hypocrisy of the EU, blaming European stakeholders. This criticism is very understandable but it is also somewhat rhetorical and only tells part of the full story. The reality is that despite rhetoric many leaders of southern governments do not necessarily maximise the value or benefits of relations with the EU to push for policies that are not in the interests of the local population.

As Spanish Ambassador to Morocco Alberto Navarro commented on the UfM that what the EMP attempted to do was very meritorious. However Sarkozy's project so far did not produce any result:

["In fact today I have been speaking with the Moroccan ambassador to the UfM, Amrani, who starts tomorrow acting as the Secretary General in Barcelona. I said to him that is necessary to initiate the UfM on the 6 or 7 aspects that are integrated in the process. It has to been done following a communitarian method. Doing things, small steps, and step by step you can do a lot. It is necessary to impulse projects in all the proposed ambits. And I have told him that his legitimacy is going to be granted if he acts and if he works"] (Interview with Navarro, 2011).

Bearing these considerations in mind it is valuable to examine the actual projects that were underway as part of the UfM by late 2011. The following table compiled by the author shows these projects, the beneficiary countries, their status and the allocated budget.

Table 1. Distribution and Status of UfM's Projects, August 2012.

| Programme | Project | Year | Budget | Beneficiaries/ Partners | Status |
|---|---|---|---|---|---|
| Transport and Urban Development | "The Euro-Mediterranean Sustainable Urban Strategy" | Nov. 2011 | Not specified. | Euro-Mediterranean Cities. Not specified. | In preparation. Not specific data. |
| | Logismedtda | Nov. 2011 | Not specified. | Euro-Mediterranean Partners. | In preparation. Not specific data. |
| Energy | Mediterranean Solar Plan Project | 2011 | Not specified. | Algeria, Egypt, Israel, Jordan, Lebanon, Morocco, Syria, Tunisia, and West Bank & Gaza. | In preparation. Not specific data. |
| Environment and Water | "Desalinization Facility for the Gaza Strip" | June 2011 (First UfM Project) | Estimated 455 m$ from 2012 to 2017. | Gaza Strip. 1–.6 million inhabitants (beneficiaries). | In preparation. Not specific data. |
| Higher Education and Research | 1 MA, 3 EMUNI Masters Programmes 3 areas of EMUNI PhD. | Sept. 2011. | Not specified. | Students from different Euro-Mediterranean Countries. | In preparation. Not specific data available. |
| Social and Civil Affairs. | "Promoting Women Entrepreneurship in Universities". | Sept 2011. | Not specified. | Jordan, Morocco, Palestine and Spain. | In preparation. Not specific data. |

Source: Compiled by author. UfM official website and other sources.

This data demonstrates the limited action that the UfM had been engaged in terms of submission, evaluation, funding and execution of projects over this time period. In most of these there is not the available information about specific objectives, costs, and execution to make substantive assessments of their value. One of the most representative projects in terms of the large number of beneficiaries is the desalinization facility for the Gaza strip. It was costed at US$455 million. But that is the exception rather than the norm.

As Ambassador Cecilia Attard-Pirotta, UfM's deputy secretary-general reflected in an interview, between the Barcelona Process and the UfM: ["The tangible results have been very little, but on the diplomatic front it has been acknowledged the importance of meeting"] (Interview Attard-Pirotta, 2012).

Despite such sentiments the actual practical role of the UfM does not appear to justify its existence. Certainly, the impact of dissolving the UfM would not be high in developmental, economic, political and social terms across the Mediterranean.

## 4.8 Europe and the Future of the UfM

EU's political discourse helps to understand further UfM's developments. In order to better understand and evaluate the evolution of the UfM it has been analysed again the conclusions of the European Council. For the purpose of this analysis it has been considered the period 2009–2013. As the following graphic shows, after 2009 it is possible to appreciate a general trend where analysed variables curb their presence and frequency.

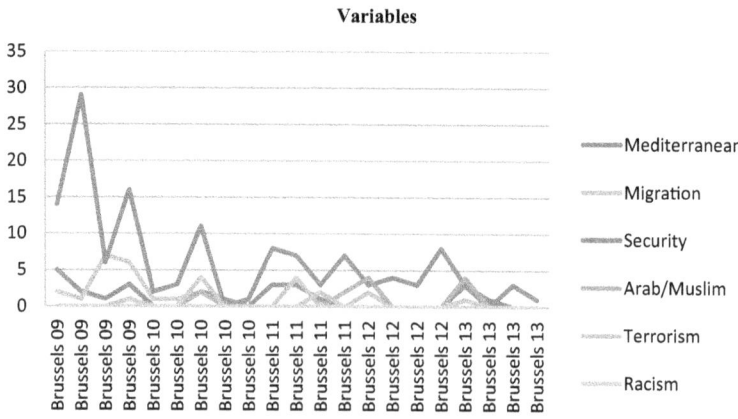

**Graphic 11.** European Council. Conclusions of the Presidency 2009–2013.
Source: European Council.

Overall the most cited variable remains "security". However, in analysing possible correlations, the use of "security" within this period of time is not correlated to issues such as "terrorism". There is a strong correlation between "security" and energy related issues. That reveals a special interest for ensuring the supply of energy to the EU. Conversely to what happened during the three "Mediterranean" waves – 1994 to 1996, 1999 to 2000 and 2005–2006 – after the presentation and institutionalization of the UfM, explicit references to the "Mediterranean" were very scarce as the graphic 22 shows. "Migration", "Mediterranean" and "Security" are also correlated within 2009, 2010 and 2011 but in a very slight way.

It is interesting to appreciate, however, how the variable "Arab" was proportionally high, especially from 2011 to 2012. This coincided with the Arab Spring and the role the Arab League should have to play to solve –or mediate – these uprisings. The tense and delicate episodes of the Arab uprising and aftermaths would have represented a golden opportunity –and justification – for the UfM to develop projects within the region. References to the role of the UfM within this context were very limited. There is a reference in 2011 underlining the potential contribution of the UfM in solving or mediating certain aspects derived from the Arab Spring (European Council, 2011).

Summarizing, European Council's public speech confirms the decadence of the Euro-Mediterranean process –UfM – and its potential as an agent to promote collaboration and cooperation between European and Southern Mediterranean countries. In analysing through the CL approach these conclusions, the Mediterranean lost political and diplomatic momentum. Therefore, political and diplomatic brokers and entrepreneurs like Spain and France sold the Mediterranean as a commodity to gain greater diplomatic stature within the EU, mostly pursuing short and medium term national interests. The following chapter will build upon the precedent chapters that have discussed how mostly Spain and also France deployed their Mediterranean policies and diplomatic initiatives.

In line with the expressed decadence of the Euro-Mediterranean institutional and diplomatic building at large, it is necessary to assess one of the most relevant aspects that challenged the consistency and coherence of these policies almost from their inception onward. The migratory issue and migratory policies managed by the EU have jeopardised the possibility of establishing win-win policies with Southern Mediterranean stakeholders. Therefore this has generated the basic elements to understand the lack of mutual trust among Euro-Mediterranean partners and the failure of Euro-Mediterranean policies.

# 5 Migration, Security and Public Opinion in the Euro-Mediterranean Region: Challenging Political Entrepreneurs and Brokers

After the assessment of the roles of Spain and France as political entrepreneurs and brokers, this chapter aims at assessing two inter-related aspects. First the most representative elements that have had to address these challenges and how they have been challenging Euro-Mediterranean politics and diplomatic action within the short, medium and long term. Second, how the EU's initial hypotheses and objectives have clashed and thus contradicted both with the development of such elements and with the particular interests of certain nations that have shifted and changed their policies and priorities due to economic, social and political difficulties.

The second objective is going to be demonstrated by analyzing European public speech and its influence is shaping European public opinion. This objective will also address and show how the EU's rhetoric in favor of the Euro-Mediterranean dialogue has clashed and has being challenged by national right-wing parties that have pushed EU member states' public opinion towards more intolerant stances during the 1990s and more intensively from 2002 onward due to immigration related issues (Oesch, 2008; Lucassen and Lubbers, 2012).

Migratory movements are essential to understand history and the way societies, political structures, economic relations and cultural patterns have been challenged and modified. It is possible to say that migration and mobility itself, represents the most representative and single socio-political, economic and cultural phenomena modifying and challenging contexts. Therefore, understanding its transforming power is crucial to explain: How politicians, political entrepreneurs and brokers deal with it; how it does affect political communication strategies; how public opinion reacts, digests and accommodates political messages and information; as well as understanding the role of migration political management in exacerbating or moderating existing conflicts or cultural cleavages.

There is strong scholarly evidence supporting the fundamental role of migration and mobility in setting and impacting agenda setting. As it has been explained in the introduction where it has been discussed political communication and sensitive issues –mostly immigration – political entrepreneurs and brokers – have found in immigration the most profitable opportunity to gather public opinion's consensus.

In considering the American case, Brown studied how the voting behaviour was conditioned by the ways politicians successfully used immigration as a central message of their campaigns (Brown, 1998). Pojmann assessed the linkages between migration and political activism in Europe highlighting the fact that immigration generates intense debates at every level of society and that ["the media, policy makers, and politicians have entered into a discourse that examines immigration from seemingly every possible angle"] (Pojmann, 2008).

Richmond studied the consequences of post-industrialism, globalization forces and international migration in boosting racial conflicts and reviving ethnic nationalism (Richmond, 1994). Betz and Swank have acknowledged that globalization processes and forces contribute to the electoral success of new far-right movements across Western Europe (Betz and Swank, 2003). This vision has been also shared by Castles and Davidson in acknowledging that globalization represents one of the most challenging forces in questioning the meaning and the boundaries of citizenship and participation. That is why immigration related issues represent a strong opportunity window for political entrepreneurs aiming at gathering public consensus by manipulating sensitive issues (Castles and Davidson, 2000).

The interest in discussing migratory related issues as an opportunity structure approach for politicians –including political entrepreneurs and brokers – was studied by Koopmans and Statham (Koopmans and Statham, 2000). Following a similar approach, Arzheimer and Carter have also confirmed that migration related issues represent a central part of political opportunity structures leaded by right-wing extremist parties –political entrepreneurs – (Arzheimer and Carter, 2006). This view has been confirmed for Western European countries by authors like Lubbers, Gjsbert and Scheepers, while they studied voting behaviour and political strategies developed by extreme right-wing parties in Europe (Lubbers, Gjsberts and Scheepers, 2002).

Summarizing the common grounds share by these scholars, Knigge stressed that increasing levels of immigration associated with raising levels of public dissatisfaction with existing political contexts and regimes, significantly facilitate right-wing extremism (Knigge, 1998). These studies validate this hypothesis by testing it from 1984 to 1993 and from 2002 onward.

The success of right-wind political parties in identifying political opportunities is related with their capacity of managing collective fears. In line with the aforementioned authors, Huysmans considers that immigration related issues represent the most representative element paying back huge dividends to political entrepreneurs.

Immigration being manipulated by political entrepreneurs and brokers, especially from far-wing factions, defines the contours of ["existential politics" by "administering inclusion and exclusion"] (Huysmanns, 2008).

Mudde coincides with this thesis and brings it further by considering that immigration has been a catalyst for most of contemporary extreme right parties (Mudde, 1999). He has even defined this theory as the single-issue party thesis. I share this point of view, considering that migration related issues are key to understand the limitations, inconsistencies and probably the failure of policies and mechanism used to promote a new strategy for the Mediterranean. This is due to the fact that primordially, those policies and mechanisms are communicational strategies that may allow or block Euro-Mediterranean dialogue and understanding. Migration related issues are very sensitive and within Euro-Mediterranean dialogue a wrong communicational strategy may lead to blocking more technical mechanisms and prevent the success of complex political and diplomatic interactions.

Euro-Mediterranean policies and mechanisms –as well as political entrepreneurs and brokers – had to deal with a fundamental contradiction. On one hand, the EU wanted to develop mechanisms to enhance trade relations and improve living standards in North African countries considering that this hypothesis would have contributed to limit and control immigration flows. In fact, as it is going to be demonstrated below, the only specific date that was contained in the documents of the EMP was 2010, moment where the FTA between the EU and North Africa would have entered into force. On the other hand EU immigration policies became increasingly restrictive from 2002

This approach shows the mercantilist standpoint promoted by the EU, whereas rhetorically speaking, the EU's discourse was addressing the importance of fostering the Mediterranean dialogue. Being politically coherent, for the success of every economic integration process, it is necessary to consider free movement of people as well. This contradiction represents the major failure point of the EMP as it is going to be demonstrated in this chapter.

In considering the traditional trade theory developed by Heckscher-Ohlin, both free trade and free migration are equivalent measures and elements of economic integration (Leamer, 1995). However as Wellisch and Walz have demonstrated, this theory does not correspond to the choices of industrialized countries that prefer free trade over free migration (Wellisch and Walz, 1998).

In line with this evidence, Schiff has demonstrated that free trade is preferred to free movement, because the later generates attachments ["with those with whom they share social capital, including norms, language, customs, values and culture"] (Schiff, 2002). Bearing in mind Euro-Mediterranean politics, these approaches are even more evident and significant as the divide between North Africa and the EU is the deepest in the world in terms of income, industrial development and institutional sophistication. On top of that immigration rates – as it is going to be demonstrated throughout this chapter – have been the most crucial aspect defining EU-Maghreb relations.

As de Haas recognizes, ["persistent and increasing migration from and through North Africa has put relations with European countries under considerable stress. In particular the EU has attempted to 'externalize' its restrictive e immigration policies through putting Maghreb states under pressure to adopt restrictive immigration laws and regulations and to intensify –joint – border controls"] (De Haas, 2011).

This artificial and intentional construction of a "buffer zone" in North Africa belongs to the EU's policy of entering into association agreements with Maghreb countries with the intention of creating a free trade area by 2010. These mechanisms were driven by a belief in the hypothesis –following a neo-liberal approach – that an open economy would not only reduce incentives for migration but also foster democracy, democratic peace as well as sustainable socio-economic changes in those countries.

However, it is arguable that this hypothesis is incorrect and did not take into account other factors such as the communication processes between more and less industrialized countries, policy coherence and consistency, and a real understanding of persistent socio-economic challenges. According to the Zelinky's model, also known as "migration hump", the improvement of socio-economic conditions would stimulate more migration within the short and medium term (De Haas, 2008).

The initial diplomatic and communicational strategies to set up the objectives of an Euro-Mediterranean dialogue coincided, as shown previously, with increasing migration flows on one hand and, on the other hand, with the development of the EU in a context of international globalization. This mixed phenomenon raised both directly and indirectly discussions on the traditional concept of nation-state and its sovereignty (Martiniello, 1995; Silverman, 1992). As Balibar, Wallerstein and Sassen have highlighted, these challenging scenarios based on discussing core issues like citizenship and nationality have forced political agendas to respond to these changing contexts in a never-ending process of reconstructing inter-state relations (Ballibar and Wallerstein, 1991).

As it has been demonstrated in Chapter 1, the initial diplomatic movements to develop Euro-Mediterranean comprehensive policies were based on a threatening communication strategy influenced by thinking on the risks that a less industrialized region like the North-African would represent for Europe. Subsequently, the theoretical justification of such policies shifted orientation and win-win situations –rhetorically speaking – were structured and designed in order to achieve a better understanding between European and Arab neighbors.

The success of these policies and rhetoric argumentations, therefore, were linked to three main theoretical and operational aspects: the understanding of long-standing problematic issues – such as socio-economic underdevelopment, security, post-colonialism, human mobility and more industrialized-less industrialized labor dynamics; the consistency of such policies and the degree of commitment of key decision makers and stakeholders; the course of parallel and complicated political situations like the Arab-Israeli conflict, the aftermaths of the 9/11 and the global economic crisis.

The 1990s were years of political and socio-cultural experimentation within the realm posed by the post-cold war scenario. These experimentations were framed and challenged by migration, security and socio-economic development related issues. All of them increasingly challenged Euro-Mediterranean relations, policies, diplomatic mechanisms and communicational processes. As it was demonstrated throughout the precedent chapters, these issues topped EU's political agenda as well as European public concerns. It was also the decade when Euro-Mediterranean politics were broadly defined and implemented following the theoretical and practical avenues defined by the Barcelona Process also called EMP.

## 5.1 General Migratory Trends

The percentage of international migrants as part of global population rose from 2.2 percent in 1970 to 2.9 percent in 2005 (Martin, 2008). However, over the same period, the concentration of international migration in OECD countries rose from 4.5 percent to 8.3 percent. Net migration from outside OECD to OECD countries from 1956 to 1976 amounted to 790,000 per year; 1.24 million per year from 1977 to 1990 and 2.73 million per year from 1990 to 2005.

According to UN and International Organization of Migration (IOM) estimates, the number of international migrants moved shifted from 150 million in 2000 to 214 million in 2012 (UN, 2008). These figures raise two fundamental questions that must be answered in order to understand possible manipulations, and inconsistencies with existing policies and generally accepted assumptions: Are politicians and the media over-stating this problem? Does irregular migration really threaten the state's sovereignty and security, or are these worries hugely exaggerated? (Koser, 2005). Along with these two initial questions, one should also ask how this phenomenon affects the Euro-Mediterranean region?

### 5.1.1 Migration in the Mediterranean

The Mediterranean, as a central pivot for Europe, North Africa and the Middle East constitutes one of the most dynamic regions in the entire world in relation to labor migration flows (Baldwin-Edwards, 2005). This dynamism is particularly evident in the Maghreb region. North African countries, mainly Morocco, Tunisia and Algeria have become some of the most active exporters of labor to Europe as De Haas and Skeldon have shown (De Haas, 2007).

Spanish and French colonization and decolonization philosophy differs in the case of North Africa from other types, such as British decolonization. Whereas the Anglo-Saxon model established the British Commonwealth, Mediterranean decolonization models in North Africa were violent and damaging to all parties. This explains why both France and Spain were reluctant to allow "former" dependent countries to become sovereign states (Perkins, 2004).

The French presence in North Africa especially in Morocco, Tunisia and Algeria since the mid-nineteenth century laid the first bricks of the constant interconnection among these countries. Algeria was the country that suffered this linkage more than the others as Naylor has studied (Naylor, 2000). The Algerian French protectorate was established in 1830 and incorporated into the French state. The Moroccan French protectorate started in 1881 and the Tunisian in 1912. During the first half of the twentieth century the French labor market had high demand during WWI and WWII as Muus and Bidwell have analyzed (Muus, 1995).

After WWII migration from the Maghreb to France continued until 1968 as noted in Chapter 4. Following the country's move to independence in 1962, Algerians were allowed to move freely between France and Algeria (Collier, 2003). This helped France to sustain and shore up its economic and industrial boom until 1973. During the Algerian war between 1954 and 1962, Moroccans workers filled the gap left by Algerians.

Broadly speaking during the first decade of post-colonialism between 1962 and 1973, Maghreb countries participated in the Euro-Mediterranean migration (De Haas, 2005 a). This notably occurred in Belgium, The Netherlands and the German Democratic Republic (GDR) (Baduel, 1980) were "guest workers", – also known as "*gastarbeiter*" – agreements were introduced.

Despite the formal channels in which this circular economic migration occurred, especially during the first years of the 1960s, irregular migration accompanied the regular process. This system was designed to promote and encourage circular migration but the majority of migrants were entitled with permanent residence permits through legalization campaigns in 1975 in The Netherlands and Belgium and in 1981–1982 in France (Muss, 1995). That is why it is difficult to estimate the exact number of migrants who moved over this decade.

The 1973 oil crisis and the global economic downturn that followed impacted severely on migration into industrial Europe, a main victim of the rapid rise in the oil price during the mid-1970s. Since then, European migration policies have been linked to the economic cycle, and thus unavoidably to the national and international macroeconomic situation (Papademetrius and Terrazas, 2005).

The subsequent period of economic and industrial stagnation generated an increasing structural unemployment leading to a reduction of the demand of the traditional immigrant labor. As De Haas points out, large number North African immigrants stayed permanently as visa restrictions pushed immigrants to remain in receiving countries.

This cause-effect approach might be at the root of the failure to manage migration, and are also (as subsequent chapters will address), potentially, at least in part, the reason for the common linkage of migration with other issues such as security, terrorism, criminality or unemployment.

The effects of the raising of oil prices provoked varied responses in the Maghreb. As an oil producer, Algeria was able to take advantage of the new situation for resetting relations with France. The government of Houari Boumédiène –in office between 1965 to 1976 – suspended immigration agreements with France because he considered emigration and those policies as ["a form of post-colonial dependence"] (Fargues, 2004).

On the other hand, as De Haas also argues that other North African countries suffered much more intensively from the 1973 oil crisis. Moroccan immigration in Europe grew steadily since 1972 due to family reunification, family formation, new labor migration and undocumented migration. According to official figures, the number of Moroccan immigrants rose from 300,000 in 1972 to nearly 2.7 million by 2005. France was the top recipient with 1 million Moroccans, followed by Spain, 500,000, Italy, 350,000, Belgium, 350,000, The Netherlands 325,000 and Germany, 108,000 (De Haas, 2009). The same trend can be witnessed for the Tunisian population. According to Gammoudi the Tunisian population abroad doubled between 1977 and 1992 and between 1987 and 2007 (Gammoudi, 2006; Zekhri, 2010). By 2007 France was the main destination for both Tunisian and Algerian migrants with 54.5 percent of Tunisians in Europe living in France. At the same time the number of Algerians residents in France was estimated 1.5 million (Goddard and Taussig, 2007).

France's colonial past and current economic power explain this but so does its cultural links. Spain, on the other hand, was not such an attractive prospect for much of the same period due to decades of economic stagnation, political dictatorship and institutional and democratic under-development. From the early 1980s onward as Spain moved from being a sending to a receiving country from migrants this all changed.

Seventy percent of the immigrants coming from the Maghreb came to Spain between 1980 and 1990 as González Yanci and López García and Berriane have shown (López García and Berriane, 200; Yanci González, 1995). Moroccans and Algerians migrated to Spain more than Tunisians. This new wave of immigrants from the Maghreb was defined by one of the most notable Spanish experts on migration as ["the return of the Moors"] (López García, 1993).

These trends have been replicated all over the Mediterranean. The graphics below show the evolution of the migrant population in Europe and in the Mediterranean area, for 4 countries: Spain, France, Italy and Malta. This first graph shows how international migration evolved between 1990 and 2010. The Spanish case has been the most dramatic given its growth from 2000 onwards, whereas France has been experiencing a very discreet rise although until 2004 it still led regarding the number of international migrants as a percentage of the population. With the exception of France, the country with largest labor migration, the inflexion point for the other Mediterranean countries began between 2000 and 2005. As it is possible to appreciate in the following graphic, between 2005 and 2005 Spain overcame France with regards to the international migrants as a percentage of the national population.

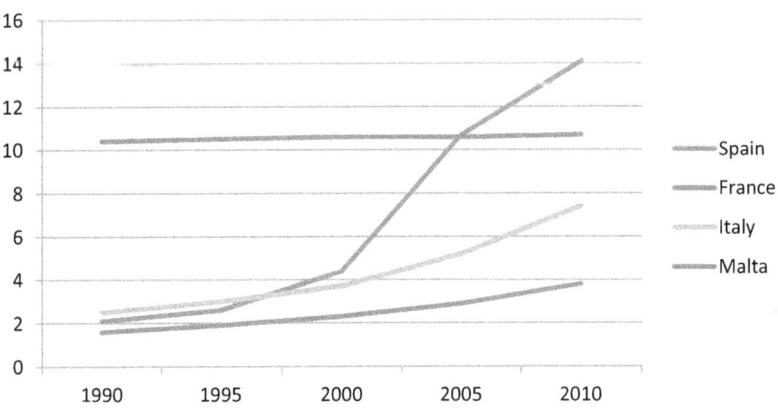

**Graphic 12.** International Migrants as a Percentage of the Population
**Source:** UN. Elaborated by the author.

In the following graphic, one can observe the annual change of the migrant stock in Southern European countries. Clearly, Spain has experienced again a very sharp growth between 2000 and 2005, whereas in Italy and Malta this growth has been much more reduced. The French case is almost irrelevant due to the fact of its long tradition attracting labor over the *treinte glorieuses*.

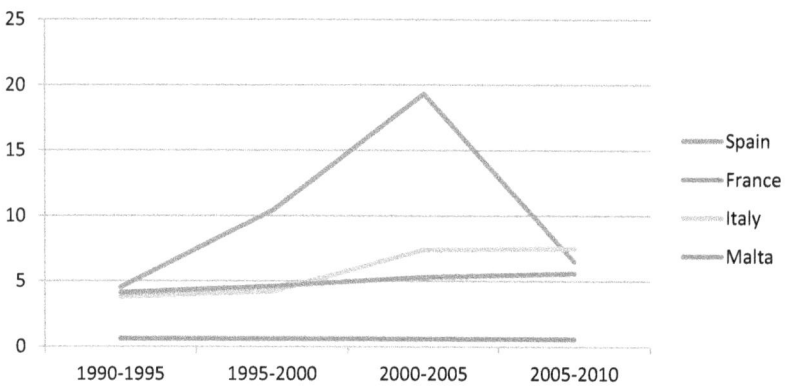

**Graphic 13.** Annual Rate of Change of the Migrant Stock % in Spain, Italy, France and Malta.
Source: UN. Elaborated by the author.

Going beyond the Mediterranean rim, the following two graphics focus on Europe. They show that the most important period in terms of migrants' inflow was between 2000 and 2005. From 1990 to 2010 the percentage of migrants as a percentage of the population in Europe grew from 7 percent to 10 percent. These two graphics below number 4 evidence the notable differences between the Mediterranean Europe and northern European countries as the aggregated values are much lower than the others displayed before. Therefore, these differential trends justify the fact that southern European countries like Spain, France and Italy have been acting as political entrepreneurs and brokers. They have been naturally raising awareness of these increasing flows and the potential risks they would entail for the entire European security.

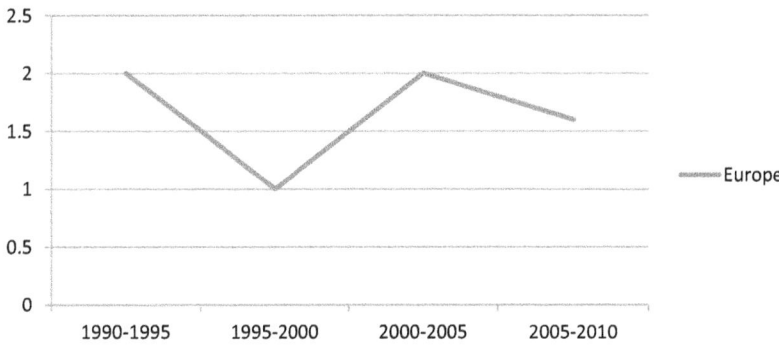

**Graphic 14.** Annual Rate of Change of the Migrant Stock % in Europe
Source: UN. Elaborated by the author.

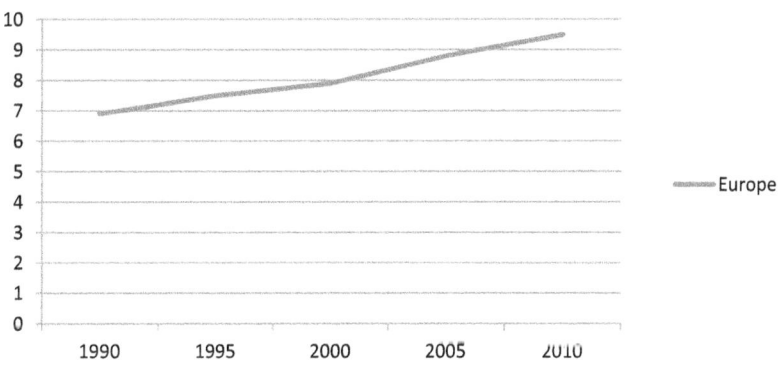

**Graphic 15.** International Migrants as a Percentage of the Population in Europe.
Source: UN. Elaborated by the author.

## 5.2 Gambling on the Needs and Problems of Southern Mediterranean Countries

The EU was created and developed to increase the economic power of member states and this economic interest established the ground for future political and diplomatic initiatives. Understanding this is fundamental to understanding how Euro-Mediterranean politics have evolved from 1995 onward.

The decade following the end of the Cold War was characterized by a certain optimism that was translated into a common European agreement upon a number of issues of common interest (Schumacher, 2004a; Rudolph, 2003). The definition of a new World Order aside the opportunities to develop creative political, economic and diplomatic mechanisms to occupy privileged positions within this new scenario were very apparent. As Calleya has stressed, ["the growth of regional arrangements since the end of the Cold War is partly due to the fact that great powers and regional powers welcomed the opportunity to participate in collective security and cooperative frameworks in which the costs of foreign policy actions are shared among several actors"] (Calleya, 2004; Schumacher, 2004b).

This wave of agreements was characterized by a rhetoric that used expressions like "north-south dialogue", "win-win solutions", "socio-economic development" or "increasing mutual security". These concepts were diplomatic mantras to sell new strategies to create new balances and new mechanisms intended to consolidate control of southern Mediterranean countries including the Maghreb and the Mashrek. Through the CL approach this is going to be demonstrated in analyzing EU's public speech.

Within this period as it was presented in the precedent chapters, the following were created: the 5+5 Initiative, the Council of the Mediterranean launched by the Maltese government, the Mediterranean Forum initiated by the Egyptian government, the Italian-Spanish proposal to flesh out the CSCM, the AMU and the Euro-Mediterranean Partnership (the Barcelona Process) led by the EU in 1995 (Ureta, 2010).

The Barcelona Process was intended to breathe new life into the Euro-Mediterranean relationship by increasing the collaborative aspect of the relationship, boosting democratic promotion, upholding human rights, safeguarding regional security and developing economic partnerships. Regional initiatives and multilateralism were also encouraged in an attempt to overcome, and put aside, the traditional bilateralism that had characterized the region up to that point.

At a communicational level, the political discourse surrounding this was optimistic, committed and proactive. However, some pessimistic voices were raised. Authors like Khader, have been criticising Euro-Mediterranean policies and mechanisms due to their lack of consistency, coherence and the attempt to verticalize Euro-Mediterranean relations (Khader, 2001; Khader 2009). Youngs criticized the lack of vision and the limitations to prioritize strategies and actions (Youngs, 1999).

In fact, as it has been also mentioned in Chapter 1, it was evident the deployment of a double discourse from the EU since the first attempts of gathering communitarian consensus on one hand and the post-1995 political and diplomatic developments on the other hand. Probably this communicational dichotomy was the seed of the future failure. This contradictory and inconsistent public discourse has contributed to enhance and reinforce an existing feeling of fear and mistrust within the entire Mediterranean region (Malmvig, 2006). This will be demonstrated by analyzing European public discourse with regards to migration relations issues.

The details of the Barcelona Process in the three areas of politics and security; economic and financial issues and social, cultural and human aspects have been widely examined (Vasconcelos, 2000; Edis, 1998; Gillespie, 1997). However, in the context of a communicative strategy on the Mediterranean, the security aspect was fundamental to gathering communitarian consensus. As Rudolph mentions, this security-focused on discourse found much support amongst states whose priority was developing free trade (Rudolph, 2003).

## 5.3 Trying to Manage Migration: The Fundamental Gap

None of the three baskets in the Barcelona process considered the migratory issue despite its centrality to the stability of the entire region. From 1995 to 1999 the European situation with regards to migration issues changed dramatically. From 1999 to 2004, and especially from the time of the al-Qaeda attacks on the US in September 2011 (the 9/11 attacks) migration and security were indefectibly associated. As the former Spanish secretary of state Anna Terron mentioned prior to the European Council of Tampere in 1999 there was no common immigration policy for Europe and Spain played a very important role in developing the importance of this issue in response to an acceleration of migratory flows from the Southern Mediterranean (Terron, 2011).

In fact, over this period Spain played a fundamental role in leading the EU on developing its migratory policies. Terrón mentioned during an interview, Spain was able to identify this trend because ["we came from this migratory experience and I think that we realized quicker than the rest of the EU that there was an intense migratory problem coming. Everything was very visible and on top of that the conscious of Spanish people to migration issues started to awake at that time"] (Terron, 2011).

The preparation of the Council of Tampere served precisely to create the mechanisms and the concept of a unified European migratory policy. During the Council of Tampere meeting, four intertwined factors were revealed as critical for the future sustainability of the Euro-Mediterranean region as a project: first, a common EU asylum and migration policy; second, a genuine European area of justice; third, a union-wide fight against crime; and fourth, stronger external action (European Council Tampere, 1999). These measures stressed the importance of managing, in a coordinated way, both existing and future migratory flows, especially points 22, 23 and 24. Point 23, highlighted the European commitment in fighting against illegal migration. That encouraged the development and implementation of a communitarian legislation to sanction serious crimes. Point 24, stressed the importance of Euro-Mediterranean cooperation in managing and controlling migration flows, an issue that reveals European worries and desires to increase domestic security.

From this point onwards it was possible to detect migration related issues shifting from the domain of low politics to the sphere of high politics. This approach acquired political justification and social acceptance after the 9/11 attacks. Subsequently, the migration-security nexus was institutionalized. As Thieux puts it the idea of multilateralism in the "idealistic" public discourse, reverted to the earlier model of the dangers of bilateral proximity (Thieux, 2005). As Anna Terron explained in her interview for this book:

> ["In considering both the sphere of the Common Foreign and Security Policy (CFSP) policies and the Justice and Home Affairs (JHA) realm, we lived since many years ago, I would say, from mid-1990s, with a very strong tension between the fear and the need of closing and managing the Euro-Mediterranean space and migratory flows with other criteria more linked to foreign policy, cooperation and development"] (Terron, 2011).

Following Tampere, the migratory issue continued to rise in importance within the EU political space jeopardizing the possibilities of developing a consistent and holistic Euro-Mediterranean approach. In 2003, and in parallel to the Barcelona Process, the European Neighborhood Policy (ENP) was launched. This created expectations and also uncertainties (Emerson and Noutcheva, 2005).

The internal consistency of this Mediterranean project had much to do with the consistency of the interaction between previous policies and mechanisms set in the region. On the other hand, the Hague Program (2004–2009) was an EU attempt to strengthen freedom, security and justice. It gave continuity to the points that were previously established during the European Council in Tampere. It described a master plan divided into 10 main points. Four of those 10 points were related to migration issues (EU, 2005). This underlined the centrality of migratory related issues within the European political debate. Adding to this, on 3 October 2005, FRONTEX (the European Agency for the Management of Operational Cooperation at the External Border of the Member States of the EU) became operational. FRONTEX aimed at providing an "integral global response" against the roots, dynamics and consequences posed by illegal migration within the Mediterranean (Carrera, 2007).

As Neal and Lutterbeck have argued, these mechanisms defined the pathway to the securitization of migration management policies (Neal, 2009). As a consequence, this more pragmatic and security-related approach provoked mistrust and misunderstanding among the EU's Mediterranean partners.

From this point only the necessary social, cultural and intercultural communication reforms were secondary objectives or even excuses to exert control and boost cooperation with Southern Mediterranean regimes on the issues of migration and illegal immigration control, the war against terrorism and drug and human trafficking.

Between 1995 and 2005, the economic gap between the EU and its Mediterranean neighbors had widened and this caused virtually uncontrollable migratory movements. So much so, in fact that it was now possible to argue that migration related issues represented an indicator of the ineffectiveness of multilateral political projects dealing with unbalanced economies sharing a very proximate and conflicted geographical space.

## 5.4 Migration and the Economic Cycle: Triggering National Fears, Evidencing Multilateral Deficiencies

The extent that multilateral projects like those launched by the EU in relation to the Mediterranean are endangered by possible economic slowdowns is an important question.

Solimano argues that ["international migration is like a barometer of economic and societal conditions in home countries with respect to the rest of the world"] (Solimano, 2003). There is some historical evidence that corroborate this link between migration and variations in the economic cycle. The global economic crisis that began in 2008 can be compared with the two other major crises of the twentieth Century in

1907–1908 and 1929–1935. Those crises were preceded by a sustained and optimistic period of buoyancy in terms of credit growth and low risk premiums; by periods of speculation driven by a fictitious feeling of financial euphoria.

By considering the two earlier crises, it is certainly possible to observe that both resulted in socio-political and economic policies aimed at closing societies, stoking nationalist fires, and rejecting earlier internationalist engagement. Of course, those political and social measures affected directly big numbers of migrants.

As Khalid Koser has pointed out, the same occurred systematically in response to other, more limited economic crises such as the Oil Crisis, 1973, the Asian financial crisis between 1997/1999, the Russian crisis of 1998 and the Latin American Crisis between 1998 and 2000 (Koser, 2009).

However, in contradiction to what occurred in the two previous global crises, the current crisis did not impact on international migration in the predicted way. As Koser has pointed out, the last global economic slowdown ["did not last long enough to disrupt migration plans that were already prepared before it began; the underlying forces that drive contemporary migration are not only economic, and in any case are so powerful that they are relatively immune to economic cycles and policy interventions"] (Koser, 2010).

Another example that would underpin these suggestions and that stresses the fact that international migration cannot be simply stopped or punished is related to the changing of routes followed by migrants. In the period between January and September 2010, FRONTEX reported a notable reduction in illegal migration on the Central Mediterranean Route. In Italy it was down 65 percent and in Malta, 98 percent. The Western Mediterranean Route saw a reduction in Spain of 20 percent. The Western Africa Route saw a reduction in the Canary Islands by 99 percent and the Central Eastern European Route saw a reduction of 24 percent in the Western Balkans.

However, over the same period, irregular migration increased by 369 percent on the Eastern Mediterranean Route along the Greek-Turkey land border (Frontex, 2010). Preventive measures on other routes had pushed migrants to find more accessible entry points (Lutterbeck, 2006). This is a common occurrence, but the fact that it happened in this specific way does challenge, partially at least, the hypothesis that links migration to the economic cycle. The reason is that Greece during

2010 was experiencing the worst economic and financial crisis within the euro-zone and was hardly a destination of choice for would-be economic migrants. Of course, Greece may well have appealed to many of these migrants as a transit destination, but it is less clear how much time they would have to wait before feeling able to attempt to move to other European country.

## 5.5 Migration and Public Opinion: National Politics Challenging International Projects

Migration is seen and used by political forces and political entrepreneurs, across the political spectrum (Castles and Miller, 2003; Ureta, 2009; Santamaría, 2003). In more industrialized countries, public opinion overwhelmingly subscribes to the idea that migration is triggered by extreme poverty. This can cause feelings of compassion and sympathy for migrants when immigration is very present in the public's everyday consciousness. However, such feelings diminish as soon as "visible migrants" become noticeable. The difference between "visible" and "invisible" migrants is related to phenotypic and cultural issues. The fear being that these people escaping from their homelands will take local jobs and will jeopardize the welfare system and cultural identity. While such views are linked to long time notions of the nation state, as Castles and Miller have studied, they do not, as Castells says, belong to the 'reality' of a globalized environment (Castells, 2007).

During a EUROMESCO meeting in Sharm el-Sheikh in 2007, Egyptian ambassador Gamal Bayoumi criticized European stakeholders because they were trying to develop an economic dialogue, favorable to EU interests, whereas at the same time, the EU was punishing migration from the Maghreb. This argument is the seed that more intensively pollutes Euro-Mediterranean relations.

European governments and political parties have been deploying intense and increasing anti-immigration campaigns. As it has been demonstrated, anti-immigrant and anti-Islam behaviour and political campaigns intensified from 2006 onwards. In the Netherlands after Pym Fortuyn's assassination –anti-immigrant and nationalist politician – Geert Wilders identified a political window to become a political broker and opportunist establishing the *Party for Freedom,* focusing its attention on anti-migrant and anti-Islam discourses (Vossen, 2010). For instance Spain in 2007 launched ads in Africa in order to discourage emigrants.

In Switzerland, SVP (*Scheweizerische Volkspartei*) headed by Christoph Blocher and first political force since 1999, deployed intense anti-immigrant political campaigns since 2007. The proposed referendums failed –to expulse foreigners committing crime, against free circulation and against the promotion of democratic naturalizations – however SVP inseminated a strong anti-immigrant sentiment within the country (Ureta and Profanter, 2011). Following a similar trend, during 2009 Italian extreme right-wing party *Lega Nord* started to prepare a video game aiming at sinking boats. The Spanish version was also prepared by a PP member in Catalonia. These attitudes and political behaviour were propelled by the rampant global financial crisis that was declared in 2008.

Most of this political discourse and xenophobic attitudes has been targeting Islam and Muslim citizens. As it has been demonstrated by Pew Global Attitude Project in 2008, negative views against Muslim communities and groups increased between 2004 and 2008. These negative perceptions increased from 37 percent to 52 percent in Spain; 46 to 50 percent in Germany; 30 to 46 percent in Poland; 29 to 38 percent in France and; 18 to 23 percent in the UK (Ureta and Profanter, 2011).

In 2003 Jacques Chirac launched a law approved by the parliament in 2004 banning the display of the Muslim veil, large Christian crosses and Jewish Kippa (Gemmie, 2004). This trend started to consolidate from 2005 onward. In September 2005 Danish newspaper *Jyllands-Posten* published the caricatures of Prophet Mohammad provoking intense debates on the limits of freedom of expression (Sturges, 2006). After this event reactions from the Muslim world ensued and what is more important, linked to the aspect of political responsibility, these reactions were easily predictable (Hervik, 2006). So it is possible to assume that political entrepreneurs and brokers make out of differences and social turmoil a substantial political benefit. Similar political strategies playing the "Islam" card were played in Europe from then onward. As mentioned earlier Swiss SVP after developing an anti-immigrant political campaign focused on an anti-minaret campaign. This happened in 2009 and this time the referendum was successful (Stussi, 2008). In 2010 Austrian far-right wing party *Freiheitlichen Partei Osterreich* (FPO) launched a video game named "Mosche Baba" –Bye bye Mosque – which main objective was the elimination of mosques.

However, despite the aforementioned examples, it is true that opinions about either positive or negative impacts or migration are normally assumptions that are not visually demonstrated. For the purpose of identifying the most relevant risks endangering Euro-Mediterranean relations the author designed for this dissertation a multivariable quantitative analysis to show how European public opinion reacted towards migration related issues over a period of almost 10 years. The hypothesis assumed that negative concepts such as terrorism, criminality, unemployment, security/securitization, are intentionally attached by political entrepreneurs to migration issues in order to influence public opinion.

In terms of methodology data from Eurobarometer (EB) studies that monitor EU public opinion were used for the period between 1999 and 2011. 36 European reports and 52 national reports –EB standards – from Spain, France, Italy and Malta were also sued due to their geographical exposure to southern Mediterranean migration and their role in lobbying, designing and managing Euro-Mediterranean policies. From 2002 to 2009 the author has consider the two Eurobarometers published every year –that's why the years are double-, whereas from 2010 the Eurobarometer is only published once a year.

Five variables were considered: Migration, employment, security, crime and terrorism. These show potential correlations, convergences and manipulations linking public speech, political strategies and public opinion. In order to quantify these correlations the author took account of how many times these concepts appeared in those reports in order to estimate the importance they had for public opinion.

In the Spanish case over the studied period until the second half of 2008, Spanish public opinion was reacting to specific political communication strategies and parties aiming at profiting from this sensitive issue. The graphic below shows that rising concerns on migration issues coincided with a peak in illegal immigration in 2006 (Terron, 2011).

Within the following two years the situation did not improve notably due to the consequences of the economic crisis and more restrictive policies introduced by the Zapatero's government (Bastida, 2008). Since 2008 within the context framed by the global economic crisis, migration and employment were the two most important concerns for Spanish public opinion. This demonstrates that political public speech and public opinion identified migration related issues and immigrants as one of the dangers and threats against native workers.

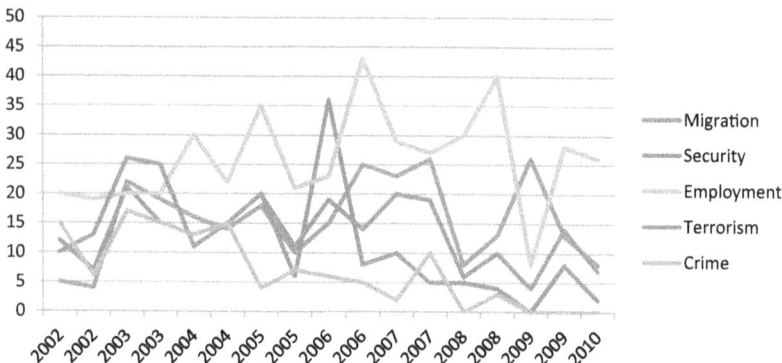

**Graphic 16.** Spain, Public Opinion
Source: Eurobarometer. Elaborated by the author.

The Italian case shows slight variations, although some patterns remain similar. That confirms the general European trend on migration related issues. On one hand migration issues threefold by 2003 and until 2007 the importance of migration related issues decreased. This happened during the pre-global crisis period. However from 2007 to 2008 migration related issues topped the concerns of Italian public opinion primarily due to the political communication strategies of Italian conservative parties like the *Lega Nord* who used migration fears to gain political consensus prior to the parliamentary elections of April 2008 (Guerra and Massetti, 2008).

Even before this, since 2001, increasing levels of migration were being linked to rising crime rates (Diamanti and Bordignon, 2001). In particular, the arrival of masses of illegal migrants from North Africa to Lampedussa contributed to creating the image of an "invasion", a word that has been widely used on populist political campaigns and mostly deployed by the *Lega Nord* and its leader Umberto Bossi.

From 2008 to 2009 illegal migrants at Lampedussa fell from 34,000 to 6,588 irregular immigrants (Maroni, 2010). But in 2011 the influx of illegal immigrants to Lampedussa skyrocketed as a consequence of the Libyan war, which led Italy to challenge the EU and raise the viability of the entire Schengen structure as will be discussed later (Koser, 2011). This evolution is demonstrated in the following graphic.

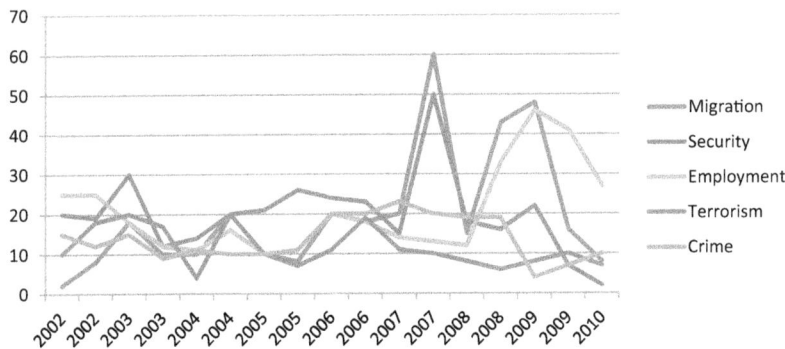

**Graphic 17.** Italy. Public Opinion.
Source: Eurobarometer. Elaborated by the author.

The French case is similar though its migration history is different. France had a much more long-standing tradition as a host country than Spain, Italy or Malta. However, despite this tradition, as Tränhardt has studied, political campaigns using migration to stir up xenophobia were already in use by political parties the end of the Cold War (Tränhardt, 1995). As the following graphic shows, like the Spanish and the Italian cases, 2003–2004 was a key period for rising fears over migration being used by politicians. It is important to note that in 2005 the riots on the outskirts of Paris in highly populated migrant areas, in the words of Kott and Duprez, posed a potential open challenge to the French Republican model of citizenship (Kott and Duprez, 2009).

At that time Nicolas Sarkozy was minister of interior and initiated a "zero tolerance" policy (Balibar, 2007). This coincided also with the French ban of headscarves in primary and secondary schools in a country where the 10 percent of the population is Muslim. From this time onward the political and social debate has been very polarized and has challenged the relationship between liberal values and religious freedom in a secular country (Joppke, 2009).

At the same time populist anti-immigration rhetoric was also deployed by French politicians like Jean Marie Le Pen, leader of far-right *National Front* (Betz and Johnson, 2004).

## 166  Migration, Security and Public Opinion

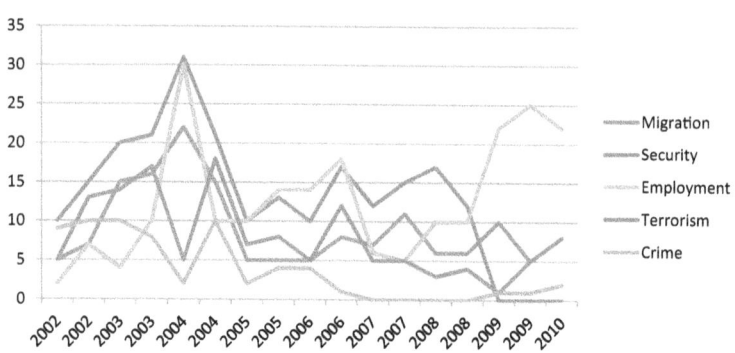

**Graphic 18.** France. Public Opinion.
Source: Eurobarometer. Elaborated by the author.

The Maltese case is also relevant due to a number of factors. On one hand the country's geographical situation placed the island very close to the North African shore. Linked to that the Malta accession to the EU in 2004 made the country much more attractive for those migrants looking to reach the EU. As Lutterbeck had shown in 2002, this ["small frontier island"] had already started to be viewed as a destination for seaborne illegal immigration (Lutterbeck, 2009). As the graph below highlights, migration has remained the second most important concern after employment for Maltese public opinion over the period under review. As Sammut has shown, the institutional influence of the media has played a major role in sustaining concerns on this issue (Sammut, 2010).

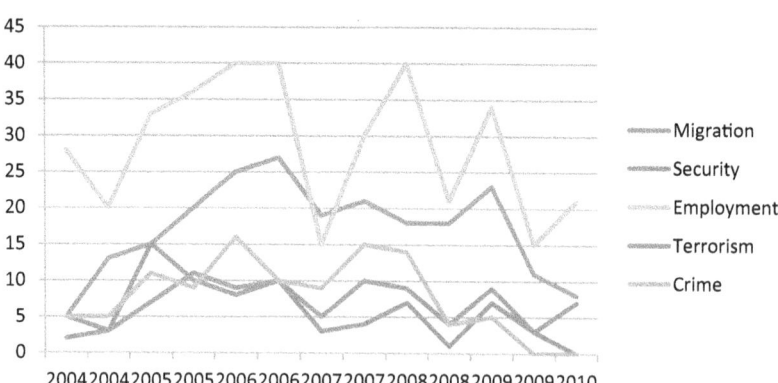

**Graphic 19.** Malta. Public Opinion.
Source: Eurobarometer. Elaborated by the author.

The following graphic shows that on the one hand French public opinion has reacted differently to immigration issues due to its long-standing tradition as a receiving country. However in comparing Italy, Spain and Malta it is possible to appreciate a particular correlation, leaving aside the 2008 Italian elections. This convergence is due to the fact that both Italy and Malta share the same geographical space and therefore they have to deal on equal basis against illegal migration coming from North-Africa.

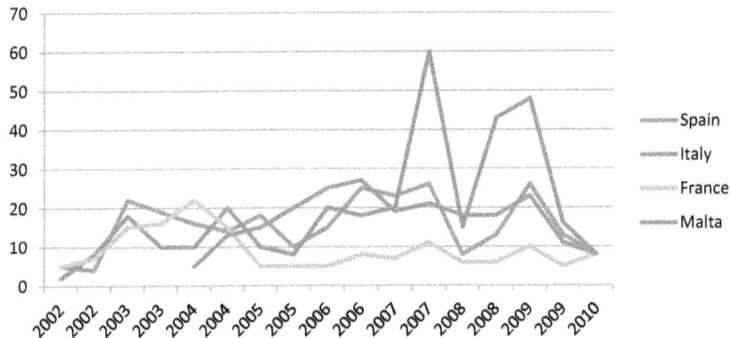

**Graphic 20.** Compared migration, Spain, Italy, France and Malta
Source: Eurobarometer. Elaborated by the author.

The following graphic represents the clearest picture showing how European public opinion has been shaped by political entrepreneurs and brokers in associating factors such as migration, crime, terrorism and security. The data confirms the hypothesis presented above that employment behaves independently and can be understood as an independent variable. This variable remains the most relevant for the public opinion and does not vary easily even over periods of good economic prospects. However, in considering the other four variables –migration, crime, security and terrorism – there is almost a linear convergence among them especially between the years 2007 and 2009. Political parties or brokers were very capable of acting irresponsibly in deploying political communications intended to make these convergences possible. As a consequence, European public opinion assimilated those images and claims and this generated a very particular social image, which in turn fuelled a hostile politico-cultural environment that has affected the entire Euro-Mediterranean building project.

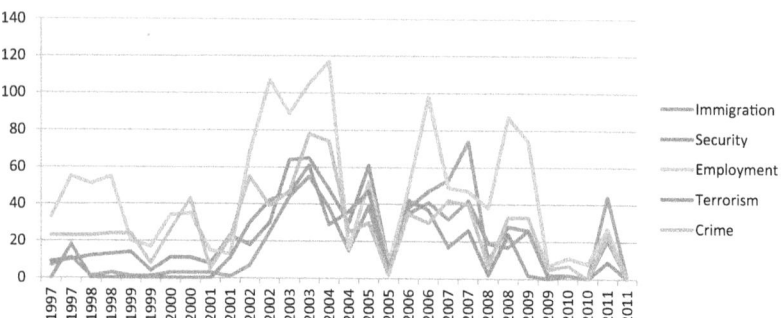

**Graphic 21.** Aggregated European Union.
**Source:** Eurobarometer. Elaborated by the author.

The following graphic shows a different perspective of the precedent one by highlighting how the trend lines –migration, security, crime and terrorism – tend to converge between 2007 and 2009.

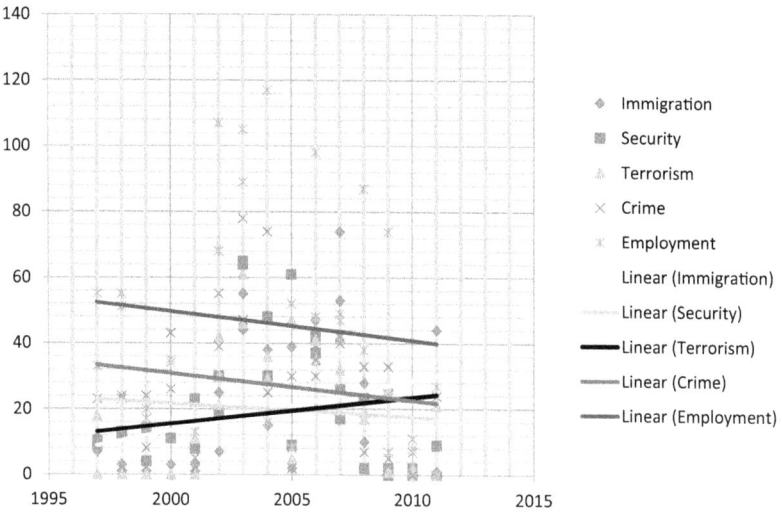

**Graphic 22.** Trend lines. Europe.
**Source:** Eurobarometer. Elaborated by the author.

Ivarsflaten has studied right-wing populist strategies to gain political support in seven western European countries by 2002, a time when migration issues started to top European concerns. He demonstrated that ["no populist right party performed well in elections around 2002 without mobilizing grievances over immigration. (...) only the appeal on the immigration issue unites all successful populist right parties"] (Ivarsflatten, 2002).

Over the following period this trend intensified as it has been also mentioned earlier. For instance in the 2009 European Parliamentary elections the EU swung to the right due to these increasing concerns. As Van Spanje, this was in part explained by a contagion effect among parties keen to be seen as holding an anti-immigration position that they believed to be popular with voters. As Van Spanje stresses, this contagion effect is not restricted to far-right wing parties but involve the entire political system ["without entering governments"] (Van Spanje, 2007).

In reality European political parties of all almost all ideological persuasions have been very active in identifying a profitable electoral opportunity in taking a stand against migration in general and against Muslim migration in particular. This general political trend that has been focusing on national politics had an international impact weakening international mechanisms and policies aiming at increasing Euro-Mediterranean dialogue and cooperation. This is central to understand how Euro-Mediterranean politics at large, have been undermined by political movements and local policies.

Given all this, the migration issue is the key and most representative variable to understand when examining the extent that EU multilateral projects or programs aimed at increasing Euro-Mediterranean dialogue and mutual relations suffer at the feet of national political interests. Without a mutually agreed and positive common migration policy neither free trade nor economic development projects are viable in the long term. Building upon these considerations, the next chapter analyses some of the most relevant long-term causes that have generated the Arab Spring. This case will also help to contextualize the impact and transformative power of the set of Euro-Mediterranean policies that were implemented over the precedent decades.

# 6 The Long Cultivation of the Arab Spring

The precedent chapters have been describing mostly the way, Spain as political entrepreneur and broker operated in order to put Mediterranean related issues on the European political and diplomatic map since its accession to EEC in 1985. The launch of the EMP represented the first achievement of that activity. On the other hand, the role played by France was also relevant and active with regards to the development of Euro-Mediterranean relations. Sarkozy tried to use the Mediterranean card to boost his political persona and propel his stature as state-man through his attempt of creating the Mediterranean Union. Their postures and attitudes as political entrepreneurs and brokers entail the possibility of assessing their views of the Mediterranean space in an instrumental way. It has been also explained that migratory issues and their management by single nation states and the EU alike, have contributed to the partial failure of these long-term policies and mechanism.

Instrumentally speaking, Euro-Mediterranean policies and mechanisms have tried to manage the differences and the long-standing challenges posed by deep economic cleavages between the north and the south of the Mediterranean. After twenty years and efforts the events of the "Arab Spring" along with the global financial crisis, have shaken the pillars that supported the Western principles of action, understanding and coordination with Southern Mediterranean government and societies. This chapter aims at explaining that the so-called "Arab Spring" has not been a phenomenon that erupted from a vacuum. The purpose of the following pages is to extract the main elements that have forged these uprisings throughout a long period of time. This period of time starts with the decolonization processes. The chapter also stresses the game of opposites and the rhetorical swifts that have differentiated a liberal discourse and the political intentions based on the principles of the *realpolitik*. Nevertheless, this chapter does not seek to blame neither Western stakeholders nor Southern Mediterranean governments. The outcome of the Arab Spring is a collaborative effort of cultivation that integrates many actors and factors.

## 6.1 Making Friends by Securing the House

On one hand, the success of Spain's initiatives, were the consequence of an active communication strategy that stressed the importance of the southern European border. On the other hand the conceptualization, design and implementation of such policies would have been impossible without the participation of other stakeholders and the EU at large. In considering this communication strategy it is possible to say that the baseline of such discourse was related to the securitization of the EU. And this argument fitted very well within a context of European expansion and integration.

The President of the European commission at that time – 1991-, Jacques Delors in referring to the Iraq war commented that, in considering security issues ["the community's influence and ability to act have not kept pace. We should interpret this as yet another argument for moving towards a form of political union embracing a common foreign and security policy"] (Delors, 1991). These words were underpinning the conclusions of the European Council of Rome that was held between the 14$^{th}$ and the 15$^{th}$ of December 1990. During the Intergovernmental Conference, the European Council gave the mandate to consolidate these policies. They crystalized one year later with the signature of the Treaty of Maastricht. Within the five pillars of the Treaty, the fifth one referred to the establishment of a common foreign and security policy (EU, 1992).

As it is possible to recall from Chapter 1, in this early 1990s, Spain was deploying a threatening discourse describing North African dangers in order to attract the attention from European stakeholders. This was the discourse strategy behind the design and consolidation of the Euro-Mediterranean partnership. Indeed, Jacques Delors defined the importance of the European southern border as the ["Community's Southern Flank"] and the relevance of both the Maghreb and the Mashrek for the European security. At that time Delors indicated that Europe was strengthening its ties with the Arab world. In so doing there was a list of protocols of financial assistance, trade agreements, technical assistance as well as environmental policies among others. And he stressed that Europe ["will have to raise its sights even higher, redoubling its efforts, if it is to create the economic conditions conducive to peace and the stability and development for the region"] (Delors, 1991). This means that the European Union was expecting that by improving socio-economic conditions in the Southern Mediterranean flank, the region would increase in security and that would contribute to improve Europe's security.

During the same years, there were also some scholarly voices theorizing about the role of the Mediterranean and Europe's security. For instance, in 1991 Aliboni interrogated about the nature of the Mediterranean. Is it considered a 'centre', a 'frontier' or a 'crossroads'? His answer was clear: It is a frontier. This appraisal has remained. While Southern European countries like Spain, Italy, Malta or Greece have been more integrated into Europe, Southern Mediterranean countries – especially the Maghreb has been increasing its political, socio-cultural and economic gap with Europe. This gap has been even deepened more due to the religious differences that dominate both the north and the south rim of the Mediterranean.

Aliboni stresses that, therefore, these differences are also the differences between: the Judaeo-Christian and Islamic world; the developed and the underdeveloped; the democratic and the authoritarian. However, this game of opposites would also represent the characteristic that allowed the development of the Euro-Mediterranean relations during the years to come. This game of opposites can be defined, on one hand as the ingredient that made possible the development of the Euro-Mediterranean relations. And, on the other hand, it was the seed that defined the essence of the so-called Arab spring. This chapter will explain this game.

Following a very similar rationale –before the signature of the Euro-Mediterranean Partnership (EMP) in 1995 – and keeping in mind the ["hazards of globalization"], Delors highlighted again that neighbouring countries of the Mediterranean constituted one of the most representative dangers for Europe's security. Associated to this risk, he mentioned Samuel Huntington's hypothesis on the clash of civilizations as an ulterior challenge that may break up in future decades (Delors, 1994).

These comments reinforce the ideas expressed throughout the precedent chapters. The most important aspect and policy pursued by a growing Europe was related to reinforce its security within an increasingly globalized world. Therefore, the interest in helping Southern Mediterranean countries was not justified by the simple fact of helping these societies *per se*. The European model of aid and policy making towards Southern Mediterranean countries was designed and instrumented to increase Europe's security and to take advantage of both its comparative and competitive advantages. The *realpolitik* was the driving –and somehow hidden – element of Europe's foreign action.

This realist discourse was evident until almost the signature of the EMP in 1995. However, once the EMP was signed the European rhetoric architecture changed. It stressed the importance of developing mutual understanding and cooperation, as well as increasing trade and socio-cultural relations. Despite this rhetorical change, the same purposes and objectives where lying behind these relations: Europe's security. This rhetorical change is also part of the aforementioned game of opposites.

Nevertheless, some European politicians voiced that this *realpolitik* approach was not an accurate definition. Štefan Füle, – European Commissioner for the Enlargement and Neighbourhood Policy – said that: "Too many of us fell prey to the assumption that authoritarian regimes were a guarantee of stability in the region. This was not even *Realpolitik*. It was, at best, short-termism – and the kind of short-termism that makes the long term ever more difficult to build" (Fule, 2011). However, according to what it has been exposed throughout the precedent chapters, a policy and an approach that started to be designed at the end of the 1980s can be difficulty defined as short termism.

## 6.2 Understanding "center/s-periphery/ies" Relations and Interactions

The abovementioned game of opposites was not unidirectional. On the contrary, somehow it represented a tacit pact between political elites from Europe and Southern Mediterranean countries. This understanding was necessary to fulfil and to achieve the objectives ambitioned by European stakeholders. This communication was also necessary to reinforce and ensure the objectives of stability and continuity demanded by North African authoritarian systems. As a matter of fact, this subtle political stability was also needed by Europe in order to facilitate the achievement of its security policy and objectives.

This approach might not be shared by large groups of politicians, activists from the civil society or by the vast majority of the public opinion. Essentially, from Western societies it is very common to study and explain North-South relations –the more industrialized and the less industrialized world – considering losers and winners. This is possible by assuming that there are absolute victims and perpetrators. Scholarly speaking a number of theories can be responsible for the creation of this mind-set. On one hand the World system theory propagated by Wallerstein explains –through a neo-Marxist approach – that inequality among nations is the product of deficiencies in power relations between core regions and peripheral states (Wallerstein, 1974). According to Wallerstein the relation between the core and the periphery is determined by differential costs structures of production (Wallerstein, 1987). In between, he also mentions the existence of semi-peripheral countries that aim at becoming core regions.

On the other hand theorists like Prebisch and Singer elaborated similar conclusions and theoretical frameworks (Prebisch, 1949; Singer, 1949). The product was defined as dependency theory. Even though this theoretical body entails some differences from Wallerstein's approach. Their approach assures that the structure of the market would be responsible for the existence of deep inequality in the World system. However, either considering the markets or states the responsible of such inequalities, the "winners-losers" scheme seems to be evident in both cases. These complementary theories were created within the post II WW era.

This was a peculiar context that boosted notable independency processes and paved the road for long and tedious post-colonial problems. It was also the moment in which Western states also started to create their aid policies as well as creating the basis of a new soft power propelled by –among others – the institutions created under the auspices of the Bretton-Woods conference (Nye, 2003; Woods, 2008). Within this context, the public opinion in general tends to associate post-colonial countries with the victims and Western countries and those trying to take advantage and abuse those peripheral areas.

In reviewing these theories, some authors like Palme, have expressed a critical view by saying that instead of speaking about theories, it would be better to speak about methodologies to analyse asymmetric contexts (Palme, 1978). Either considered theories or methodologies, what it results clear is that the vertical relation between the developed and the underdeveloped appears to be automatic.

However, this vertical and dependent description of North-South relations appears to be weaker than initially would seem. It might be possible even to consider a transversal and linked relation between these categories. Both metaphorically and materially speaking, the "core-periphery" asymmetric relation can be easily understood. In accepting these two categories –it is also possible to include here the "semi-periphery" – it would be possible to define them as –almost transversally – transactional hubs or units. In considering their asymmetric and differential power and influence, the core, the periphery and the semi-periphery would have a transactional nature and they would be naturally linked by elite interests and market forces.

In so considering, the "cores" and the "peripheries" would be dynamic and they would be connected among themselves in order to guarantee their sustainability and survival. These transactional hubs are not just dominated and shaped by market forces themselves, but by elite groups that use the market forces to define and achieve their objectives. Therefore, it is possible to speak about "cores" within the so-called "periphery". These "cores" are controlled by local politico-economic elites that have reinforced their position and influence since the postcolonial processes started. In most of cases, these "cores" are linked and their survival is connected to western interests as they ensure investments, financial aid, and politic and diplomatic support.

Therefore, in order to ensure local, regional or national influence, Western stakeholders have supported the "peripheral cores" in order to ensure political collaboration. This dynamic has strengthened the consolidation of authoritarian –and collaborative – regimes. This game has been played at the expenses of the real "periphery": the civil society.

By accepting this conceptual twist to the existing theory, it would be possible to say that the differences between the core and the periphery should not be strictly related to the degree of economic sophistication and market development. In less industrialized states the core would be integrated by politico-economic elites that control mostly those economic sectors that contribute to the formal economy. And they aim at controlling – within the long term – the socio-political and cultural mechanisms of those social groups integrating both the informal and the formal economy: the periphery. These governments do this with the help of Western stakeholders and groups of economic interest.

The existence of a clear fracture between core and periphery in Maghreb countries have been at the very base of the socio-economic unrests. On one hand it was possible that North African countries were showing sustained economic growth and improvement in its social and human indexes. On the other hand, the economic growth evidenced by the statistics at national level did not voice the regional disparities and a deficient redistribution of wealth and opportunities.

Whereas core regions enjoyed the benefits of an economy based on international transactions and investment, peripheral regions witnessed this economic growth without really participating of its benefits. As a matter of fact, as the African Development Bank (AfDB) has stated, regional disparities were at the core of the socio-economic unrest in cities like Kasserine and Thala (AfDV, 2011). This phenomenon is a constant characteristic across the region and therefore, a consistent and long-standing discriminatory policy creates resentment, insecurity and brings the main ingredients of civil unrest. As Boutayeb and Helmert have highlighted, despite the heralded economic growth, North African countries –and governments – still have to face the challenge of inequality at different levels: rural-urban and advantaged-marginalised regions and cities (Boutayeb and Helmert, 2011).

Following with this rational, Arab scholars are not surprised about the explosion of these uprisings. The limited economic trickle down from more industrialized regions to poorer areas in MENA countries as well as the limited investment in developing rural areas represents one of the most important long-term factors that have shaped the nature of the Arab Spring. Zurayk has studied and confirmed this hypothesis by studying the collapse of traditional agricultural livelihoods in the MENA region since late 1980s (Zurayk, 2012). That process of stagnation and socio-economic depression over the time, generated a very extended wave of disillusionment towards developmental policies lead by Western agencies and stakeholders.

Therefore is not only possible to accuse Western stakeholders to have acted according to the principles of the *realpolitik* which is legitimate if it is clear and is ensued by a consistent rhetoric. This *realpolitik* approach has been also played by Maghreb's and Maschrek's governments. All North African countries share commonalities with regards to their relations with Western stakeholders, although these commonalities have not coincided in the time.

## 6.3 Heirs, Political Mortgages and "forced" Allies

Multilateral projects, policies and mechanisms oblige the parts to take actions towards the definition of collaborative approaches and procedures. In considering the stakeholder-management/analysis approach it is important to recognise the role, interest and impact of each country with regards to the project. As Brugha and Varvavoszky have expressed, understanding and analysing involved stakeholders and main actors, can help to understand their future behaviour, their intentions, the nature and potential impact or interference of their agendas and the resources –and limitations – that they can contribute with (Brugha and Varvavoszky, 2000). This analysis is crucial to better define and implement decision-making processes as well as to increase efficiency and efficacy towards the achievement of durable and mutually beneficial outcomes.

As it has been mentioned in precedent chapters, while defining the scope and nature of the EMP, politicians interrogated themselves about who should integrate the partnership. Without elaborating a precise stakeholder analysis *per se,* European representatives thought that probably they should concentrate their efforts just considering the Western Mediterranean, because it was there where the EU might have a stronger voice, and most relevant politico-economic interests. However, at the end it was decided to integrate the widest approach. This understanding has generated some successes like sitting together Israel and Palestine. But on the other hand, it has generated more problems, misunderstandings and divisions that have undermined a smother evolution of the EMP as well as limiting its potential impacts.

Without offering now a detailed stakeholder analysis, it is interesting to offer a short overview of the historical and political developments of two relevant cases: Libya and Tunisia. This might help to understand the long-standing elements that are behind the long incubation of the "Arab Spring". Some of the rulers of these countries –Libya, Egypt or Tunisia – were defined as dictators after the uprisings broke up. Before they were considered friends and business partners.

### 6.3.1 Libya

After the Italian colonisation Libya started its independency in 1951. Since then the socio-economic and political history of the country has been determined by internal and external inflows of capital (Vandewalle, 1998). This unproductive and sclerotic model has been crucial for its existence. During the first years as an independent country, however, Libya relied very much on external influence. King Idris I accepted the protection offered by Great Britain in 1953 and the US one year later in exchange of technical and financial aid. However this economic and political model started to change in 1959 when oil was discovered in Libya and the country started to be less dependent from international sources.

As a matter of fact, the ruling monarch started to develop important infrastructural programmes in order to start modernising the country (Clarke, 1963). With the prospects of becoming a clearly richer country also the internal political dynamics started to change. In parallel, the increasing pan-Arabism across the region played also an important role in Libya's political change. After Egypt was defeated in the six days war against Israel in 1967, King Idris's political stance was seen as pro-Israeli and this fact contributed largely to the coup lead by Qaddafi in 1969.

Since Qaadafi overthrown the monarchy in Libya, the country launched an aggressive diplomatic campaign to eliminate any foreign presence in the country. One of the first actions following a philosophy based on the Arab nationalism, was related with the withdrawal of British troops and the liquidation of their military bases. One year later the last US troops abandoned also the country and Italian properties were confiscated and over the next years the country completed an extensive and intensive nationalization process.

From 1969 Libyan-Western relations have been experiencing ups and downs due to Qaadafi's understanding of international politics and diplomacy on one hand and Libya's economic attractiveness on the other hand. However it is possible to say that until 1999 Libyan relations with the west have been problematic in general and particularly tense with the EU. Especially the Lockerbie affair in 1988 and the UTA bombings in 1989 were determinant to shade these complicated relations (Joffè, 2001).

A similar antagonism reigned between Libya and the US due to evident accusations of cooperation with terrorist groups (Zoubir, 2002). From 1999 Libya-EU relations have twisted and clear signs of mutual understanding and cooperation have been regular. As Lutterbeck has noted since the sanctions were lifted in 1999, Libya has become increasingly important for EU's main security and economic interests. The two political entities started to develop cooperation on three main areas: immigration control, military cooperation and an intense collaboration in the energy field. However, despite the acknowledgment of Libya's violations in human rights issues for instance, little discourse and concerns were raised within the EU as Lutterbeck has stressed.

However cosmetically there have been occasions when the EU has been reluctant to collaborate with Libya. For instance, even though, by 2006 the ENPI Regulation (European Neighbourhood and Partnership Initiative) included Libya, the Regional Strategy Document 2007–2013, the Regional Indicative Programme 2007–2010 and the Regional Indicative Programme 2010–2013 did not include the North African country due to political controversies. Therefore Libya did not participate in the ongoing regional projects architected by the EMP (European Commission, 2011). In spite of similar situations, from 1999 onward and thanks to the importance of Libya's role in contributing to European overall security, the collaboration between Europe and Libya has been characterized by an economic and political realism putting aside any criticism about Qaddafi's authoritarian regime and overall socio-political deficits (Zoubir, 2009). This two-ways realism was due to Europe's interest in securing its borders on one hand and the despair of Qaddafi's pan-Arab ambitions on the other hand (Dawisha, 2002).

### 6.3.2 Tunisia

The history of the contemporary Maghreb has suffered the effects of a dilemma and a theoretical-practical contradiction that has been not solved. At a theoretical level: the desire of establishing democratic policies and processes. At a practical level: the consolidation of authoritarian regimes. This contradiction was very evident in Tunisia since the first years as an independent country. Habib Bourguiba who fought for the independence since the early 1930s and who eradicated the monarchy, acceded to the presidency in 1957. Concurring with Moore, Bourguiba's first three years in office could be defined as a ["presidential monarchy"] (Moore, 1995).

With this attitude, as soon as Bourguiba became president, he started to establish important socio-political, cultural and economic reforms. Most of these reforms were designed to work towards the progressive secularization of the nation. The 1956 Code of Personal Status that was issued in 1956 and that substituted Shari'a Law represented an important milestone (Mounira, 2001). Associated with this fundamental change, the 1958 education reform marked also a very important turn in Tunisia's future and it was a priority also during Ben Ali's government. The hypothesis was clear: An educated society would represent the basis of a developing country.

However, this hypothesis entailed an error of calculation. If a government pretends to keep an autocracy, it is not possible to launch a mass education policy without establishing a progressive and measurable democratization process where the civil society achieves higher quotas of socio-political representation. The revolution outbreak would be a matter of time. If, on top of that the demographic pyramid is mostly dominated by youngsters, that model is not sustainable. Fuller has studied these questions and has explained them through the youth bulge theory (Fuller, 1995). On top of that, as it has been discussed in the chapter on migration related issues, if within the long term due to a wider global openness and exchange, this youth fails in its ambitions to migrate to more industrialized regions –due to endogenous or exogenous reasons like the securitization of migration in the EU as a consequence of the global economic crisis – it is more likely to predict a revolt (Schomaker, 2013).

From 1963 to 1981 the Néo-Destour party was the only recognised and authorised political organization. In 1975 Bourguiba made the mistake of self-proclaim himself: president for life. The same mistake was made again by Ben Ali by seeking his presidential perpetuation although through the celebration of parliamentary elections. Therefore it is possible to say that the seeds of the revolution were planted since the establishment of the independent republic.

The revolution was a matter of time. The required time that the government would need to keep –helped by international stakeholders – an artificial image of social peace and progress. This artificial image and the imposition of the vertical imposition of this political model were promoted through a ["rhetoric of beauty"].

## 6.4 A Surprising Arab Spring?

The explosion of revolts across North Africa and the Middle East surprised experts and public opinion in general alike. Western stakeholders did not know how to react, what to say and what to expect. However this surprise factor was the consequence of a long-term denial.

In 2005 both the World Bank (WB) and the Islamic Development Bank (ISDB), defined Tunisia as a successful story (Hassan, 2005). This report mentioned among a wide array of data, that by 2005 the Tunisians enjoy more than two-and-a-half times the real incomes than their parents 30 years ago. It also mentions that the EU was the dominant partner of Tunisia – 67 percent – and that the Tunisian economic diversification and development was mostly motivated by these inflows of foreign capital. This report, despite discussing the main elements related to Tunisia's development did not mention anything about the situation of human rights or the socio-political limitations imposed by an authoritarian regime.

In following a similar trend and in focusing merely on economic and financial figures, on June 3 2008, the *Sunday Times* placed Tunisia among the best economies to invest in times of crisis. The same year, the Global Competitiveness Report elaborated by the World Economic Forum (WEF) confirmed Tunisia's leading position in North Africa accounting to the 36$^{th}$ at world level. The report also mentioned-without showing any specific criticism – that ["the country's institutions, which have been favourably assessed for a number of years, are one of its major competitive advantages"] (WEF, 2008). According to the report, in order to improve its competitiveness, the country should reform its rigid labour market.

Indeed, flexibility of the labour market represents one of the most important criteria taken into consideration by neo-liberal institutions. This is the discourse and the argumentation that has defined a new financial architecture that ended up with the global economic crisis that started in 2008. As Crotty has stated, the evolution of the pre-crisis financial system took form of cycles where deregulation accompanied by a quick financial innovation –speculation – stimulated strong and optimistic financial booms that finalised into deep crises (Crotty, 2009).

The same trend was confirmed by *Newsweek* in 2010 as well as by the Global Competitiveness Report elaborated by the World Economic Forum (WEF). Before the 17 December 2010 when the Tunisian vegetable seller Mohamed Bouzizi set himself fire the region seemed to be still attractive for international investors and tourists. According to the 2010 UNDP Human Development Report, Tunisia, Algeria and Morocco where among the top 10 movers in Human Development Index (HDI) non income HDI and GDP between 1970 and 2010 (UNDP, 2010). As a matter of fact, Francisco R. Rodríguez and Emma Samman, the authors of this classification, defined this phenomenon as the North African miracle. This definition was probably building on the same concept coined by Colton in 1996 who was mainly focusing on macroeconomic outcomes (Colton, 1996).

However as Ndikumana and Boyce have stated, this optimistic definition clashed against the long-term structural deficiencies inherent to the North African socio-economic and political systems (Ndikumana and Boyce, 2012). As a matter of fact, in considering the whole sociopolitical and economic fabric, and beyond macroeconomic figures, persistent inequalities in distribution of wealth and power paved the road to the revolutions. Before the revolts and despite the good prognosis published by economic and financial agencies, associations like Human Rights Watch were denouncing notable violations of human rights in the MENA region. For instance in 2009, Tunisian authorities refused to grant legal recognition to "every truly independent human rights organization" (Human Rights Watch, 2009).

It would be possible to say that the most miraculous part of this process is that the revolutions did not start earlier. The global financial crisis that started in 2008 precipitated the uprisings. Western countries and organizations limited their resources and budgets to fund projects in Southern Mediterranean countries and socio-politically speaking, the effects of the economic crisis fuelled "dormant" revolts.

### 6.4.1 Revolutions Propelled by the International Financial System

MENA countries and economies have been traditionally –and increasingly – affected by the international economic environment. Most of countries in the MENA region faced shortage of international currency since the 1980s onward (Kara and Hleihel, 1996). This context forced MENA countries to adopt policies especially designed to stabilize and ensure the structural adjustment of their economies. As Karshenas has pointed out, new development strategies were focused towards a higher participation in the international markets, a less interventionist state and trade liberalization (Karshenas, 2001). Countries with limited natural resources like Tunisia, Morocco or Egypt to name few, adopted these strategies with the objective of attracting foreign capital to achieve two objectives: to fund their particular process of socio-economic development and; to consolidate their ambitions to perpetuate their authoritarian regimes.

Given that North African markets where clearly dependant on foreign direct investment as well as financial aid, it would be possible to hypothesize that a retrenchment of these investments due to the crisis would affect the advancement of those markets. It would be also possible to question, to what extent economic and financial crises would affect regime change and boost democratization processes. As Gasiorowski has studied focusing on less industrialized countries, inflationary crisis inhibited democratization processes from the 1950s through early 1970s. But on the contrary may have facilitated them in the late 1980s and recessionary crises may have facilitated democratic breakdowns but did not have effect on democratic transitions during this period (Gasiorowski, 1996).

In which manners the global economic crisis that started in 2008 affected MENA markets? And, to what extent this crisis affected North

African political regimes and boosted democratization processes across the region? It is important to analyse these two questions considering first the short and the medium-long term.

Within the short term an according to the World Bank, MENA countries due to their limited integration with global financial circuits, were not deeply affected by the global financial crisis. In considering the short term, oil exporting countries were more exposed to the consequences of the global financial crisis, whereas non-oil exporting countries were not vulnerable at the same level due to a limited international exposure of their economies (Branch and Loewe, 2009).

However this short term optimism should be scrutinized with attention as within the medium and long term the effects of the crisis would have affected (Kouane, 2009). Within the short term is not accurate to say that MENA markets were limitedly impacted. As the FAO Food Price Index shows –from 2000 to 2014 – food prices increased notably in 2008 (FAO, 2014). As a consequence 2008 marked also the year where food riots spread across the MENA region and Africa in general (Lagi, Bertrand and Bar Yam, 2011).

As the OECD has mentioned, even before 2008 the MENA region faced rampant socio-economic –and also political – challenges. One of the most relevant ones was related with absorbing a growing and youth population into its labour markets. Before the crisis it was calculated that by 2020 the region should have to create 100 million new jobs to accommodate the growing population. As Joffé has noted, the main causes that provoked these events ["lie in the global economic crisis and in the neo-patrimonial political natures of regional states"] (Joffé, 2013).

## 6.5 EU's Response, Scope and Outcomes

Bearing in mind the previous sections it is possible to say that the so-called Arab Spring has multiple paternities. One paternity is obviously held by MENA countries. The other paternity on the other hand corresponds to Western stakeholders which have been also responsible for the outbreak of these events. Hollis has highlighted that EU policies helped to trigger these revolts, not intentionally but by default. More precisely Hollis mentions that EU policies such as the Mediterranean Partner Countries (MPCs) under the framework of the Barcelona Process (EMP) as well as the European Neighbourhood Policy (ENP) have contributed to generate these outcomes (Hollis, 2012).

This has happened because beyond the EU's rhetoric focused on win-win solutions and shared prosperity, these policies were merely orchestrated to prioritize Europe's security at the expenses of real developmental needs from Southern Mediterranean societies –not governments – and this was especially true considering the securitization of migration related issues as it was presented in Chapter 5. On top of that, as some economists have mentioned, the objective of shared prosperity would have only possible through the convergence of living standards, together with the increase of exports from MPCs –indicator that would represent reversing the trend of economically dependent countries – as well as the intensification of intra-regional trade (Montero Luque and Peeters, 2009). Despite the allocation of financial resources from the mechanisms designed by the EU, these conditions did not improve notably and their achievement seems to be improvable especially within the context of the global economic crisis and the aftermaths of the Arab Spring.

When the revolts in North Africa started in December 2010, the initial reactions from Western governments were ambiguous and slow. As it has been stressed by some scholars, the reaction demonstrated by Spain –for instance – towards the first steps of the Arab Spring was tepid and hesitant.

One of the factors that may surprise the general audience is that, somehow, these events were even unexpected for specialized scholars (Gause, 2011). The EU's perception towards their action to react against the episodes related to the Arab Spring is subjective. The EU considers that its institutional reaction dated on March 8 2011 was an early response. EU's answer was the publication of a document titled ["A Partnership for Democracy and Shared Prosperity with the Southern Mediterranean"] (EU, 2011). Within the text it is recognised that the EU must not be a passive spectator. This institutional conviction and strategic partnership was designed to work on three elements.

The first one is related to politico-institutional issues and addressed: Democratic transformation and institution building mainly focusing on strengthening fundamental freedoms, as well as developing constitutional and judiciary reforms while working also to fight against corruption.

The second one focused on social issues and aimed at developing stronger partnerships with the civil society and specially the youth. The third element was specifically designed to cope with educational and economic issues. It concretely would support the creation of Small and Medium Enterprises (SMES) in order to reinforce entrepreneurial activities among the youth as well as developing specific training and educational systems in poorer regions.

This document was also important because forced to the EU to re-think its approach to migration related issues because this argument is capital to strengthen good relations and communication with Southern Mediterranean countries. Therefore there were established the Dialogues for Migration, Mobility and Security, which were centred of the EU's renewed Global Approach to Migration and Mobility (GAMM). Nevertheless, as Carrera, den Hertog and Parkin have stressed, the success of this approach as well as its power to develop cooperative partnerships that might underpin the socio-economic and political transformations in North Africa, would depend on how the GAMM at the EU has been reinterpreted. Mostly because so far it was characterized by internal fragmentation, lack of transparency as well as the predominance of home affairs and security actors (Carrera, den Hertog and Parkin, 2012).

However, in analysing the theoretical postulates of this strategic partnership, is it possible to speak about a renovation of the way the EU expresses its concerns and plans? Or on the contrary there is continuity? Teti by using critical discourse analysis (CDA) concludes that this document maintains unaltered the vision of the liberal model that the EU implemented in the past in order to generate developmental processes and democratization across the region. This unmuted rhetoric would lead to the repetition of the same mistakes that generated the Arab Spring and would contribute to increase the poor image of the EU across the MENA region (Teti, 2012).

Beyond its philosophical aspects that reflect a foreign policy flooded with normative values, on the operational side very little is said about how the new approach should be implemented and propagated (Echague, Hirchov and Mikail, 2011). Also, operationally speaking it is also relevant to reflect about national interests and EU interests. For instance, whereas within the first steps of the Arab Spring both France and Britain lead the interventions in North Africa, Germany remained apart. In considering these operational limitations and leadership it is also important to assess how France and Spain reacted in front of the outbreak of the Arab Spring.

Egyptian, Libyan or Tunisian democratic transitions were expected from Western stakeholders to be "westernized" democratic transitions. In this sense the ENP would have to re-focus its objectives in order to face existent challenges within the short, medium and long term. In fact, as it has been abovementioned, the strategic partnership was in charge to promote and support these transitions and regime change. Between 2011 to the end of 2013, the available budget managed by the European Neighbourhood and Partnership Instrument amounted to EUR 4 billion. Obviously this support, as it has been highlighted by Perthes, has generated concrete expectations towards Europe, and one of those, which would be difficult to attain is freedom to travel. One of the most critical aspects characterizing EU-MENA relations (Perthes, 2011).

Within this context it was established the "more for more" conditional principle that rewarded with more support and aid for deeper and better application of democratic transformations. This principle of conditionality, however, was applied keeping the same philosophy that supported authoritarian regimes in the past, before the outbreak of the revolts. Therefore in continuing with the same philosophy, "more for more" would also represent a good excuse to buy the loyalty of new governments that were internally fragmented since the beginning. Does "more for more" means, more financial aid for more alignment and obedience? Intrinsically, this principle and its practical application reinforce the same *realpolitik* that was exhibited by the EU before the revolts.

Within the short term, these neo-liberal economic and financial formulas might have worked, especially considering the post-revolutionary optimism. However, within the medium and long term, once the new governments start their processes of consolidation the outcomes of these policies would be less clear. As recognised by Catherin Ashton ["we should offer help but not to dictate outcomes or impose solutions. As international community we will accompany the transformation if our help is welcome. But the future lies firmly in the hands of the Tunisian and Egyptian people. They own their revolution and rightly so"] (Ashton, 2011). Theoretically speaking Ashton was right. The application of such theory would be problematic within the long term.

However there are a number of elements that should be taken into consideration to better evaluate the propensity of these programmes either to success or to fail. First it is necessary to acknowledge the existence of two speeds. One speed is related to the investment schedule of such financial programmes. They have to be invested within a precise timeframe. The second speed is related to the capacity of Southern Mediterranean partners to absorb, assimilate and generate sustainable changes to their long-standing structural issues. This speed demands longer periods of time. Second, it was clear the mechanisms –either considering bilateral or multilateral relations – that would prevent the stakeholders from imposing certain recipes and practices that comply with Western standards and expectations.

For the EU and the rest of Western stakeholders, one of the most relevant worries was related to the terrorism and the "re-Islamization" of the society in North African countries. As a matter of fact, Europe was worried when Ennahda won the elections in Tunisia and some European countries like Spain made statements about this new situation demonstrated fear and lack of understanding. José María Margallo, Spain's minister of Foreign Affairs asked to the Tunisian authorities to keep control of those political groups that wanted to establish the Shari'a. After long discussions, Tunisia's minister of Foreign Affairs Rafik Ben Abdesalem, confirmed on the 26 March 2012 that the government would not apply the Shari'a law.

The precedent comments show that the so-called Arab spring tested the coherence and consistency of Euro-Mediterranean policies. They also demonstrate that the same patterns exhibited by Western countries over the precedent decades are present in the way the managed the crises and faced the new "democratic" processes. Therefore, the collective actions guided by the principle of the *realpolitik* will continue to be present in the way EU stakeholders understand and manage their relations with either Maghreb and Mashrek countries.

# Conclusions

Since 1985 and with its accession to the EEC Spain played the Mediterranean political card to increase its diplomatic stature and influence in Europe. As it has been explained in precedent chapters Spain's initiative facilitated the design and implementation of Euro-Mediterranean policies from 1995 onward. Beyond the EMP and after the political twist lead by José María Aznar, Zapatero tried to regain diplomatic presence by launching the AoC. Despite these efforts, Spain did not achieve in a sustainable way the objectives marked by its ambitions. The reaction towards Sarkozy's impulsive proposal to create a Union for the Mediterranean evidenced lack of preparedness and diplomatic agility. And even in the case of winning UfM's headquarters in Barcelona, it is not possible to say Spain consolidated a leading position as a relevant diplomatic player. Prior to outbreak of the Arab Spring, on one hand the global financial impacted negatively on Spain, with the subsequent loss of international respect. But despite the rigidity of Spain's migration policies towards Southern Mediterranean neighbours, the diplomatic relations with North African regimes remained stable.

This book concludes that rhetorically speaking it would be possible to consider, within the short term, that all studied governments behaved and justified their political communication strategies following the characteristics of political entrepreneurs and brokers. However, in considering the medium and long run, almost of them have been acting as political opportunists speculating, irresponsibly, on international threats and existing myths, globally speaking, in order to better defend national interests.

Following on from this political entrepreneurs and brokers like Spain and France identified opportunities, designed projects and worked towards their institutionalization on the basis of a competitive and non-cooperative approach. Rhetorically speaking they sold Euro-Mediterranean problems as European problems, but the strongest interest behind this strategy was related to the defence and protection of national objectives.

Political communication strategies deployed first by France or Spain and later by the EU were characterized by a double discourse. On one hand, once a political entrepreneur and broker identified a political window, in order to convince potential partners the "selling" and "marketing" discourse raised questions related to common European security issues. Once the policy was designed, in order to attract the consensus from Southern Mediterranean partners, the discourse was defined by the necessity of implementing win-win and cooperative mechanisms. However southern Mediterranean countries were not actively involved in the process of design and implementation. That generated an asymmetrical Euro-Mediterranean relation and encouraged economic and political dependency.

The EU and national political entrepreneurs and brokers alike hypothesized that improving socio-economic standards – through trade, investments (FDI), development aid (ODA) – in southern Mediterranean countries, would reduce incentives to migrate. This, in turn would bring more security to Europe. This hypothesis proved wrong as an improvement of socio-economic standards in sending countries accelerated migration within the short and medium term.

Beyond the aforementioned double discourse, that entailed an operational and instrumental dimension, European priorities continued to be European security, broadly understood, regional stability and increasing trade opportunities. Cultural, educational, socio-economic projects remained relegated to a secondary position. In that sense changing socio-economic and political contexts –like the global economic crisis or increasing migration flows from Southern Mediterranean countries – compromised the continuity of those programmes and the consistency of the policies and mechanisms.

In considering these changing contexts, along with economic issues, migration-management policies and their evolution represent one of the most relevant aspects to analyse the consistency and coherence of multilateral and multicultural projects, policies and mechanisms.

If political and trade interests and objectives are not accompanied by an integrative common migration policy, the sustainability of common projects, mechanisms and policies is weak and within the medium and long term they are doomed to fail.

The EU's international politics, policies, mechanisms and diplomacy are strictly bound to local, regional and national levels. The EU can design, institutionalize and implement policies and mechanisms but their overall performance will depend on how local, regional and national politics evolve and adapt according to changing scenarios on the ground.

## Conclusions 191

From 2006 onwards a more restrictive attitude towards migration, culminating in the "criminalization" of the issue across Europe occurred. This increasing tendency of political parties to display negative attitudes towards migrants in general and against Muslim migrants in particular resulted in the deterioration of Euro-Mediterranean relations. This, in turn led to a progressive deterioration in Euro-Mediterranean cooperation and confidence building and associated policies and mechanisms.

Western leaders, political entrepreneurs and brokers, have been trying to find and support cooperative and collaborative regimes. In parallel, leaders from Southern Mediterranean countries have been playing that game in order to consolidate their leadership.

Despite the number of Euro-Mediterranean initiatives, projects and mechanisms European partners did not show a commitment to choosing the right objectives and expectations for the challenges they faced. Therefore, at a managerial level, these policies have been ambiguous and scarcely productive.

In line with this lack, the EU's political discourse was dominated by the term "will". On one hand this connotates the political "will" needed to develop and build mechanisms and policies. On the other hand there is a notable absence of rhetoric formulas indicating accomplished strategies, policies or objectives.

In these terms, this book has attempted to compare, understand how Spanish and French leaders have acted as entrepreneurs and brokers in creating, designing, implementing and institutionalizing –also communicating – Euro-Mediterranean politics. In order to do this it has developed 12 factors that are relevant to achieving these objectives. One of these factors is contextual, whereas the rest are transversal. The contextual factor is "Europeanism". Transversal factors are: opportunism, individualism, originality, entrepreneurship, brokerage, consistency, negotiation, cooperative and competitive behaviour, analytic skills, charisma and, communication skills. All are ranked on a scale from 1 to 5, with 1 being the minimum and 5 the maximum.

The graph below – number 23 – shows the ideal representation of a political broker and entrepreneur. Nevertheless in applying this approach it is necessary to explain how "entrepreneurs", "brokers" and "opportunists" are interpreted. In considering this graphic, "entrepreneurs" and "brokers" are defined by a positive connotation. Therefore, "entrepreneurs" and "brokers" would start new ideas and projects and broker them on the basis of socio-political and cultural responsibility.

They would aim to produce sustainable change, establish win-win situations and pursue their objectives consistently and coherently. They would work towards the completion of short, mid and long term objectives.

Conversely, "opportunists" are defined here by their short term-speculative behaviour. There are also two variables that have to be explained: cooperative and competitive behaviour. With regards to multilateral political projects involving heterogeneous partners, cooperative behaviour would be expected from political brokers and entrepreneurs. This behaviour would ensure the design, implementation, institutionalization and development of win-win political projects. A competitive behaviour would be linked to an "opportunist" approach that seeks to maximize individual gains. This attitude is counterproductive for the achievement of common strategic goals. The graphic number 23 displays the ideal image of a political broker and entrepreneur bearing in mind the aforementioned comments and specifications.

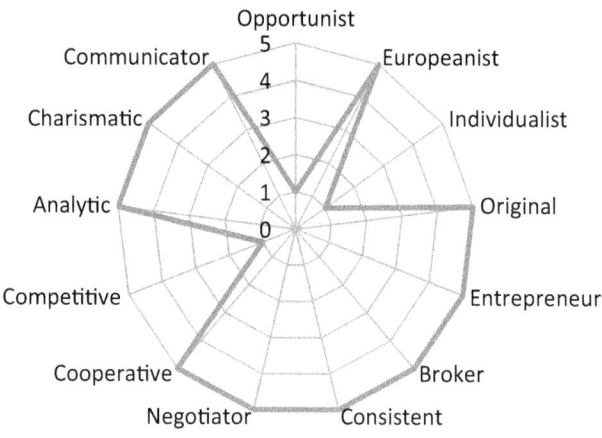

**Graphic 23.** Ideal Political Broker/Entrepreneur.
Source: Elaborated by the author.

The graphic number 24 compares the political profiles of: Felipe González, José María Aznar, José Luis Rodriguez Zapatero and Nicolas Sarkozy. On this point it was not possible to gain access to more French senior politicians and diplomats that would have allowed a more balanced appraisal of Franco-Spanish competition and cooperation. With regards to Spanish politicians and diplomats, it is possible to appreciate a higher number of personalities affiliated to the PSOE. However, on the other hand politicians and diplomats from the PSOE were more involved than those affiliated to the PP in developing a Euro-Mediterranean approach.

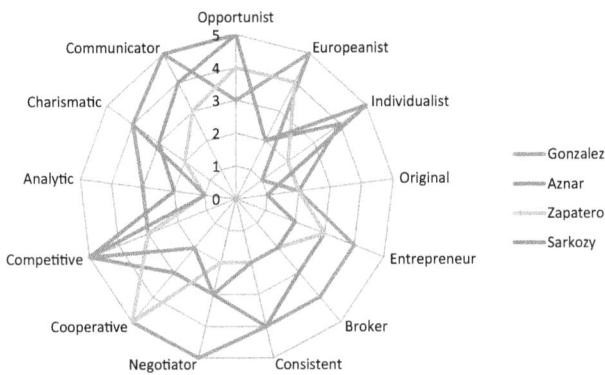

**Graphic 24.** Leaders. Behaviour and Characteristics.
**Source:** Elaborated by the author.

In considering the four leaders, Felipe González is the one who is closer to the ideal of political entrepreneur and broker considering abovementioned comments and specifications. In line with this, González was the most consistent and coherent political entrepreneur in designing, negotiating and lobbying for creating a cooperative and European project that would also serve Spanish interests. This resulted in the launch of the Barcelona Process.

Aznar and Sarkozy were typical examples of opportunists and individualists deploying a competitive and non-Europeanist attitude. Whereas Zapatero coincided more with González's style. However he did not display the negotiating and communication skills or strong charisma of his predecessor as Spanish leader. However, Sarkozy, Aznar and Zapatero all acted more like opportunists in terms of launching initiatives without ensuring strong planning.

## Political Entrepreneurship Cycle (PEC)

The Political Entrepreneur Cycle (PEC) can be applied to a number of contexts where the role of political brokers, entrepreneurs and other kind of socio-political actors and agents has to be analysed. The PEC should be applied to a number of different socio-cultural, economic and political contexts in order to better identify transversal –constant – and contextual variables. From this point of view, next steps aimed at developing the PEC should focus on the elaboration of a replicable and scalable system –or a sort of metrics – to measure the five stages of the cycle. The PEC using the CL a CDA approach will be useful to assess long cycles and micro-cycles alike. In considering both multilateral and bilateral political projects and mechanisms, the PCE will be also useful to determine political responsibilities and identify in advance potential failures. As was defined in the first section of this thesis, political entrepreneurs follow a four-stage process to develop their interest and ambitions. This process is linear because it considers the creation, design, implementation and institutionalization of policies and mechanisms. However, this process should be circular not a mere linear description and figure number 1 shows.

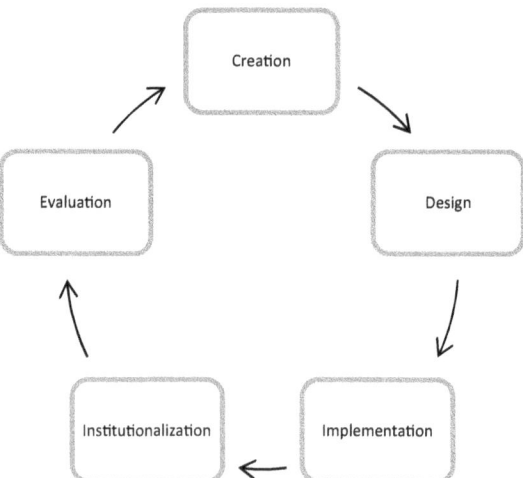

**Figure 1.** Political Entrepreneurship Cycle Elaborated by the author.
**Source:** Elaborated by the author.

## Creation

The creation of Euro-Mediterranean policies and mechanisms –from the EMP to the UfM– was led by political entrepreneurs and brokers, notably France and Spain, who had particular national interests. Beyond these political brokers and entrepreneurs were also interested in increasing their political and diplomatic stature and influence within the international system. During this first stage, political entrepreneurs and brokers lobbied massively with European partners –especially key ones like Germany – in order to gather the necessary support.

## Design

The stage of design did not correspond strictly to political entrepreneurs and brokers. The design stage entailed the Europeanization of the project. Within this stage small and medium powers like Spain tried to collaborate with major powers like Germany in order to get support and influence in the design process in the service of their own interests. During this stage both the debate on and the design of Euro-Mediterranean policies and mechanisms were mostly concentrated on the European side. Although these policies included the participation of southern Mediterranean countries, their involvement and participation were hardly considered. At the same time the planning and design was very abstract and was not considered in terms of clear short, medium or long term goals.

## Implementation

The implementation of these mechanisms and policies were problematic due to the above bad planning and design. Once initiated these policies were inefficient and vulnerable to contextual socio-economic and political changes due to a lack of objectives and benchmarks. However, the division between northern and southern Mediterranean partners was also very apparent in this stage. This absence of multilateral coordination, horizontal communication and clear shared objectives and tasks contributed to the weak implementation that ended up with the failure of the processes within the medium and long term. In considering this stage, the political entrepreneurs and brokers that launched these projects and mechanisms did not actively engage in correcting these deficiencies. Therefore their role was secondary and barely operative.

## Institutionalization

These common mechanisms were designed to defend EU's interests and overall security. The institutionalization established the structure, the budget and the official procedures to put into motion the objectives and ideas developed over the previous stages. However, institutionalized mechanism to evaluate the fulfilment of objectives and milestones were not available. That contributed to generate more ambiguity and institutional weakness. On top of that, within this institutionalization, again, southern Mediterranean countries were not fully integrated. This occasioned the verticalization of communication processes.

The decision-making processes were mostly concentrated on the EU side for two reasons. First it was easier to institutionalize these policies and mechanisms within the EU due to its higher socio-cultural, political and economic homogeneity. Second, southern Mediterranean countries were not organized around strong common institutional bodies and therefore their organizational and negotiation capacities were very limited. This prevented the possibility of solving problems and facing contextual challenges.

## Evaluation

Analysing the EU's public speech is important in understanding how political brokers and entrepreneurs have been impacting and shaping the EU's political agenda. With regards to Euro-Mediterranean politics the graph below –number 25 – enables us to appreciate the cycle that started in 1992 and ended in 2013. One can see how relevant issues such as migration, Mediterranean, Security, Arab/Muslim, terrorism and racism, have all played a role over this period of time. This is reflected in graphic number 25.

Indeed, within this 20 years cycle it is possible to identify three micro-cycles. The first micro-cycle lasted between 1993 and 1996. That represented the inception and launch of the Barcelona process and within this first micro-cycle it is possible to appreciate the convergence of the topics security and Mediterranean. This reveals that the interest in developing this Euro-Mediterranean mechanism was mostly due to strict security issues and concerns.

The second micro-cycle spanned the period between 1999 and the beginning of 2002. Again the convergence between Mediterranean and security is evident, especially after the 9/11 al-Qaeda attacks on the

United States. The third and last micro-cycle extended from 2004 to 2008. Within this last micro-cycle the converging variables were: terrorism, migration and security, whereas Mediterranean started to lost momentum. However, this micro-cycle coincided with the evaluation of the Barcelona process in 2005. The last year of this micro-cycle, 2008, coincided both with the start of the global financial crisis and the launch of the UfM. The last part of the cycle between 2009 and 2013 shows that Euro-Mediterranean politics declined and its presence within the EU's public speech almost disappeared.

In analysing these factors it is possible to say that Euro-Mediterranean politics as a communitarian project failed. The three micro-cycles show the peaks where political entrepreneurs and brokers were more active. This also shows that there was political inconsistency and coherence. This trend also shows that political entrepreneurs and brokers were mostly interested in short-medium term results, rather than developing a consistent and cooperative –and responsible – political and diplomatic project.

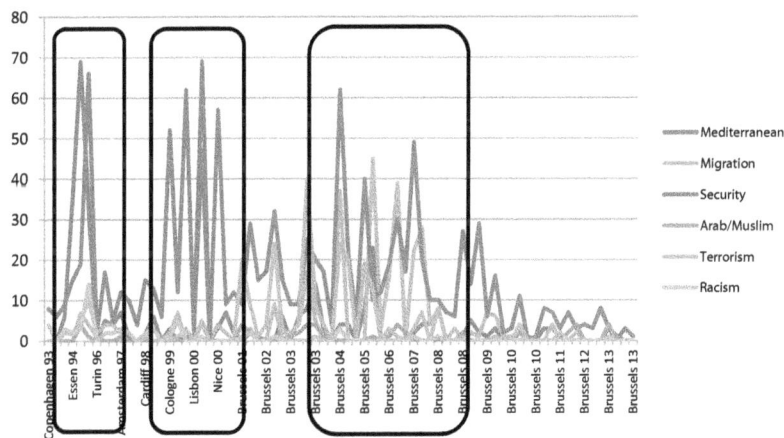

**Graphic 25.** Long-Term Comparative Analysis Council of Europe, Public Speech. 1993–2013
Source: European Council. Elaborated by the author.

Connected to the graphic number 25, it is also important to understand how European public opinion integrated and understood the EU's public speech. The analysed variables in this case were immigration, security, terrorism, crime and unemployment. Whereas unemployment played an independent role because in reality it is not linked to other contextual variations, the other variables tended to converge between 2005 and 2009. This coincides with the third micro-cycle presented above and it is represented in graphic number 26.

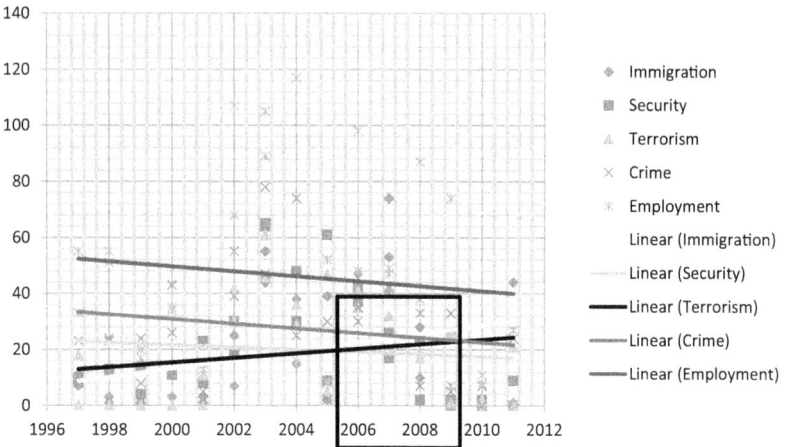

**Graphic 26.** Trend line. European Public Opinion, 1997–2011.
Source: Eurobarometer. Elaborated by the author.

The connections between the EU's public speech and EU public opinion crossover. This convergence is also important in evaluating why Euro-Mediterranean mechanisms and platforms failed. It is not possible to try to develop multilateral political, diplomatic, economic and socio-cultural projects and mechanisms involving heterogeneous stakeholders, while at local, regional and national levels, political brokers and entrepreneurs try to gather socio-political consensus manipulating sensitive variables such as migration, terrorism, security and crime that would contribute to generate mistrust and misunderstandings between European and Southern Mediterranean countries.

With the ongoing financial global crisis that started in 2008, multilateral projects devoting particular attention to the Mediterranean commenced to suffer a notable stagnation. The long-standing problems separating the North and Southern rim of the Mediterranean started to deepen and the badly managed root-problems finally favoured the explosion of the revolts baptised as the Arab Spring demonstrating the incapacity of Western stakeholders to react in due time and with sustainable recipes. Given that the revolts have signaled a shift in the understanding of Euro-Arab relations, it could be argued that the true revolutions are still to come unless public servants adopt clearly defined ethical and responsible communication and management policies.

# References

## A Primary Sources

Central Historic Archives. Council of Europe. Adhesion of Spain. 07.15 1 (46):7. Dossiers 1–12. Box 1.

Commission of the European Communities. (1978): List of Main EEC Agreements with Other Countries. Europe Information, Spokesperson Group and Directorate General for Information. 6/78.

Council of Europe. Resolution 640 (1976) 1. 28th Assembly. 21–22 September 1976. Brussels.

Eurobarometer Standards. European Union. From 1999 to 2013. Numbers: 51, 52, 53, 54, 55, 56, 57, 58, 59, 60, 61, 62, 63, 64, 65, 66, 67, 68, 69, 70, 71, 72, 73, 74, 75, 76, 77, 78, 79, 80.

Eurobarometer Standard. Spain. From 2002 to 2011. 57, 58, 59, 60, 61, 62, 63, 64, 65, 66, 67, 68, 69, 70, 71, 72, 73, 74, 75, 76, 77, 78, 79, 80.

Eurobarometer Standard. France. From 2002 to 2011. 57, 58, 59, 60, 61, 62, 63, 64, 65, 66, 67, 68, 69, 70, 71, 72, 73, 74, 75, 76, 77, 78, 79, 80.

Eurobarometer Standard. Italy. From 2002 to 2011. 57, 58, 59, 60, 61, 62, 63, 64, 65, 66, 67, 68, 69, 70, 71, 72, 73, 74, 75, 76, 77, 78, 79, 80.

Eurobarometer Standard. Malta. From 2004 to 2011. 61, 62, 63, 64, 65, 66, 67, 68, 69, 70, 71, 72, 73, 74, 75, 76, 77, 78, 79, 80.

European Council. Conclusions of the Presidency. From 1993 to 2013: Copenhagen, Brussels (1993), Corfu, Essen (1994), Cannes, Madrid (1995), Turin, Florence, Dublin (1996), Amsterdam, Luxembourg (1997), Cardiff, Vienna (1998), Berlin, Cologne, Tampere, Helsinki (1999), Lisbon, St. María, Biarritz, Nice (2000), Stockholm, Goteborg, Brussels, Laeken (2001), Copenhagen, Brussels, Seville, Barcelona (2002), Brussels, Brussels, Thessaloniki, Brussels (2003), Brussels x 4 (2004) Brussels x 3 (2005), Brussels x 3 (2006), Brussels x 3 (2007), Brussels x 4 (2008), Brussels x 4 (2009), Brussels x 4 (2009), Brussels x 5 (2010), Brussels x 4 (2011), Brussels x 4 (2012), Brussels x 4 (2013).

Historic Archives. Council of the European Union. Brussels. Archival EEC and EAEC, CM2/1970–851. Dossier relative to the signing of the commercial agreement between Spain and the EEC.

Historic Archives. Council of the European Union. Brussels. Archival. EEC and EAEC, CM2/1970–851. Dossier relative to the signing of the commercial agreement between Spain and the EEC.

Historic Archives. Council of the European Union. Brussels. Archival. EEC and EAEC, CM2/1970–851. Dossier relative to the signing of the commercial agreement between Spain and the EEC. Letter sent by P.H. Spaak to Castiella. 2 June 1964.

National Institute of Demographic Studies. (INED). Spain. Demographics.

National Institute of Statistics and Economic Studies (INSEE). France. Demographics.

Opinion on the Spain's Application for Membership. Bulletin of the European Community. September 1978. N. Supplement 9/1978. P.14–21. Brussels.

OSCE. Official Monthly Bulletin of Foreign Trade. February 1978.

# B Printed Books

Aarts, J., and Keijs, W. (Eds.) (1990): *Theory and Practice in Corpus Linguistics*. Rodopi, Amsterdam.

Abulafia, D. (1994): *A Mediterranean Emporium: The Catalan Kingdom of Majorca*. Cambridge University Press, Cambridge.

Abulafia, D. (Ed.) (2003): *The Mediterranean in History*. Thames and Hudson, London.

Abulafia, D. (2011): *The Great Sea: A Human History of the Mediterranean*. Oxford University Press.

Ackrill, R. (2000): *The Common Agricultural Policy*. Sheffield Academic Press, Sheffield.

Aeschiman, E., and Boltanski, C. (2007): *Chirac d'Arabie. Les Mirages d'Une Politique Française*. Grasset, Paris.

Ageron, C.R. (1991): *Modern Algeria. A History from 1930 to Present*. Hurst and Co. London.

Aliboni, R., Joffé, J., Lannon, E., Mahjoub, A., Saaf, A., and Vasconcelos, A. (2008): *Union for the Mediterranean: Building on the Barcelona Acquis*. European Union Institute for Security Studies, Brussels.

Allison, G. (1971): *Essence of Decision: Explaining the Cuban Missile Crisis*. Little Brown, Boston.

# References

Allison, G., and Szanton, P. (1976): *Remaking Foreign Policy*. Basic Books, New York.

Andersen, R. (2006): *A Century of Media, A Century of War*. Peter Lang, Oxford.

Aristegui, G. (2000): "Nuestra Postura Ante los Conflictos Cercanos, Oriente Medio, Balcanes, Terrorismo y Narcotráfico". In Anon. (Eds.): *España, Un Actor Destacado en el Ámbito Internacional*. FAES, Madrid. Pp. 1–81–247.

Aristegui, G. (2003): "El Terrorismo y las Nuevas Amenazas". In Valle Gálvez, A. (Ed.): *Los Nuevos Escenarios Internacionales y Europeos del Derecho y la Seguridad*. Madrid. Escuela Diplomática. Pp. 1–09–124.

Arostegui, J. (1996): *La Guerra Civil 1936–1939: La Ruptura Democrática*. Temas de Hoy, Madrid.

Ayache, G. (1981): *Les Origines de la Guerre du Rif*. Publications de la Sorbonne, Paris.

Aziza, M. (2003): *La Sociedad Rifeña frente al Protectorado Español en Marruecos*. Bellaterra, Barcelona.

Aznar, J.M. (1992): "Principales Problemas Que Afectan al Sur de Europa: Política de Seguridad y Cooperación en el Mediterráneo". In Trillo Figueroa, J. et Al.: *El Fundamentalismo Islámico*. Fundación Cánovas del Castillo, Madrid. Pp. 8–9–100.

Babbie, E.R. (1990): *Survey Research Methods*. Wadsworth Publishing, Belmont.

Babbie, E.R. (2012): *The Practice of Social Research*. Cengage Learning.

Babiano, J., and Fernández A. (1998): *El Asociacionismo Como Estrategia Cultural: Los Emigrantes Españoles en Francia. 1956–1974*. Fundación 1 de Mayo, Madrid.

Babiano, J., and Fernández A. (2002): *El Fenómeno de la Irregularidad en la Emigración Española de los Años 60*. Fundación 1 de Mayo, Madrid.

Baduel, P.R. (1980): *Societe et Emigration Temporaire au Netzaoua. Tunisie*. CNRS, Paris.

Baker, P. (2006): *Using Corpora in Discourse Analysis*. Continuum, London.

Baker, P. (2010): "Corpus Methods in Linguistics". In Litosseliti, L. (Ed.): *Research Methods in Linguistics*. Continuum, London.

Baldwin-Edwards, M. (2005): *Migration in the Middle East and the Mediterranean.* Commission Mondiale sur les Migrations Internationales. PAntheion University, Greece.

Balfour, S. (2005): "The Reinvention of Spanish Conservatism: The Popular Party Since 1989". In Balfour, S. (Ed.): *The Politics of Contemporary Spain.* Routledge, London. Pp. 1–46.

Balibar, E., and Wallerstein, I.M. (1991): *Race, Nation, Class: Ambiguous Identities.* Verso, London.

Ball, S. (1994): "Political Interviews and the Politics of Interviewing". In Walford, G. (Ed.): *Researching the Powerful in Education.* University College London Press, London.

Baon, R. (2001): *Historia del Partido Popular.* Ibersaf. Editores, Madrid.

Bardají, R.L. (1992): *España En El Nuevo Entorno Estratégico.* Incipe, Madrid.

Basora, A. (2009): "US-Spain Relations from the Perspective of 2009". In CIDOB: *International Yearbook 2009.* Bellaterra, Barcelona.

Beer, F.A., and Hariman, R. (1996): Post Realism, Just War on the Gulf War Debate". In Feldman, O., and De Landtsheer, O. (Eds.): *Politically Speaking: A Worldwide Examination of Language Used in the Public Sphere.* Praeger. New York. Pp. 1–85–194.

Beer, F.A., and Hariman, R. (1998): *Post-Realism: The Rhetoric Turn in International Relations.* Michigan State University, Michigan, Ann Arbor.

Bennet, L.W. (2008): *News: The Politics of Illusion.* Longman, London.

Berg, B.L. (2001): *Qualitative Research Methods for the Social Sciences.* Pearson Publishing, Boston.

Bernstein, S. (1993): *The Republic of De Gaulle, 1958–1969.* Cambridge University Press, Cambridge.

Biber, D., Conrad, S., and Reppen, R. (1998): *Corpus Linguistics: Investigating Language and Use.* Cambridge University Press, Cambridge.

Bicchi, F. (2007): *European Foreign Policy Making Toward the Mediterranean.* Palgrave Macmillan, London.

Bidwell, R. (1973): *Morocco Under Colonial Rule: French Administration of Rural Areas 1912–1956.* Frank Cass, London.

Borchard, K., and Buchheim, C. (1991): "The Marshall Plan and Key Economic Sectors: A Microeconomic Perspective". In Maier, C., and Bischof, G. (Eds.): *Marshall Plan and Germany.* Oxford, Berg.

Brauch, H.G., Marquina, A., Brad, A., and Liotta, P. (Ed.) (2000): *Euro-Mediterranean Partnership for the 21st Century*. Palgrave MacMillan, London.

Braudel, F. (1995): *The Mediterranean and the Mediterranean in the Age of Phillip II*. University of California Press, Berkeley and Los Angeles.

Braudel, F. (1996): *The Mediterranean and The Mediterranean World in the Age of Philip II*. University of California Press. Vols. 1 and 2.

Breyer, Y.A. (2011): *Corpora in Language Teaching and Learning. Potential, Evaluation, Challenges*. Peter Lang, Oxford.

Brink, P.J. (1989): "Issues in Reliability and Validity". In Morse, J.M. (Ed.): *Qualitative Nursing Research: A Contemporary Dialogue*. Sage, Thousands Oaks, CA. Pp. 5-2-74.

Brown, C. (2005): *Understanding International Relations*. Palgrave Macmilllan, London. 3rd Edition.

Brown, T.A. (1988): *Migration and Politics: The Impact of Population Mobility on American Voting Behaviour*. University of North Carolina Press.

Calleya, S. (2004): *Evaluating Euro-Mediterranean Relations*. Routledge, London.

Cánovas del Castillo, A. (1854): *Historia de la Decadencia de España, Desde el Advenimiento de Felipe III al Trono Hasta la Muerte de Carlos II*. Ruiz, Madrid.

Caron, J. (1983): *Les Régulations du Discours. Psycholinguistique et Pragmatique du Languague*. PUF, Paris.

Carr, R. (1982): *Spain, 1808-1975*. Oxford University Press, Oxford. 2nd Edition.

Carr, R. (2007): *Historia de España*. Península, Madrid.

Carty, K.R., and Cross, W. (2010): *Political Parties and the Practice of Brokerage Politics*. The Oxford Handbook of Canadian Politics, Oxford.

Castells, M. (1997): *The Information Age: Economy, Society and Culture: The Power of Identity*. Oxford Blackwell, Oxford. 2nd Edition.

Castles, S., and Davidson, P. (2000): *Citizenship and Migration: Globalization and the Politics of Belonging*. Routledge, London.

Castles, S., and Miller, J.M. (2003): *The Age of Migration*. Palgrave Macmillan, London. 3rd Edition.

Cebrián, J.L. (2011): *El Fundamentalismo Democrático*. Santillana Ediciones Generales, Madrid.

Cembrero, I. (2006): *Vecinos Alejados. Los Secretos de la Crisis entre España y Marruecos*. Galaxia Gutenberg, Barcelona.

Chafer, T. (2002): *The End of the Empire in French West Africa: France's Successful Decolonization?* Berg, Oxford.

Chambers, I. (2008): *Mediterranean Crossings: The Politics of an Interrupted Modernity*. Duke University Press.

Charles, M., Pecorar, D., and Hunston, S. (2009): "Introduction: Exploring the Interface between Corpus Linguistics and Discourse Analysis". In Charles, M., Pecorar, D., and Hunston, S. (Eds.): *Academic Writing. At the Interface of Corpus and Discourse*. Continuum. London.

Chicote, J. (2012): *Socialistas de Élite. Felipe y los Felipistas: De Suresnes al Club del Millón de Euros*. La Esfera, Madrid.

Cobb, R.W., and Elder, C.D. (1983): *Participation in American Politics: The Dynamics of Agenda Building*. Allyn and Bacon, Boston.

Cole, A. (1998): *French Politics and Society*. Hertforshire, Prentice Hall.

Cook, T.E. (2005): *Governing With the News: The News Media as a Political Institution*. University of Chicago Press, Chicago.

Curran, J., and Seaton, J. (Eds.) (2003): *The Press, Broadcasting and New Media in Britain*. Routledge, London. 6th Edition.

Dahlgren, P., and Sparks, C. (Eds.) (1991): *Communication and Citizenship: Journalism and the Public Sphere in The New Media Age*. Routledge, London.

Danrit, C. (1889): *La Guerre de Demain*. Rossignol, Paris.

De Long, J., and Eichengreen, B. (1993): "The Marshall Plan: History's Most Successful Structural Adjustment Programme". In Dornbuch, D. et Al. (Ed.): *Post-war Economic Reconstruction and Lessons for the East Today*. MIT Press, Cambridge. Pp. 1–89–230.

Del Arenal, C. (2011): *Política Exterior de España y Relaciones con América Latina. Iberoamericanidad, Europeización y Atlantismo en la Política Exterior Española*. Fundación Carolina, Madrid.

Delaisi, F. (1911): *La Force Allemand et la Guerre Qui Vient*. Nemrich, Paris.

Delanty, G. (1995): *Inventing Europe: Idea, Identity, Reality*. Palgrave Macmillan, New York.

Delmas, P. (1999): *De la Prochaine Guerre Avec l'Allemagne*. Odile Jacob, Paris.

Denzin, N.K. (1978): *The Research Act: A theoretical Introduction to Sociological Methods.* McGraw Hill, New York.

Destler, I.M. (1972): *Presidents, Bureaucrats and Foreign Policy: The Politics of Organizational Reform.* Princeton University Press, USA.

Deutsch, K. (1969): *Political Community in the North Atlantic Area: International Organization in the Light of Historical Experience.* Greenwood, New York.

Douglas, J.D. (1984): *Creative Interviewing.* Sage, Thousand Oaks.

Drever, E. (1995): *Using Semi-Structured Interviews in Small Scale Research: A Teacher's Guide.* Scottish Council for Research in Education, Edinburgh.

Eisenstadt, S.N. (1972): "Social Institutions". In Sill, D. (Ed.): *International Encyclopaedia of Social Sciences.* Macmillan, New York. Pp. 4–09-429.

El Moustaoui, F. (2011): *Mitterrand et le Moyen Orient.* L'Harmattan, Paris.

Ellinas, A. (2010): *The Media and Far Right in Western Europe: Playing the Nationalistic Card.* Cambridge University Press, Cambridge.

Emerson, M., and Noutcheva, G. (2005): "From Barcelona Process to Neighbourhood Policy". In Iemed (Ed.): *Iemed 2005 Yearbook.* Iemed, Barcelona.

Entman, R.M. (2003): *Projection of Power: Framing News, Public Opinion and US Foreign Policy.* University of Chicago Press, Chicago.

Escudé, C. (2011): *¿Cuánto Valen Estas Bases? El Tira y Afloja Entre Estados Unidos y España, 1951–1953.* Cuadernos de Historia Contemporánea. Universidad Complutense de Madrid, Madrid.

Esdaile, C. (2003): *The Peninsular War: A New History.* Palgrave Macmillan, London.

European Commission. (2011): *Europe and the Mediterranean: Towards a Closer Partnership. An Overview of the Barcelona Process in 2002.* Dictus Publishing

Fairclough, N., Mulderrig, J., and Wodak, R. (2011): "Critical Discourse Analysis". In Van Dijk, T. (Ed.): *Discourse Studies: A Multidisciplinary Introduction.* Sage, London. 2$^{nd}$ Edition. Pp. 357–378.

Farré, S. (2001): *Spanische Agitation: Emigración Española y Antifranquismo en Suiza.* Fundación 1 de Mayo, Madrid.

Fenby, J. (2010): *Charles de Gaulle and the France He Saved.* Simon and Schuster, Paris.

Fernández Molina, I. (2009): "Los Partidos Políticos y la Política Exterior Española Hacia el Maghreb. Los Casos del PSOE y del PP." In Hernando de Larramendi, M.H. and Mañe, A. (Eds.): *La Política Exterior Española Hacia el Magreb*. Real Instituto Elcano. Ariel, Barcelona. Pp. 4–2–61.

Ferrer, A. (1996): *Historia de la Globalización. II*. Fondo de Cultura Económica, Buenos Aires.

Finnemore, M. (1996): *National Interests in International Society*. Cornell University Press. Ithaca.

Flowerdaw, L. (2012): "Corpus-Based Discourse Analysis". In Gee, J.P. and Handford, M. (Eds.): *The Routledge Handbook of Discourse Analysis*. Routledge, London. Pp. 1–74–187.

Folmer, H. (1953): *Franco-Spanish Rivalry in North America. 1524–1763*. A.H. Clark Co., California.

Fourastié, J. (1979): *Les Trente Glorieuses, ou, La Révolution Invisible de 1946 à 1975*. Fayard, Paris.

Gammoudi, T. (2006): *L'Impact de L'Emigration sur la Région de Départ : Cas de l'Oasis Continentale de Fatnasse*. Master Dissertation. Université du 7 Novembre. Carthage, Tunisia.

Gaulle, de. C. (1970): *Discours et Messages. Volume III: Avec le Renouveau 1958–1962*. Plon, Paris.

Gänzle, S. (2007): "The European Neighbourghood Policy: A Strategy for Security in Europe?" In Gänzle, S. (Ed.): *The Changing Politics of European Security*. Palgrave Mamillan. London. Pp. 110–134.

Geddes, A. (2003): *The Politics of Migration and Immigration in Europe*. Sage, London.

Glaseerfeld, E.U. (1984): "An Intro to Radical Constructivism". In Watzlawick, P. (Ed.): *The Invented Reality: How do We Know What We Believe We Know*. W.W. Norton. New York. Pp. 1–7–40.

Glick-Schiller, N. (1998): *Towards a Transnational Perspective on Migration: Race, Class, Ethnicity and Nationalism Reconsidered*. New York Academy of Sciences, New York.

Godard, B., and Taussig, S. (2007): *Les Musulmans en France: Courants, Institutions, Communautés*. Pluriel, Paris.

Godicheau, F. (2006): *La Guerre d'Espagne: De la Démocratie à la Dictature*. Gallimard, Paris.

Goldstein, J., and Keohane, R.O. (Eds.) (1993): *Ideas and Foreign Policy: Beliefs, Institutions and Political Change*. Cornell University Press, Ithaca.

Gómez, R. (2003): *Negotiating the Euro-Mediterranean Partnership. Strategic Action in EU Policy?* Ashgate Publishing House, London.

González Alcantud, J.A., and Martin Corrales, E. (Eds.) (2007): *La Conferencia de Algeciras en 1906: Un Banquete Colonial.* Bellaterra, Barcelona.

González del Miño, P. (1991): *La Heterogeneidad de las Relaciones Bilaterales Hispano-Francesas Durante el Cambio Político Español: 1969–1986: Sus Constantes y Sus Variables.* Universidad Complutense de Madrid, Madrid.

González del Miño, P. (1994): "Las Relaciones Bilaterales Hispano-Francesas" In Calduch, R. (Ed.): *La Política Española en el Siglo XX.* Ediciones de las Ciencias Sociales, Madrid. Pp. 2–23–235.

González, M.J. (1979): *La Economía Española del Franquismo. 1940–1970: Dirigismo, Mercado y Planificación.* Tecnos, Madrid.

Gordon, P.H. (1993): *A Certain Idea of France: French Security Policy and the Gaullist Legacy.* Princeton University Press, New Jersey.

Gottweis, H. (2007): "Rhetoric in Policy Making: Between Logos, Ethos and Pathos". In Fisher, F., Miller, G.J., and Sidney, M.S. (Eds.): *Handbook of Public Analysis: Theory, Politics and Methods.* Taylor and Francis, New York. Pp. 2–37–250.

Graber, D.A. (2009): *Mass Media and American Politics.* CQ Press.

Graber, D.A., McQuail, D., and Norris, P. (2007): *The Politics of News: The News of Politics.* CQ Press, Thousands Oaks.

Güell, C. (2009): *Las Potencias Internacionales Ante la Dictadura Española, 1944–1955.* Aresta, Madrid.

Guillen, M.F. (2005): *The Rise of Spanish Multinationals: European Business in the Global Economy.* Cambridge University Press, Cambrige.

Guillespie, R. (2000): *Spain and the Mediterranean. Developing a European Policy towards the South.* Palgrave Macmillan, London.

Guillespie, R. (Ed.) (1997): *The Euro-Mediterranean Partnership: Political and Economic Perspectives.* Routledge, London.

Hahn, M. (2009): *The Euro-Mediterranean Partnership: The Barcelona Process since 1995.* Diplomica Verlag, Amsterdam.

Halperin, M. (1974): *Bureaucratic Politics and Foreign Policy.* Brookings, Washington.

Hammar, T. (Ed.) (1995): *European Immigration Policy: A Comparative Study.* Cambridge University Press, Cambridge.

Harbi, M. (1998): *1954, La Guerre Commence en Algérie*. Editions Complexe, Paris. 3rd Edition.

Hayes, M. (2006): "The Transmed and Maghreb Projects: Gas to Europe from North-Africa" In Victor, D.G., Jaffee, A.M., and Hayes, M.H. (Eds.): *Natural Gas and Geopolitics. From 1970 to 2040*. Cambridge University Press, Cambridge. Pp. 1–34–167.

Hazareensingh, S. (2010): *Le Mythe Gaullien*. Gallimard, Paris.

Hegel, G.W.F. (1955): *Sämtliche Werke Sistem Der Philosophier Ertedt Terl*. Hoffmeister Hamburg. Lectures.

Hegel, G.W.F. (2001): *The Philosophy of History*. Batoche Books. Kitchener. Ontario, Canada.

Herman, E.S., and Chomsky, N. (1998): *Manufacturing Consent: The Political Economy of the Mass Media*. Pantheon, New York.

Hilsman, R. (1967): *To Move a Nation*. Doubleday, New York.

Hoey, M., Mahlberg, M., Stubbs, M., and Teubert, W. (2007): *Text, Discourse and Corpora. Theory and Analysis*. Continuum, London.

Holstein, J.A., and Gubrium, J.F. (1995): *The Active Interviewing*. Sage, Thousands Oaks.

Holsti, R.O. (1968): *Content Analysis: A Handbook with Applications for the Study of International Crisis*. Northwestern University Press, Chicago.

Hopkin, J. (1999): *Party Formation and Democratic Transition in Spain: The Creation and Collapse of the Union of Democratic Centre*. Palgrave Macmillan, London.

Horden, P., and Purcell. N. (2000): *The Corrupting Sea: A Study of Mediterranean History*. Blackwell Publishers, London.

Hugh, T. (2001): *The Spanish Civil War*. Modern Library, New York.

Huneens, C., and Nohlen, D. (1985): *La UCD y la Transición a la Democracia en España*. Editorial Siglo XXI, Madrid.

Huntington, S. (1961): *The Common Defence*. Columbia University Press, New York.

IOM. (2010): *World Migration Report 2010*. International Organization for Migration, Geneva.

Iyengar, S., and McGrady, J. (2006): *Media Politics: A Citizen's Guide*. W.W. Norton and Co. New York.

Jervis, R. (1976): *Perceptions and Misperceptions in International Politics*. Princeton University Press.

Jiménez Redondo, J.C. (2006): *De Suárez a Zapatero: La Política Exterior de la España Democrática*. Dílex, Madrid.

Jiménez Redondo, J.C. (2006): *De Suárez a Zapatero: La Política Exterior de la España Democrática*. Dilex, Madrid.

Joffe, G. (Ed.) (1999): *Perspectives on Development: The Euro-Mediterranean Partnership*. Frank Cass, London.

Joffe, G., and Vanconcellos, A. (2000): *The Barcelona Process: Building a Euro-Mediterranean Regional Community*. Frank Cass, London.

Joppke, C. (2009): *Veil, Mirror of Identity*. Polity Press, London.

Jordi, J.J. (1962): *De L'Exode à L'Exil. Rapatriés et Pieds-Noirs en France*. L'Harmattan, Paris.

Katz, M.B., Doucet, M.J., and Stern, M.J. (2002): *The Social Organization of Early Industrial Capitalism*. Harvard University Press, USA.

Keohane, R.O., and Martin, L.L. (2003): "Institutional Theory as a Research Program". In Elman, C., and Elman, M.F. (Eds.): *Progress in International Relations Theory: Appraisal in the Field*. MIT, Cambridge, USA.

Khader, B. (1995): *Europa y el Mediterráneo*. Icaria. Barcelona.

Khader, B. (2001): *Le Partenariat Euro-Méditerranéen vu du Sud*. L'Harmattan, Paris.

Khader, B. (2009): *L'Europe pour la Méditerranée. De Barcelone a Barcelone, 1995–2008*. L'Harmattan, Paris.

Khan, H., and Ghazali, K. (2011): "Critical Discourse Analysis" In Azirah, H., Khemlani, D., and McLellan, J. (Eds.): *Text, Discourse and Society: Functional and Pragmatic Approaches to Language in Use*. Peter Lang, Oxford. Pp. 164–181.

King, N., and Horrocks, C. (2010): *Interviews in Qualitative*. Sage, New York.

King, R., and Wood, N. (Eds.) (2001): *Media and Migration. Constructions of Mobility and Difference*. Routledge, London.

Kingdon, J.W. (1984): *Agendas, Alternatives and Public Policies*. Little Brown, Boston.

Kingdon, J.W. (1995): *Agendas, Alternatives and Public Policies*. Longman, London, 2nd Edition.

Koller, V. (2004): *Metaphor and Gender in Business Media Discourse. A Critical Cognitive Study*. Palgrave Macmillan, London.

Koopmans, R., and Statham, P. (2000): "Migration and Ethnic Relations as a Field of Political Contention: An Opportunity Structure Approach" In Koopmans, R. and Statham, P. (Eds.): *Challenging Immigration and Ethnic Relations Politics: Comparative European Perspectives.* Oxford University Press.

Koser, K. (2009): *The Impact of Financial Crises on International Migration: Lessons Learned.* International Organization for Migration, Geneva.

Kupchan, C.A. (1994): *The Vulnerability of Empire.* Cornell University Press, Ithaca.

Legendre, M. (1913): *La Guerre Prochaine et la Mission de la France.* Marcel Riviere, Paris.

Leguineche, M. (1996): *Annual 1921, El Desastre de España en el Rif.* Ediciones Alfaguara, Madrid.

Lesser, I.O., Larrabee, F.S., Green, J., and Zanini, M. (1998): *NATO's Mediterranean Initiative: Policy Issues and Dilemmas.* Rand.

Levy, J. (1989): "Domestic Politics and War". In Rotberg, R. and Rabb, T. (Eds.): *The Origin and Prevention of Major Wars.* Cambridge University Press.

Liedtke, B. (1998): *Embracing a Dictatorship: US Relations with Spain, 1945–1953.* St. Martin's Press, New York.

Locke, T. (2004): *Critical Discourse Analysis.* Continuum, Amsterdam.

López García, B., and Berriane, M. (Eds.) (2004): *Atlas de la Inmigración Marroquí en España.* Taller de Estudios Internacionales Mediterráneos. Universidad Autónoma de Madrid. Secretaría de Estado de Inmigración y Emigración. Madrid.

Lopez García, B. (1993): *Inmigración Maghrebí en España: El Retorno de los Moriscos.* Editorial Mapfre, Madrid.

Lorite, N. (2002a): *Comunicación, Inmigración y Dinamización Socio-Cultural en el Ámbito Local.* Migracom. Universidad de Barcelona, Barcelona.

Lorite, N. (2002b): *Tratamiento Informativo de la Inmigración en España.* Migracom. Universidad de Barcelona, Barcelona.

Lorite, N. (2006): *Tratamiento Informativo de la Inmigración en España.* 2 Migracom. Universidad de Barcelona, Barcelona.

Lynch, J. (1989): *Bourbon Spain.* Oxford University Press, Oxford.

Lynch, J. (1992): *The Spanish World in Crisis and Change. 1598–1700.* Oxford University Press, Oxford.

MacEnery, T., and Wilson, A. (2001): *Corpus Linguistics: An Introduction*. University of Edinburg, Edinburgh. 2nd Edition.

MacEnery, T., Xiao, R., and Yukio Tono, Y. (2006): *Corpus-Based Language Studies. An Advanced Resource Book*. Routledge, London.

Macmaster, N. (1997): *Colonial Migrants and Racism. Algerians in France. 1900–1962*. Palgrave Macmillan, London.

Magone, J.M. (2009): *Contemporary Spanish Politics*. Routledge, London. 2nd Edition.

Marks, G. (1996): "Exploring and Explaining Variation in EU Cohesion Policy" In Hooghe, L. (Ed.): *Cohesion Policy and European Interpretation Building Multilateral Governance*. Oxford University Press, Oxford. Pp. 3–88–422.

Martin, P.L., and Taylor, J.E. (1996): "The Anatomy of a Migration Hump" In Taylor, P.L. (Ed.): *Development Strategy, Employment and Migration: Insights from Models*. OECD Development Centre, Paris. Pp. 4–3–62.

Martiniello, M. (1995): "European Citizenship, European Identity and Migrants: Towards the Post-National State?" In Miles R., and Thrändhart, D. (Eds.): *Migration and European Integration: The Dynamics of Inclusion and Exclusion*. Pinter, London. Pp. 3–7–52.

Matés Barco, J.M. (2007): La Economía Durante el Franquismo : La Década de la Transición. 1950–1959. In González Enciso, A., and Matés Barco, J.M. (Eds.): *Historia Económica de España*. Ariel, Madrid. Pp. 707–744.

Mathison, S. (1988): Why Triangulate? *Educational Researcher*. March.

Mattelart, T. (2007): *Médias, Migrations et Cultures Transnationelles*. Lavoisier, Paris.

Mayer, S. (2011): "Die NATO Nach Dem 11. September: Aufgoben, Strategien und Institutionelles Design" In Jäger, T. (Ed.): *Die Welt Nach 9/11*. University of Bremen, Bremen. Pp. 4–89–507.

McEnery, T., and Hardie, A. (2012): *Corpus Linguistics*. Cambridge University Press, Cambridge.

Mearsheimer, J. (2001): *The Tragedy of Great Power Politics*. Norton, New York.

Mercer, J. (1996): *Reputation and International Politics*. W.W. Norton. New York.

Meyer, T. (2002): *Media Democracy: How the Media Colonize Politics*. Polity, Cambridge.

Meynier, G. (2000): *Histoire Intérieure du FLN, 1954–1962*. Lavoisier, Paris.

Milward, A. (1984): *The Reconstruction of Western Europe: 1945–1951*. Methuen, London.

Momsem, T. (2006): *The History of Rome*. Indy Publishing. 3rd Edition.

Monroe, E. (1938): *The Mediterranean in Politics*. Oxford University Press, Oxford.

Morán Blanco, S. (1996): *La Cooperación Hispano-Francesa en la Lucha Contra ETA*. Universidad Complutense de Madrid. Doctoral dissertation. Madrid.

Moravcsik, A. (1998): *The Choice for Europe: Social Purpose and State Power from Messina to Maastricht*. Cornell University Press, Ithaca.

Mortimer, B.A. (1999): "The Maghreb Union: Myth and Reality". In Zoubir, Y.H. (Ed.): *North Africa in Transition: State, Society and Economy Transformation in the 1990s*. University Press of Florida. Pp. 3–6–61.

Moyo, D., and Ferguson, N. (2010): *Dead Aid: Why Aid Is Not Working and How There's a Better Way for Africa*. Farrar, Strans and Giroux, London.

Murray, D. (1980): *Odious Commerce: British, Spain and the Abolition of the Cuban Slave Trade*. Cambridge University Press, Cambridge.

Muus, P. (1995): *L'Emigration Marocaine Vers L'Europe. Changement et Continuitè*. Universitè Mohammed V Press, Rabat.

Naylor, P.C. (2000): *France and Algeria: A History of Decolonization and Transformation*. University Press of Florida.

Neal, L. (1993): *The Rise of Financial Capitalism: International Capital Markets in the Age of Reason*. Cambridge University Press, Cambridge.

Neudstadt, R. (1960): *Presidential Power: The Politics of Leadership*. Wiley, New York.

Newman, B.I. (Ed.) (1991): *The Handbook of Political Marketing*. Sage, London.

Nolan, M.E. (2005): *The Inverted Mirror: Mythologizing the Enemy in France and Germany. 1898–1914*. Berghan Books, New York.

Norwich, J.J. (2007): *The Middle Sea: A History of the Mediterranean*. Doubleday. First edition, 1929.

Núñez Villaverde, J.A. (2001): "The Mediterranean: A Firm Priority of Spanish Foreign Policy?". In Gillespie, R. and Youngs, R.

(Eds.): *The European and International Challenges*. Frank Cass, London. Pp. 1–29–147.

Nuttall, S. (1997): "Two Decades of EPC Performance". In Regelsberger, P., De Schoutheete, P., and Wessels, W. (Eds.): *Foreign Policy of the European Union*. Lynne Rienner. Pp. 2–4–42.

Ogden, P.E. (1995): "Labour Migration to France". In Cohen, R. (Ed.): *The Cambridge Survey of World Migration*. Cambridge University Press, Cambridge. Pp. 1–89–296.

Oñate, J. (Ed.) (2005): *Portugal y España. Veinte Años de Integración en Europa 1985-2005*. Asociación de Periodistas Europeos. Muñoz Vergara Ediciones, Madrid.

Ostrander, S. (1995): "Surely you are not in this just to be helpful; Access, Rapport and Interviews in Three Studies of Elites". In Hertz, B., and Imber, J.B. (Eds.): *Studying Elites Using Qualitative Methods*. Sage, Thousand Oaks. Pp. 1–30–174.

Papademetriou, D.G., and Terrazas, A. (2009): *Immigrants and the Current Economic Crisis: Research Evidence, Policy Challenges and Implications*. Migration Policy Institute, Washington, D.C.

Parra Luna, F. (1981): *La Emigración Española en Francia. 1962-1977*. Instituto Español de Emigración, IEE, Madrid.

Parsons, T. (1934): *The Structure of Social Action*. Free Press, New York.

Parsons, T. (1951): *The Social System*. Free Press, New York.

Patton, M.Q. (1990): *Qualitative Evaluation and Research Methods*. Sage, Newbury Park. 2nd Edition.

Pennell, C.R. (1986): *A Country with a Government and a Flag: The Rif War in Morocco, 1921-1926*. Middle East and North African Studies Press.

Pereira, D. et Al. (Eds.) (2004): *Las Zonas Rurales: Un Diagnóstico Desde la Perspectiva de las Desigualdades Territoriales y los Cambios Sociales y Económicos*. Fundación Fondesa, Madrid.

Pereira, J.C. (Ed.) (2009): *La Política Exterior de España, 1800-2003*. Ariel, Barcelona. 2nd Edition.

Perkins, H. (2004): *History of Modern Tunisia*. Cambridge University Press, Cambridge.

Perse, E.M. (2001): *Media Effects and Society*. Taylor and Francis, London.

Pettit, P. (1997): *Republicanism: A Theory of Freedom and Government*. Oxford Clarendon Press, Oxford.

Philpott, D. (2001): *Revolutions in Sovereignty: How Ideas Shaped Modern International Relations*. Princeton University Press, New Jersey.

Picasso, J. (1976): *Expediente Picasso*. Frente de Afirmación Hispanista. Mexico.

Pielke, R. (2007): *The Honest Broker: Making Sense of Science in Policy and Politics*. Cambridge University Press, Cambridge.

Pojmann, W. (Ed.) (2008): *Migration and Activism in Europe since 1945*. Palgrave Macmillan.

Pollack, B., and Hunter, G. (1987): *The Paradox of Spanish Foreign Policy: Spain's International Relations from Franco to Democracy*. Pinter. London.

Polsby, N. W. (1984): *Political Innovation in America: The Politics of Policy Initiation*. Yale University Press, New Haven.

Powell, C. (2000): "Cambio de Régimen y Política Exterior: España, 1975–1989". In Tussell, J., Avilés, J., and Pardo, R. (Eds.): *La Política Exterior de España en el Siglo XX*. Universidad Nacional de Educación a Distancia, UNED, Madrid. Pp. 4–13–453.

Press and Information Office of the Government of the Federal Republic of Germany. (1977): *Texts Relating to the European Political Co-Operation*. PIOGFRG, Bonn.

Preston, P. (2007): *The Spanish Civil War: Reaction, Revolution and Revenge*. W.W. Norton and Co., New York.

Pridham, G. (1987): "Interviewing Party-Political Elites in Italy". In Moyser, G., and Wagstaffe, M. (Eds.): *Research Methods for Elite Studies*. Allen and Unwin, London.

Prieto, A.P., and Hall, C.A. (2013): *Spain's Photovoltaic Revolution. The Energy Return on Investment*. Springer, London.

Prochaska, D. (1990): *Making Algeria French: Colonisation in Bone, 1870–1920*. Cambridge University Press, Cambridge.

Pujol, J. (2006): *Idees I Records*. Galaxia Guttenberg, Barcelona.

Putnam, R. (1993): *Making Democracy Work: Civic Traditions in Modern Italy*. Princeton University Press, New Jersey.

Remiro Brotóns, A. (2004): "Espagne: Les Années Aznar". In Moderne, F., and Bon, P. (Eds.): La Politique Étrangère. *La Documentation Française*. Paris.

Renouf, A., and Kehoe (Eds.) (2009): *Corpus Linguistics: Refinements and Reassessments*. Rodopi, Amsterdam.

Richard, J.L., and Tripier, M. (1999): "Les Travailleurs Immigrès en France, des Trente Glorieuses á la Crisse". In Dewitte, P. (Ed.): *Immigration et Integration: L'Etat des Savoirs*. La Dècourverte, Paris. Pp. 1–73–184.

Richmond, A.H. (1994): *Global Apartheid: Refugees, Racism and the New World Order*. Oxford University Press.

Riddell, R.C. (2007): *Does Foreign Aid Really Work?* Oxford University Press, Oxford.

Romero, F. (1999): *Spain 1914–1918: Between War and Revolution*. Routledge. London

Rosencrance, R. (1986): *The Raise of Trading State: Commerce and Conquest in the Modern World*. Basic Books, New York.

Rosencrance, R.N. (1986): *Rise of the Trading State*. Basic Books, New York.

Rosenholm, A., Nordenstreng, K., and Trutina, E. (Ed.) (2010): *Russian Mass Media and Changing Values*. Routledge, London.

Rubio, J. (1974): *La Emigración Española a Francia*. Madrid.

Ruggie, J.G. (1983): "International Regimes, Transactions, and Change". In Krasner, S. (Ed.): *International Regimes*. Cornell University Press, Ythaca.

Ruggie, J.G. (1998): *Construction of the World Polity: Essays on International Institutionalization*. Routledge, London.

Rule, C.J. (1999): "The Enduring Rivalry of France and Spain ca. 1462–1700". In Thompson, W.R. (Ed.): *Great Power Rivalries*. University of South Carolina, USA.

Russet, B. (1995): *Grasping the Democratic Peace: Principles for a Post-Cold War World*. Princeton University Press.

Sabry, T. (Ed.) (2004): Media and Migration. *Westminster Papers on Communication and Culture*. University of Westminster, London.

Sahlins, P. (1989): *Boundaries: The Making of France and Spain in the Pyrenees*. University of California Press, USA.

Sammut, C. (2010): "Producing Immigration News in Receiving Countries: Beyond Journalists' Professional Ideology and Cultural Explanations". In Ureta, I. (Ed.): *Media, Migration and Public Opinion. Myths Prejudices and the Challenge of Attaining Mutual Understanding Between Europe and North Africa*. Peter Lang, Bern. Pp. 2–15–238.

Sanz, C. (2004): *Clandestinos Ilegales, Espontáneos. La Emigración Ilegal de Españoles a Alemania en el Contexto de las Relaciones*

*Hispano-Alemanas. 1960–1973*. Comisión Española de Relaciones Internacionales, Madrid.

Sassen, S. (1996): *Losing Control: Sovereignty in an Age of Globalization*. Columbia University Press, New York.

Sayad, A. (1999): *La Double Absence: Des Illusions de l'Émigré aux Souffrances de l'Immigré*. Seuil, Paris.

Schalk, D.L. (1991): *War and the Ivory Tower: Algeria and Vietnam*. University of Nebraska Press.

Schilling, W.R., Hammond, P.Y., and Snyder, G.H. (Eds.) (1962): *Strategy, Politics and Defense Budgets*. Columbia University Press, New York.

Schroeder, P.W. (1999): "A Pointless Enduring Rivalry: France and the Habsburg Monarchy: 1715–1918". In Thompson, W.R. (Ed.): *Great Power Rivalries*. University of South Carolina. Pp. 6–0–85. USA.

Silverman, M. (1992): *Deconstructing the Nation: Immigration, Racism and Citizenship in Modern France*. Routledge, London.

Silverstein, A. (2004): *Algeria in France: Transpolitics, Race and Nation*. Bloomington, Indiana.

Sistiaga, G. (2003): "Terrorismo y Seguridad Internacional en Europa". In Valle Gálvez, A. (Ed.): *Los Nuevos Escenarios Internacionales y Europeos del Derecho Internacional y Relaciones Internacionales*. BOE, Madrid. Pp. 8–7–92.

Siune, K., and Treutzchler, W. (Eds.) (1992): *Dynamics of Media Politics: Broadcast and Electronic Media in Western Europe*. Sage, London.

Skeldon, R. (1997): *Migration and Development*. Prentice Hall, New York.

Smith, B. (1978): *The French Stake in Algeria*. Cornell University Press, Ithaca.

Smith, J.G. (1972): *Political Brokers; People, Organisations, Money and Power*. National Journal Book.

Solimano, A. (2003): *Development Cycles, Political Regimes and International Agents: Argentina in the $20^{th}$ Century*. CEPAL, United Nations, New York.

Sorum, P. (1977): *Intellectuals and the Decolonization in France*. Chapel Hill, Ithaca.

Statham, P. (Ed.) (2010): *Political Communication, Media and Constitution Building in Europe. The Search for a Public Sphere*. Routledge, London.

Steinbrunen, J.D. (1974): *The Cybernetic Theory of Decision*. Princeton University Press, USA.

Stewart, D. (1965): *Assimilation and Acculturation in Seventeenth-Century Europe: Roussillon and France, 1959–1745*. Greenwood Publishing Group, USA.

Stokes, C.S., Dunning, T., and Nazareno, M. (2013): *Brokers, Voters and Clientelism: The Puzzle of Distributive Politics*. Cambridge University Press, Cambridge.

Stora, B. (1992): *Ils Renaient d'Algerie: L'Immigration Algérienne en France 1912–1992*. Fayard, Paris.

Stora, B. (2001): *Algeria 1830–2000. A Short History*. Cornell University Press, Ithaca.

Study Prepared for the Global Commission on International Migration. Panteion University, Athens.

Temple-Patterson, A. (1960): *The Other Armada: The Franco-Spanish Attempt to Invade Britain in 1779*. University of Manchester Press, UK.

Thieux, L. (2005): *The Democratic Deficit: A Pending Objective for the Barcelona Process*. Peace Research Centre, Madrid.

Tognini-Bonelli, E. (2001): *Corpus Linguistics at Work*. John Benjamins, Amsterdam.

Tortella, G. (1975): *Los Orígenes del Capitalismo Español*. Tecnos, Madrid.

Touraine, A. (1981): *The Voice and the Eye: An Analysis of Social Movements*. Cambridge University Press, Cambridge.

Tryandafylliou, A., Wodala, A., and Krzyzanowski, M. (Eds.) (2009): *The European Public Sphere and the Media: Europe in Crisis*. Palgrave MacMillan, New York.

Tsoluakis, L. (1997): Revisited. Oxford University Press.

Ünven Noi, A. (2011): *The Euromediterranean Partnership and the Broader Middle East and North Africa Initiative: Competing or Complementary Projects?* University Press of America, USA.

Ureta, I. (2003): *Hidroeléctrica Española y el Desarrollo de la Industria Eléctrica España 1907–1977*. Universidad de Deusto. PhD dissertation, Bilbao.

Ureta, I. (2010): "Migration, Development and Policy Coherence in the Mediterranean". In Ureta, I., and Lutterbeck, D. (Eds.): *Migration, Development and Diplomacy: Perspectives From the Southern Mediterranean*. Africa World Press, New Jersey. Pp. 1–69–190.

Ureta, I. (Ed.) (2010): *Media, Migration and Public Opinion. Myths Prejudices and the Challenge of Attaining Mutual Understanding Between Europe and North Africa*. Peter Lang, Bern.

Valencia, M. M. (2000): "España y la Diplomacia Económica". In Ferrè, J.M. (Ed.): *España, Un Actor Destacado En El Ámbito Internacional*. FAES, Madrid. P. 303–331.

Valenzuela, A. (1977): *Political Brokers in Chile: Local Government in a Centralized Polity*. Duke University Press, USA.

Van Dijk, T. (Ed.) (2011): *Discourse Studies: A Multidisciplinary Introduction*. Sage, London. 2nd Edition.

Vasconcelos, A. (Ed.) (2000): *The Barcelona Process: Building a Euro-Mediterranean Regional Community*. Routledge, London.

Viñas, A. (1999): "Breaking the Shackles from the Past: Spanish Foreign Policy from Franco to Felipe González". In Balbour, S., and Preston, P. (Eds.): *Spain and the Great Powers in the Twentieth Century*. Routledge, New York. Pp. 4–3–67.

Viñas, A. (1999): "Breaking the Shackles from the Past: Spanish Foreign Policy from Franco to Felipe González". In Balfour, S., and Preston, P. (Eds.): *Spain and the Great Powers in the Twentieth Century*. Routledge, London. Pp. 121–146.

Viroli, M. (2002): *Republicanism*. Hill and Wang. New York.

Volpi, F. (2003): *Islam and Democracy: The Failure of Dialogue in Algeria*. Pluto Press, London.

Wais, F. (1974): *Historia de los Ferrocarriles Españoles*. Editora Nacional, Madrid.

Walker, J.L. (1981): "The Diffusion of Knowledge, Policy Communities and Agenda Setting: The Relationship of Knowledge and Power". In Tropman, J.E., Dluhy, M.J., and Lind, R. (Eds.): *New Strategic Perspective on Social Policy*. Pergamon Press. New York. Pp. 7–4–96.

Waltz, K.N. (1979): *Theory of International Politics*. McGraw Hill, New York.

Webb, E.J. et Al. (1966): *Unobstrusive Measures*. Rand McNally, Chicago.

Weber, M. (1958): *The Protestant Ethic and the Spirit of Capitalism*. Charles Scribner and Sons, New York.

Wendt, A. (1999): *Social Theory of International Politics*. Cambridge University Press.

Wodak, R. (2004): "Critical Discourse Analysis" In Seale, C., Gobo, G., Gubrium, J.F., and Silverman, D. (Eds.): *Qualitative Research Practice.* Sage, New York. Pp. 1–85–202.

Ybarra Enríquez, N.C. (1998): *España y la Descolonización del Magreb: Rivalidad Hispano-Francesa en Marruecos 1951–1961.* UNED, Madrid.

Zank, W. (Ed.) (2009): *Cooperation or Clash of Civilizations? Overlapping Integration and Identities.* Ashgate Publishing House, London.

Zapata, R., and Van Dijk, T.A. (2007): *Discursos Sobre la Inmigración en España. Los Medios de Comunicación, Los Parlamentos y Las Administraciones.* Bellaterra, Barcelona.

Zekri, A. (2010): "Migration and Development: Socio-Economic Impacts of Emigration in Tunisia" In Ureta, I., and Lutterbeck, I. (Eds.): *Migration, Development and Diplomacy: Perspectives from the Southern Mediterranean.* Africa World Press, New Jersey. Pp. 2–9.

# C Printed Journals

Aghrout, A., and Sutton, K. (1990): Regional Economic Union in the Maghreb. *The Journal of Modern African Studies.* Vol. 28. Issue 1. Pp. 1–15–139.

Al Dajani, A.S. (1980): The PLO and the Euro-Arab Dialogue. *Journal of Palestine Studies.* Vol. 9. N°3. Pp. 8–1 98.

Aliboni, R., and Ammor, F.M. (2009): Under the Shadow of 'Barcelona': From the EMP to the Union for the Mediterranean. *Euromesco Paper.* N°77.

Allen, D. (1977): The Euro-Arab Dialogue. *Journal of Common Market Studies.* Vol. 16. Issue 4. Pp. 3–23–342.

Allison, G., and Halperin, M. (1972): Bureaucratic Politics: A Paradigm and Some Policy Implications. *World Politics.* N°.24. Pp. 4–0–79.

Alpher, J. (1998): The Political Role of the European Union in the Arab-Israel Peace Process: An Israeli Perspective. *The International Spectator.* Pp. 80–81.

Ammor, F.M., and Aliboni, R. (2009): Under the Shadow of "Barcelona": From the EMP to the Union for the Mediterranean. *Euromesco.* Working Paper 77.

Anon. (1977): Communiqué de l'Èlisée à l'issue de la Visite à Paris du Premier Ministre Espagnol Adolfo Suarez. *La Politique Étrangère de la France*. 3rd Semester.

Antolín, F. (1988): Electricidad y Crecimiento Económico: Los Inicios de la Electricidad en España. *Revista de Historia Industrial*. N°3.

Aoun, E. (2003): European Foreign Policy and the Arab-Israeli Dispute: Much Ado About Nothing? *European Foreign Affairs Review*. N°8. Pp. 2–38–312.

Art, R.J. (1973): Bureaucratic Politics and American Foreign Policy: A Critique. *Political Sciences*. N°4. Pp. 4–67–490.

Arzheimer, K., and Carter, E. (2006): Political Opportunity Structures and Right Wing Extremist Party Success. *European Journal of Political Research*. Vol. 45. Issue 3. Pp. 4–19–443.

Assenburg, M. (2003): The EU and the Middle East Conflict: Tackling the Main Obstacle to Euro-Mediterranean Partnership. *Mediterranean Politics*. Vol. 8. Issue 2–3. Pp. 1–74–193.

Baker, P., and MacEnery, T. (2005): A Corpus-Based Approach to Discourses of Refugees and Asylum Seekers in UN and Newspaper Texts. *Journal of Language and Politics*. N°4. Issue 2. Pp. 1–97–226

Baker, P., Gabrielatos, C., Khovravinik, M., Krzyzanovski, M., and Wodak, R. (2008): A Useful Methodological Synergy? Combining Critical Discourse Analysis and Corpus Linguistics to Examine Discourses of Refugees and Asylum Seekers in the UK Press. *Discourse and Society*. N°19. Pp. 2–73–305.

Balch, A. (2010): Economic Migration and the Politics of Hospitality in Spain: Ideas and Policy Change. *Politics and Policy*. Vol. 38. Issue 5. Pp. 1–037–1065.

Balci, A. (2009): The Alliance of Civilizations: The Poverty of the Clash/Alliance Dichotomy. *Insight Turkey*. Vol. 11. N°9. Pp. 9–5–108.

Balci, A., and Mis, N. (2008): Turkey's Role in the Alliance of Civilizations: A New Perspective in Turkish Foreign Policy? *Turkish Studies*. Vol. 9. Issue 3. Pp. 3–87–406.

Balfour, R. (2009): The Transformation of the Union for the Mediterranean. *Mediterranean Politics*. Vol. 14. N°1. Pp. 9–9–100.

Balfour, R., and Schmid, D. (2008): Union for The Mediterranean, Disunity for the EU? *European Policy Centre*. Policy Brief. February 2008.

Balfour, S. (2004): Civil Military Relations in the Spanish Protectorate in Morocco: The Road to the Spanish Civil War 1912–1936. *Armed Forces and Society*. Vol. 30. N°2. Pp. 2–03–226.

Balibar, E. (2007): Uprisings in the Banlieues. *Constellations*. Vol. 14. N°1.

Ball, D.J. (1974): The Blind Man and the Elephant: A Critique of Bureaucratic Politics Theory. *Australian Outlook*. Vol. 28. Issue 1. Pp. 7–1–92.

Barbaro, F. (1972): Political Brokers. *Society*. Vol. 9. Issue 10. Pp. 4–2–54

Barbé, E. (1996): The Barcelona Conference: Launching Pad of a Process. *Mediterranean Politics*. Vol. 1. Issue 1. Pp. 2–5–42.

Barbé, E., Mestres I Camps, L., and Soler I Lecha, E. (2007): La Política Mediterránea de España: Entre el Proceso de Barcelona y la Política Europea de Vecindad. *Revista Cidob d'Afers Internacionals*. N°79–80. Pp. 3–5–51.

Bardají, R., and Portero, F. (2007): La España Menguante...Menguada. *FAES*. N°46.

Barkin, J.S. (2003): Realist Constructivism. *International Studies Review*. Vol. 5. Issue 3. Pp. 3–25–342.

Barreñada, I. (2006): Alliance of Civilizations: Spanish Public Diplomacy and Cosmopolitan Proposal. *Mediterranean Politics*. Vol. 11. N°1. Pp. 9–9–104.

Barreñada, I., Martín, I., and Sanahuja, J.A. (2004): L'Espagne et la Guerre en Iraq: Ruptures Dans la Politique Extérieure. *Critique Internationale*. N° 23. Pp. 9–21.

Barribal, I..K., and While, A. (1994): Collecting Data Using a Semi-Structured Interview: A Discussion Paper. *Journal of Advanced Nursing*. N°19. Pp. 3–28–335.

Bauchard, D. (2008): L'Union Pour la Mediterranée : Un Défi Européen. *Politique Étrangere* Spring. Pp. 5–1–64.

Baun, M.J. (1995): The Maastricht Treaty as High Politics: Germany and France and European Integration. *Political Science Quarterly*. Vol. 110. N°4. Pp. 6–05–624.

Bazen, S., and Martin, J.P. (1991): L'Incidence du Salaire Minimum sur les Gains et L'Emploi en France. *Revue Economique de l'OCDE*. N°16. Spring.

Bensassi, S., Márquez Ramos, L., and Martínez Zarzano, I. (2012): Economic Integration and the two Margins of Trade: The Impact of the Barcelona Process on North African Countries. *Journal of African Economies*. 21(2) Pp. 2–28–268.

Betz, H.G., and Johnson, C. (2004): Against the Current Stemming the Tide: The Nostalgic Ideology of the Contemporary Radical Populist Right. *Journal of Political Ideas*. Vol. 9. Issue 3. Pp. 3–11–327.

Bicchi, F. (2002): Actors and Factors in European Foreign Policy Making: Insights from the Mediterranean Case. *EUI. Working Paper* N°47. Pp. 4–5.

Bocquillon, P., Confavreux, P., and Voionmaa, O. (2009): L'Union pour la Méditerranée, Une Vrai Chance pour le Sud d l'Europe? *Pollens. Association pour la Politique à l'ENS.* Pp. 3–4.

Bulmer, S.J. (1983): Domestic Politics and European Community Policy Making. *Journal of Common Market Studies.* N°21. Pp. 3–49–363.

Bustos, R. (2003): Economic Liberalization and Political Change in Algeria, Theory and Practice. 1988-1992 and 1994-1999. *Mediterranean Politics.* Vol. 8. Issue 1. Pp. 1–26.

Butler, C.S. (2004): Corpus Studies and Functional Linguistics Theories. *Functions of Language.* N°11. Issue 2. Pp. 1–47–186.

Byman, D.L., and Pollack, K.M. (2001): Let Us Now Praise Big Men. *International Security.* Vol. 25. N°24. Pp. 1–07–146.

Cairns, J.C. (1961): Algerian Progress: Towards Reality and Negotiation. *International Journal.* Vol. 16. N°2. Pp. 158–168.

Cajal, M. (2009): The Alliance of Civilizations: A Spanish View. *Insight Turkey.* Vol. 11. N°3. Pp. 4–5–55.

Calabrese, J. (1997): Beyond Barcelona: The Politics of the Euro-Mediterranean Partnership. *European Security.* Vol. 6. Issue 4. Pp. 8–6–110.

Caldwell, D. (1977): Bureaucratic Foreign Policy Making. *American Behavioural Scientist.* Vol. 21. Pp. 8–7–110.

Calleja, J. (1992): Security and Cooperation in the Mediterranean. *International Journal of World Peace.* Vol. IX. N°1. March. Pp. 2–6.

Calvo, O. (2001): Bienvenido Mr. Marshall! La Ayuda Económica Americana y la Economía Española en la Década de 1950. *Revista de Historia Económica.* N°19. Pp. 2–53–275.

Campbell, D.T., and Fiske, D.W. (1959): Convergent and Discriminant Validation by the Multitrait-multimethod matrix. *Psychological Bulletin.* Vol. 56. N°2. Pp. 8–1–105.

Carman, J. (1973): On the Universality of Marketing. *Journal of Contemporary Business.* N°2. 4.

Celso, A. (2009): Spanish Post-3/11 Antiterror Policy: Zapatero's Tyranny of Circumstances and the Dashing of Good Intentions. *Mediterranean Quarterly.* Vol. 20. N°2. Pp. 1–1–25.

Christiansen, T., Knud, E.J., and Wiener, A. (1999): The Social Construction of Europe. *Journal of European Public Policy.* Vol. 6. Issue 4. Pp. 5–28–544.

Christopoulos, D.C. (2006): Relational Attributes of Political Entrepreneurs : A Network Perspective. *Journal of European Public Policy.* Vol. 5. N°13. Pp. 7–57–778.

Clark, G.L. (1998): Stilized Facts and Close Dialogue: Methodology in Economic Geography. *Annals of the Association of American Geographers.* Vol. 88. N°1. Pp. 7–3–87.

Collyer, M. (2003): Explaining Change in Established Migration Systems: The Movement of Algerians to France and the UK. *Sussex Migration Working Paper.* N°16. University of Sussex.

Connors, R.S. (1979): The Differences Between Speech and Writing: Ethos, Pathos and Logos. *College Cognition and Communication.* Vol. 30. N°3. Pp. 2–85–290.

Copeland, D. (2000): The Constructivist Challenge to Structural Realism. *International Security.* Vol. 25. N°2. Pp. 1–87–212.

Craner, L. (2006): Will US Democratization Policy Work? Democracy in the Middle East. *Middle East Quarterly.* Summer. Pp. 3–10.

Dalacoura, K. (2005): US Democracy Promotion in the Arab Middle East Since 11 September 2001: A Critique. *International Affairs.* Vol. 81. Issue 5. Pp. 9–63–979.

Dalacoura, K. (2011): The 2011 Uprisings in the Arab Middle East: Political Change and Geopolitical Implications. *International Affairs.* Vol. 88. Issue 1. Pp. 6–5–66.

Dallmayr, F.R. (2002): Globalization and Inequality: A Plea for Global Justice. *International Studies Review.* Vol. 4. Issue 2. Pp. 1–37–156.

De Haas, H. (2005a): International Migration, Remittances and Development Myths and Facts. *Third World Quarterly.* Issue 26. N°8. Pp. 1–269–1284.

De Haas, H. (2007): Between Courting and Controlling: The Moroccan State and 'It's' Emigrants. *Centre on Migration, Policy and Society.* University of Oxford.

De Haas, H. (2007): The Myth of Invasion. Irregular Migration from West Africa to the Maghreb and the European Union. *International Migration Institute and James Martin 21$^{st}$ Century School.* University of Oxford.

De Haas, H. (2008): Migration and Development: A Theoretical Perspective. *IMI.* N°9. University of Oxford.

Del Arenal, C. (2004): La Política Exterior del Gobierno Socialista. *Política Exterior.* Vol. 18, N°100.

Del Sarto, R., and Schumacher, T. (2005): From EMP to ENP: What's at Sake with the Southern Neighbourhood Policy towards the Southern Mediterranean? *European Foreign Affairs Review.* N°10. Pp. 1–7–38.

Derisbourg, J.P. (1997): The Euro-Mediterranean Partnership Since Barcelona. *Mediterranean Politics.* 2:1. Pp. 1–9.

Desmond, R.T. (1927): Dictatorship in Spain. *Foreign Affairs.* Vol. 5. N°2. Pp. 2–79–284.

Diamanti, I., and Bordignon, F. (2001): Sicurezza e Opinione Pubblica in Italia. *Rassegna Italiana di Sociologia.* N°1. Pp. 1–13–131.

Diez Cárcamo, A. (2006): El PSOE. De Suresnes a la Democracia: 1974–1982. *Revista Clio.* N°32.

Dussel, E. (1994): Eurocentrism and Modernity. *The Postmodernist Debate in Latin America.* Vol. 3. Pp. 65–70.

Echeverría, C. (2007): La Unión Mediterránea del Presidente Nicolás Sarkozy: ¿La Superación del Proceso de Barcelona? *UNISCI Discussion Papers.* N. 15. Universidad Nacional de Educación a Distancia.

Edis, R. (1998): Does the Barcelona Process Matter? *Mediterranean Politics.* Vol. 3. Issue 3. Pp. 93–105.

Edis, R. (1998): Does the Barcelona Process Matter? *Mediterranean Politics.* Vol. 3. Issue 3. Pp. 9–3–105.

Emerson, M. (2008): Making Sense of Sarkozy's Union for the Mediterranean. *CEPS Policy Brief.* N°155.

Emerson, M., and Noutcheva, G. (2005): From the Barcelona Process to Neighbourhood Policy: Assessment and Open Issues. *CEPS Working Documents.* N°220. 1. March.

Erdogan, R.T. (2007): A Union of Civilizations. *New Perspectives Quarterly.* Vol. 24. Issue 3. Pp. 2–7–29.

Esdaile, C. (1988): War and Politics in Spain, 1808–1814. *The Historical Journal.* Vol. 31. Issue 2. Pp. 2–95–317.

Fargues, P. (2004): Arab migration to Europe: trends and policies. *International Migration Review.* N° 38. Pp. 1348–1371.

Fearon, J. (1994): Domestic Audience Costs and the Scalation of International Disputes. *American Political Science Review.* Vol. 88. N°5. P. 92.

Feliú, L. (2005): España y el Magreb Durante el Segundo Mandato del Partido Popular. Un Período Excepcional. *FRIDE.* Working Paper. N°9.

Fernández Árias, L. (2005): Sahara Occidental: Un Año Después Baker. *Política Exterior.* Vol. 19. N°107. Pp. 7–3–82.

Fernández Asperilla, A. (1998): La Emigración como Exportación de Mano de Obra: El Fenómeno Migratorio a Europa Durante el Franquismo. *Historia Social.* N°30. Pp. 6–3–81.

Fernández Molina, I. (2007): El Partido Popular y la Política de España Hacia el Magreb. *Revista CIDOB d'Afers Internacionals.* La política Árabe y Mediterránea en España. N°. 79–80. Pp. 5–3–71.

Fernández, D. (2006): El Antiamericanismo en la España del Primer Franquismo, 1939–1953. *Ayer.* N° 62. Pp. 2–57–282.

Ferrer-Gallardo, X. (2008): The Spanish-Moroccan Border Complex: Processes of Geopolitical, Functional and Symbolic Rebordering. *Political Geography.* Vol. 27. Issue 3. Pp. 3–01–321.

Fied, B.N. (2009): A "Second Transition" in Spain? Policy, Institutions and Interparty Politics under Zapatero (2004–2008) *South European Society and Politics.* Vol. 14. Issue 4. Pp. 3–79–397.

Finaish, M., and Bell, E. (1995): Strategy of Integration, Future Changes. *Middle East Executive Reports.* December.

Fleming, S.E., and Fleming, A.K. (1977): Primo de Rivera and Spain's Moroccan Problem, 1923–1927. *Journal of Contemporary History.* Vol. 12. N°1. Pp. 8–5–99.

Fogg, T., and Wightman, C.W. (2000): Improving Transcription of Quality Research Interviews with Speech Recognition Technology. Paper Presented at the Annual Meeting of *The American Educational Research Association.* New Orleans.

Fontela, E.M. (1995): El Marco de las Nuevas Relaciones Europa-Maghreb. *Revista Española de Economía Agraria.* N°172.

Freedman, L. (1976): Politics and Foreign Policy Processes: A Critique of the Bureaucratic Politics Model. *International Affairs.* Vol. 52. N°3. Pp. 4–34–449.

French Government. (1976): Mémorandum sur la Réforme des Réglements Communautaires Concernant les Productions Agricoles Méditerranées. *La Politique Étrangère de la France.* 3$^{rd}$ Quarter. 26 July 1976.

Furlong, A. (2010): Cultural Integration in the European Union: A Comparative Analysis of the Immigration Policies of France and

Spain. *Transnational Law and Contemporary Problems.* Vol. 19. Pp. 6–81–703.

Gänzle, S. (2009): EU Governance and the European Neighbourhood Policy: A Framework for Analysis. *Europe-Asia Studies.* Vol. 61. N°10. Pp. 1–715–1734.

Gerecht, R.M., and Schmitt, G. (2006): A Post-Gaullist, Pro-American France? *American Entreprise Institute for Policy Research.* N°1.

Gfeller, A.E. (2011): A European Voice in the Arab World: France, the Superpowers and the Middle East, 1970–1974. *Cold War History.* Vol. 11. Issue 4. Pp. 6–59–676.

Gheciu, A. (2005): Security Institutions as Agents of Socialization? NATO and the "New Europe". *International Organization.* N°59. Pp. 9–73–1012.

Gil Bazo, M. (1998): The Role of Spain as a Gateway to the Schengen Area: Changes in the Asylum Law and their Implications for Human Rights. *International Journal of Refugee Law.* Oxford University Press. Vol. 10. N°1/2. Pp. 214–229.

Gillespie, R. (1995): Northern European Perceptions on the Barcelona Process. *Afers Internacionals.* N°37.

Gillespie, R. (1997): Spanish Protagonismo and the Euro-Med Partnership Initiative. *Mediterranean Politics.* Vol. 2. N°1. Pp. 3–3–48.

Gillespie, R. (1997): Northern European Perceptions of the Barcelona Process. *Revista CIDOB.* Pp. 6–5–75.

Gillespie, R. (2003): Reshaping the Agenda? The Internal Politics of the Barcelona Process in the Aftermath of September 11. *Mediterranean Politics.* Vol. 8. Issue 2–3. Pp. 2–2–36.

Gillespie, R. (2006): "This Stupid Little Island": A Neighbourhood Confrontation in the Western Mediterranean. *International Politics.* N°43. Pp. 1–10–132.

Gillespie, R. (2008): A 'Union for the Mediterranean' … or For the EU? *Mediterranean Politics.* Vol. 13. N°2. Pp. 2–77–286.

Goldstein, K. (2002): Getting in the Door: Sampling and Completing Interviews. *Political Science and Politics.* Vol. 35. N°4. Pp. 6–69–672.

González del Miño, P. (1988): Las Cumbres Hispano-Francesas: Nueva Diplomacia Entre Vecinos. *Cuadernos de la Escuela Diplomática.* N°1. Pp. 1–59–174.

González González, I. (2007): La "Hermandad Hispano-Árabe" en la Política Cultural del Franquismo. *Anales de Historia Contemporánea.* Universidad de Murcia. N°23.

Guerra, S., and Massetti, E. (2008): The Italian Parliamentary Election of April 2008. *EPERN.* Election briefing N°41. University of Sussex.

Guillespie, R., and Youngs, R. (2007): Spain's International Challenges at the Turn of the Century. *Mediterranean Politics.* Vol. 5. N°2. Pp. 1–13.

Guitta, O. (2005): The Chirac Doctrine. *Middle East Quarterly.* Vol. XII. N°4. Pp. 4–3–53.

Guldbrandsson, K., and Fossum, B. (2009): An Exploration of the Theoretical Concepts Policy Windows and Policy Entrepreneurs at the Swedish Public Health Arena. *Health Promotion International.* Vol. 24. N°4. Pp. 4–34–435.

Halliday, F. (1991): The Gulf War and its Aftermath: First Reflections. *International Affairs.* Vol. 67. N°2. Pp. 2–23–234.

Harvey, W.S. (2010): Methodological Approaches for Interviewing Elites. *Geography Compass.* N°4/3. Pp. 1–93–205.

Hoffman, P. (1984): The Chicora Legend and Franco-Spanish Rivalry in La Florida. *The Florida Historical Quarterly.* Vol. 62. N°4. Pp. 4–19–438.

Hollis, M., and Smith, S. (1986): Roles and Reasons in Foreign Policy Decision Making. *British Journal of Political Science.* Vol. 16. Pp. 2–69–286.

Hollis, R. (1997): Europe and the Middle East. Power by Stealth? *Foreign Affairs.* Vol. 73. N°1.

Holmes, J.W. (1996): Italy: In the Mediterranean but *of* it? *Mediterranean Politics.* Vol. 1. N°2. Pp. 1–76–192.

Hualde Amunarriz, X. (2010): La Question Basque. Un Factor de Tensión entre Francia y la España Franquista, 1945–1975. *Revista de la Fundación Sancho el Sabio.* N°32. Pp. 9–5–116.

Huber, J.D., and Martinez-Gallardo, C. (2004): Cabinet Instability and the Accumulation of Experience: The French Fourth and Fifth Republics in Comparative Perspective. *British Journal of Political Science.* Vol. 34. Issue 1. Pp. 2–7–48.

Huysmans, J. (2008): *The Politics of Insecurity: Fear, Migration and Asylum in the EU.* Routledge, London. Pp. 4–5–54.

Iglesias Cavicchioli, M. (2007): A Period of Turbulent Change: Spanish-US Relations Since 2002. *The Whitehead Journal of Diplomacy and International Relations*. Vol. 8. N°. 2. Pp. 1–17.

Ivarsflaten, E. (2002): What Unites Right-Wing Populists in Western Europe? Re-Examining Grievance Mobilization Models in 7 Successful Cases. *Comparative Political Studies*. Vol. 31. N°1. Pp. 3–23.

Jackson, P.T., and Nexon, D.H. (2004): Bridging the Gap: Toward a Realist-Constructivist Dialogue. *International Studies Review*. N°6. Pp. 3–37–352.

Jamet, J.F. (2008): Intégration Régionale: Processus de Barcelone et Union pour la Méditerranée, Quels Scénarios d'avenir? *Questions d'Europe*. N°105. Foundation Robert Schuman.

Jentleson, B.W. (2002): The Need for Praxis: Bridging Policy Relevance Back In. *International Security*. Vol. 26. N° 4. Pp. 1–69–183.

Joffé, G. (1997): Europe and North Africa. *Cambridge Review of International Affairs*. Vol. 10. N°2. Pp. 8–4–103.

Johansson-Nogués, E. (2004): Profiles: A 'Ring of Friends'? The Implications of the European Neighbourhood Policy for the Mediterranean. *Mediterranean Politics*. Vol. 9. Issue 2. Pp. 2–40–247.

Jordan Gandulf, J.M. (1997): Spanish Moroccan Economic Relations. *Mediterranean Politics*. Vol. 2. Issue 1. Pp. 4–9–63.

Kaarbo, J. (1998): Power Politics in Foreign Policy: The Influence of Bureaucratic Minorities. *European Journal of International Relations*. Vol. 4. N°1. P.70.

Kausch, K. (2010): El Declive de la Política de España en el Mediterráneo. *FRIDE*. Policy Brief. N°26. Pp. 1–8.

Kausch, K., and Young, R. (2009): The End of the "Euro-Mediterranean Vision". *International Affairs*. N°. 85.

Kelley, J. (2006): New Wine in Old Wineskins: Promoting Political Reforms through the New European Neighbourhood Policy. *Journal of Common Market Studies*. Vol. 44. N°1. Pp. 2–9–55.

Khatib, K. (2010): The Union for the Mediterranean: Views from the Southern Shores. *The International Spectator: Italian Journal of International Affairs*. Vol. 45:3. Pp. 4–1–50.

Knigge, P. (1998): The Ecological Correlates of Right-Wing Extremism in Western Europe. *European Journal of Political Research*. Vol. 34. Issue 2. Pp. 2–49–279.

Kodmani-Darwish, B. (1995): La Frane et le Moyen-Orient: Entre Nostalgie et Réalisme. *Politique Etrangere*. Vol. 60. N°4. Pp. 9–41–962.

Kolbe, H. R,. and Burnett, M.S. (1991): Content Analysis Research: An Examination of Application with Directives for Improving Reliability and Objectivity. *Journal of Consumer Research*. Vol. 18. N°2. Pp. 2–43–250.

Koliris, P. (1984): Global Mediterranean Policy Implications in View of the New EEC Enlargement. *Journal of Agricultural Economics*. Vol. 35. Issue 3. Pp. 3–19–329.

Koser, K. (2005): Irregular Migration, State Security and Human Security. *Global Commission on International Migration*.

Koser, K. (2010): Why Didn't the Global Economic and Financial Crisis Have More of an Impact on International Migration. GCSP, Geneva. Paper n°6. P.1.

Koser, K. (2011): Responding to Migration from Complex Humanitarian Emergencies: Lessons Learned from Libya. *Global Health Security*. 2011/2.

Kotler, P., and Sidney, J.L. (1969): Broadening the Concept of Marketing-Too Far. *Journal of Marketing*. N°33. 1. Pp. 1–0–15.

Kott, H., and Duprez, D. (2009): The 2005 Riots in France: The International Impact of Domestic Violence. *Journal of Ethnic and Migration Studies*. Vol. 35. Issue 1. Pp. 7–13–730.

Kubicek, P. (2005): Turkish Accession to the EU: Challenges and Opportunities. *World Affairs* 168, N°2 Platinum Periodicals.

Kull, S., Ramsay, C., and Lewis, E. (2003): Misperceptions, the Media and the Iraq War. *Political Sciences Quarterly*. Vol. 118. Issue 4. Pp. 5–69–598.

Lachmann, N. (2011): In the Labyrinth of International Community: The Alliance of Civilizations Programme at the UN. *Cooperation Conflict*. Vol. 46. Issue 2. Pp. 1–85–200.

Lario Bastida, M. (2008): Crónica Crítica del Debate Sobre las Políticas Migratorias en España en 2008. *Discurso y Sociedad*. Vol. 2. N°4. Pp. 769–798.

Larreguy, H.A. (2013): Monitoring Political Brokers: Evidence from Clientelistic Networks in Mexico. EPSA Annual General Conference. MIT.

Lavenex, J. (2004): EU External Governance in 'Wider Europe'. *Journal of European Public Policy*. Vol. 11. Issue 4. Pp. 6–80–700.

Lavenex, S. (2006): Immigration Policy in Europe: The Politics of Control. *West European Politics*. Vol. 29. Issue 2. Pp. 3–29–350.

Leamer, E.E. (1995): The Heckscher-Ohlin Model in Theory and Practice. *Princeton Studies in International Finance*. N°77.

Lees-Marshment, J. (2008): Political Marketing. *Journal of Political Marketing*. Vol. 2. N° 1. Pp. 2–3.

Leonard, S. (2010): EU Border Security and Migration into the European Union: FRONTEX and Securitisation Through Practices. *European Security*. Vol. 19. Issue 2. Pp. 2–31–254.

Lilleker, D.G. (2003): Interviewing the Political Elite: Navigating a Potential Minefield. *Politics*. N°23. Vol. 3. Pp. 2–07–214.

Lubbers, M., Gjsberts, M., and Scheepers, P. (2002): Extreme Right-Wing Voting in Western Europe. *European Journal of Political Research*. Vol. 41. Issue 3. Pp. 3–45–378.

Ludena, J. (2003): El Plan Baker II: ¿Solución Para el Sahara Occidental? *Papeles de Cuestiones Internacionales*. N°84. Pp. 1–21–127.

Lutterbeck, D. (2006): Policing Migration in the Mediterranean. *Mediterranean Politics*. Vol. 11. N°1. Pp. 59–82.

Lutterbeck, D. (2009): Small Frontier Island : Malta and the Challenge of Irregular Immigration. *Mediterranean Quarterly*. Vol. 20. N°1. Pp. 1–19–144.

Maghraoui, A. (2003): Ambiguities of Sovereignty: Morocco, The Hague and The Western Sahara Dispute. *Mediterranean Politics*. Vol. 8. Issue 1. Pp. 1–13–126.

Malmvig, H. (2006): Caught Between Cooperation and Democratization: The Barcelona Process and the EU's Double Discursive Approach. *Journal of International Relations and Development*. Vol. 9. N°4. Pp. 343–370.

Mann, S. (1984): Brokers as Entrepreneurs in Pre-Socialist China. *Comparative Studies in Society and History*. Vol. 26. Issue 4. Pp. 6–14–636.

Marks, J. (1996): High Hopes and Low Motives: The New Euro-Mediterranean Partnership Initiative. *Mediterranean Politics*. Vol. 1. Issue 1. Pp. 1–24.

Mautner, G. (2005): Time to Get Wired: Using Web-Based Corpora in Critical Discourse Analysis. *Discourse and Society*. N°16. Issue 6. Pp. 8–09–828.

Mays, N., and Pope, C. (2000): Qualitative Research in Healthcare: Assessing Quality in Quality Research. *British Medical Journal*. 330 (7226). Pp. 5–0–52.

McDonough, P., Barnes, S.H., and Pina, A. (1986): The Growth of Democratic Legitimacy in Spain. *The American Political Science Review*. Vol. 80. N°3. Pp. 753–760.

McDowell, L. (1998): Elites in the City of London: Some Methodological Considerations. *Environment and Planning*. A. 30. Pp. 2–133–2146.

McEvoy, J. (2006): Elite Interviewing in a Divided Society: Lessons from Northern Ireland. *Politics*. Vol. 26. N°3. Pp. 1–84–191.

Mearsheimer, J. (1994): The False Promise of International Institutions. *International Security*. Vol. 19. N°3. Pp. 5–49.

Mearsheimer, J.J. (1989): Assessing the Conventional Balance: The 3:1 Rule and the Future of Security Studies. *International Security*. Vol. 13. N°4. Pp. 5–4–89.

Mestres I Camps, L. (2005): Veinte Años de Cooperación Entre España y Francia: Amigos, Socios o Aliados? *Revista CIDOB d'Afers Internacionals*. N°75. Pp. 1–51–172.

Mikecz, R. (2012): Interviewing Elites: Addressing Methodological Issues. *Qualitative Inquiry*. Vol. 18. N°6. Pp. 4–82–493.

Mohsen-Finan, K. (2002): The Western Sahara Dispute and UN Pressure. *Mediterranean Politics*. Vol. 7. Issue 2. Pp. 1–12.

Moisi, D. (1982): La France de Mitterrand et le Conflict du Proche-Orient: Comment Concilier Emotion et Politique. *Politique Etrangere*. Vol. 47. N°2. Pp. 3–95–402.

Monar, J. (1998): Institutional Constraints of the European Union's Mediterranean Policy. *Mediterranean Politics*. Vol. 3. N°2. Pp. 3–9–60.

Montanari, M. (2007): The Barcelona Process and the Political Economy of Euro-Mediterranean Trade Integration. *Journal of Common Market Studies*. Vol. 45. Issue 5. Pp. 1–011–1040.

Montobbio, M. (2002): The Spanish Presidency of the Council of the EU 2002 and the Relaunching of the Barcelona Process. *Real Instituto Elcano*. Working Paper WP5–2000.

Moratinos, M.A. (2004): Una Nueva Política Exterior para España. *Política Exterior*. N°99. May/June. P. 65.

Moratinos, M.A. (2009): España por fin en su Sitio. Cuatro Cumbres para la Historia. *Política Exterior*. N°120. May/June. Pp. 1–9–23.

Moravcsik, A. (1993): Preferences and Power in the European Community: A Liberal Inter-Governmentalist Approach. *Journal of Common Market Studies*. N°31. Pp. 1–9–56.

Mortimer, R. (1993): Regionalism and Geopolitics in the Maghrib. *Middle East Report*. N°184. Special Number on New Orders: The Middle East in a Realigned World.

Mudde, C. (1999): The Single-Issue Party Thesis: Extreme Right Parties and the Immigration Issue. *West European Politics*. Vol. 22. Issue 3. Pp. 1–82–197.

Natorski, M. (2007): Explaining Spanish and Polish Approaches to the European Neighbourhood Policy. *European Political Economy Review*. N°7. Pp. 6–3–101.

Neal, A.W. (2009): Securitization and Risk at the EU Border. The Origins of Frontex. *Journal of Common Market Studies*. Vol. 47. Issue 2. Pp. 3–33–356.

Nichols, R.F. (1933): Trade Relations and the Establishment of the United States Consulates in Spanish America, 1779–1809. *The Hispanic American Historical Review*. Vol. 1. N°3.P. 289–313

O'Halloran, K. (2007): Critical Discourse Analysis and the Corpus-Informed Interpretation of Metaphor at the Register Level. *Applied Linguistics*. N°28. Issue 1. Pp. 1–24.

Orpin, D. (2005): Corpus Linguistics and Critical Discourse Analysis: Examining the Ideology of Sleaze. *International Journal of Corpus Linguistics*. N°10. Issue 1. Pp. 3–7–61.

Paasi, A. (2001): Europe as a Social Process and Discourse: Considerations of Place, Boundaries and Identities. *European Urban and Regional Studies*. Vol. 8. N°1. Pp. 7–28.

Pace, M. (2005): Conclusion, Cultural Democracy in Euro-Mediterranean Relations. *Mediterranean Politics*. Vol. 10. N°3. Pp. 427–437.

Peabody, R.L. et Al. (1990): Interviewing Political Elites. *Political Science and Politics*. Vol. 23. N°23. Pp. 4–51–455.

Perlmutter, A. (1974): The Presidential Political Center and Foreign Policy: A Critique of the Revisionist and Bureaucratic-Political Orientations. *World Politics*. Vol. 27. Pp. 8–7–106.

Pero, M. (2001): Kissinger e la Politica Estera Americana nel Mediterraneo: Il Caso Portoghese. *Studi Storici*. N°4.

Peters, J. (1998): The Arab Israeli Multilateral Peace Talks and the Barcelona Process: Competition or Convergence? *The International Spectator: Italian Journal of International Affairs*. Vol. 33. Issue 4. Pp. 6–3–76.

Petito, F. (2007): The Global Political Discourse among Civilizations: Mohammed Khatami and Václav Havel. *Global Change, Peace and Security*. Vol. 19. Issue 2. Pp. 1–03–126.

Pomfret, R. (1981): The Impact of the EEC Enlargement on Non-Member Mediterranean Countries' Exports to the EEC. *The Economic Journal*. Vol. 1. N°363. Pp. 7–26–729.

Portero, F. (2005): La Democracia Como Amenaza. *Cuadernos de Pensamiento Político*. FAES. N°8.

Pujante, D., and Morales López, E. (2008): A Political Action against Popular Opinion: Aznar's Final Speech before the Spanish Parliament Justifying the War in Iraq. *Journal of Language and Politics*. Vol. 7. N°1. Pp. 7–1–96.

Pye, L.W. (1958a): Administrators, Agitators and Brokers. *The Public Opinion Quarterly*. Vol. 22. N° 3. Pp. 3–42–348.

Pye, L.W. (1958b): The Non-Western Political Process. *The Journal of Politics*. Vol. 20. Issue 3. Pp. 4–68–486.

Razoux, P. (2008): The NATO Mediterranean Dialogue at a Crossroads. *NATO Research Division*. Defence College, Rome. N°35.

Reinares, F. (2010): The Madrid Bombings and Global Jihadism. *Survival. Global Politics and Strategy*. Vol. 52. Issue 2. Pp. 8–3–104.

Roberts, N.C., and King, P. (1991): Policy Entrepreneurs: Their Activity Structure and Function in the Policy Process. *Journal of Public Administration Research and Theory*. N°2. Pp. 1–47–175.

Rosati, J.A. (1981): Developing a Systematic Decision-Making Framework: Bureaucratic Politics in Perspective. *World Politics*. Vol. 33. N°2. P. 234–252

Royo, S. (2009): After the Fiesta: The Spanish Economy Meets the Global Financial Crisis. *South European Society and Politics*. Vol. 14. Issue 1. Pp. 1–9–34.

Rudolph, C. (2003): Security and the Political Economy of International Migration. *American Political Science Review*. Vol. 97. N°4. November. Pp. 603–620.

Ruggie, J.G. (1998): What Makes the World Hang Together? Neo-Utilitarianism and the Social Constructivism Challenge. *International Organizations*. N°52. Pp. 8–87–917.

Ruiz Miguel, C. (2006): Sáhara Occidental: Independencia, Paz y Seguridad. *Cuadernos de Pensamiento Político*. N°12.

Ruiz Miguel, C. (2007): La Conveniencia de Pensar el Giro de Nuestra Política Exterior. *GEES*.

Runge, C.F., and Von Witzke, H. (1987): Institutional Change in the Common Agricultural Policy of the European Community. *American Journal of Agricultural Economics*. Vol. 69. N°2. Pp. 2–13–222.

Sánchez Mateos, E. (2005): Libya's Return to the International Scene. *Mediterranean Politics*. Special Issue. Conceptualizing Cultural and Social Dialogue in the Euro-Mediterranean Area: A European Perspective. Vol. 10. Issue 3. Pp. 4–39–445.

Sand Holtz, W. (1993): Choosing Union: Monetary Politics and Maastricht. *International Organization*. N°47. Pp. 1–39.

Santamaria, E. (2002): Immigración y Barbarie. La Construcción Social y Política del Inmigrante Como Amenaza. *UAB*. Vol. 66.

Sartre, J.P. (1955): L'Algerie n'est pas la France. *Temps Modernes*. May.

Sartre, J.P. (1956): Le Colonialism est un Système. *Temps Modernes*. March.

Sasse, G. (2008): The European Neighbourhood Policy: Conditionality Revisited for the EU's Eastern Neighbours. *Europe-Asia Studies*. Vol. 60. Issue 2. Pp. 2–95–316.

Scammell, M. (1999): Political Marketing: Lessons for Political Science. *Political Studies*. N°47: 4. Pp. 7–18–739.

Schiff, M. (2002): Love thy Neighbor: Trade, Migration and Social Capital. *European Journal of Political Economy*. Vol. 18. Issue 1. P. 87.

Schimmelfennig, F. (2001): The Community Trap: Liberal Norms, Rhetorical Action and the Eastern Enlargement of the European Union. *International Organization*. Vol. 55. N°1. Pp. 4–7–80.

Schimmelfennig, F., and Scholtz, H. (2008): EU Democracy in the The European Neighbourhood: Political Conditionality, Economic Development and Transnational Exchange. *European Union Politics*. Vol. 9. N°2. Pp. 1–87–215.

Schmid, D. (2008): La Turquie et l'Union pour la Méditerranée: Un Partenariat Calculé. *Politique Étrangere*. 2008/1. Primptemps. Pp. 6–6–79.

Schneider, C.L. (2008): Police Power and Race Riots in Paris. *Politics and Society*. Vol. 36. N°1. Pp. 1–33–159.

Schumacher, T. (2004): Riding on The Wings of Change: The Future of the Euro-Mediterranean Partnership. *The International Spectator*. Vol. 38. N°2. Pp. 8–9–103.

Schumacher, T. (2004a): "Riding the Wings of Change": The Future of the Euro-Mediterranean Partnership. *The International Spectator.* Vol. 2. Issue 39. Pp. 89–103.

Schumacher, T. (2004b): Survival of the Fittest: The First Five Years of Euro-Mediterranean Economic Relations. *EUI Working Papers.* European University Institute. Florence.

Semetko, H.A., and Valkenburg, P.M. (2000): Framing European Politics: A Content Analysis of Press and Television News. *International Communication Association.* Vol. 50. Issue 2. Pp. 9–3–109.

Share, D. (1986): The Franquist Regime and the Dilemma of Succession. *The Review of Politics.* Vol. 46. Issue 48. Pp. 546–575.

Sharp, J. M. (2005): The Broader Middle East and North Africa Initiative: An Overview. *US Military.*

Shenton, A., and Hayter, S. (2004): Strategies for Gaining Access to Organizations and Informants in Qualitative Studies. *Education for Information.* N°22. Pp. 2–23–231.

Sjursen, M. (2004): On the Identity of NATO. *International Affairs.* Vol. 80. Pp. 6–87–703.

Skinner, Q. (2002): Machiavelli on Virtú and the Maintenance of Liberty. *Visions of Politics.* N°2. Pp. 1–60–185.

Smith, K. (2005): The Outsiders: The European Neighbourhood Policy. *International Affairs.* Vol. 81. Issue 4. Pp. 7–57–773.

Smith, M.E. (2000): Conforming to Europe: The Domestic Impact of EU Foreign Policy Co-Operation. *Journal of European Public Policy.* Vol. 4. N°7. Pp. 6–13–631.

Soler I Lecha, E. (2008): España y el Mediterráneo. En Defensa del Proceso de Barcelona. Monografía del *Observatorio de Política Exterior Europea.* N°14.

Soler i Lecha, E., and Weltner-Puig, R. (2002): "Dialogo Euromediterráneo: ¿Una Segunda Oportunidad? In Barbé, E. (Ed.): *España y la Política Exterior de la UE. Entre las Prioridades Españolas y los Desafíos del Contexto Internacional.* Institut Universitari d'Estudis Europeus. Working Paper. N°40. Pp. 5–3–71.

Soumille, P. (1991): Rivalites Franco-Spagnoles Avant et Pendant la Revolution Français. *Awraq.* Estudios Sobre el Mundo Árabe e Islámico Contemporáneo. N°12. Pp. 1–79–195.

Staton, C.D. (1994): Democracy's Quantum Leap. *Demos Quarterly.* N°3.

Sterling-Folker, J. (2002): Realism and the Constructivist Challenge: Rejecting, Reconstructing or Re-reading. *International Studies Review.* Vol. 4. N°1. Pp. 7–3–97.

Strang, D. (1990): From Dependency to Sovereignty: An Event History Analysis of Decolonization 1870–1987. *American Sociological Review.* Vol. 55. Pp. 8–48–860.

Sudriá, C. (1997): La Restricción Energética al Desarrollo Económico de España. *Papeles de Economía Española.* N°73.

Swank, D., and Betz, H.G. (2003): Globalization, the Welfare State and Right Wing Populism in Western Europe. *Socio-Economic Review.* Vol. 1. N°2. P. 215.

Swindler, A. (1986): Culture in Action: Symbols and Strategies. *American Sociological Review.* Vol. 51. N°2. Pp. 2–73–286.

Taheri, A. (2003): France's "Arab" Policy: Time for Debate. *American Foreign Policy Interests.* Vol. 25. Issue 4. Pp. 3–23–336.

Tailleur, J.P. (2002): Many French Newspapers Have Been Shy on Inmigration Questions When Related to Islam and Islamism. *Bévues de Presse*

Taittinger, J. (1977): Intervention 20 September 1977. *La Politique Étrangère de la France.* 3rd Quarter. Pp. 66–67.

Taliaferro, J.W. (2000): Security Seeking Under Anarchy: Defensive Realism Revisited. *International Security.* Vol. 25. N°3. Pp. 128–161.

Teece, D.J. (1993): The Dynamics of Industrial Capitalism: Perspectives on Alfred Chandler's Scale and Scope. *Journal of Economic Literature.* Vol. 31. N°1. Pp. 1–99–225.

Telhami, S. (1993): Arab Public Opinion and the Gulf War. *Political Sciences Quarterly.* Vol. 108. N° 3. Pp. 4–37–452.

Telhani, S. (2003): A View from the Arab World: A Survey in Five Countries. *The Brookings Institution.*

Tovias, A. (2003): Israel and the Barcelona Process: The First Five Years. *Israel and Europe.* Pp. 3–7–51.

Tränhardt, D. (1995): The Political Uses of Xenophobia in England, France and Germany. *Party Politics.* N°1. Pp. 3–23–345.

Tsoukalis, L. (1977): EEC and the Mediterranean: Is `Global' Policy Misnomer? *Royal Institute of International Affairs.* Vol. 53. N°3. Pp. 422–438.

Tucker, W.T. (1974): Future Directions in Marketing Theory. *Journal of Marketing.* N°38. 2. Pp. 3–0–35.

Van der Steen, M., and Groenewegen, J. (2008): Exploring Policy Entrepreneurship. Discussion Paper Series on the Coherence between Institutions and Technologies in Infrastructures. WP0801. École Polytechnique Fédéral de Lausanne and Delft University of Technology.

Van Dijk, T. (2005): War Rhetoric of a Little Ally: Political Implicatures and Aznar's Legitimation of the War in Iraq. *Journal of Language and Politics*. Vol. 4. N°1. Pp. 6–5–91.

Van Spanje, J. (2010): Anti-Immigration Parties and their Impact on Other Parties' Immigration Stances in Contemporary Western Europe. *Party Politics*. Vol. 26. N°5. P. 563.

Vaquer I Fanes, J. (2003): The Domestic Dimension of EU External Policies: The Case of EU-Morocco 2000–2001 Fisheries Negotiations. *Mediterranean Politics*. Vol. 8. Issue 1. Pp. 5–9–82.

Wagner, R.H. (1974): Dissolving the State: Three Recent Perspectives on International Relations. *International Organization*. Vol. 28. Pp. 4–35–466.

Wallace, W. (1996): Truth and Power, Monks and Technocrats: Theory and Practice in International Relations. *Review of International Studies*. N°22. Pp. 3–01–321.

Walt, S.M. (2005): The Relationship Between Theory and Policy in International Relations. *Annual Review of Political Science*. Vol. 8. Pp. 2–3–48.

Waltz, K.N. (1996): International Politics is not Foreign Policy. *Security Studies*. Vol. 6. N°1. Pp. 5–4–57.

Wansbrough, J. (1968): The Decolonization of North African History. *The Journal of African History*. Vol. 9. Issue 4. October. Pp. 6–43–650.

Weil, G.L. (1967): The Merger of the Institutions of the European Communities. *The American Journal of International Law*. Vol. 61. N°1. Pp. 5–7–65.

Weiner, M. (1993): Security, Stability and International Migration. *International Security*. Vol. 17. N°3. Pp. 9–1–126.

Wellard, S., and McKenna, L.G. (2000): Turning Tapes into Text: Issues Surrounding the Transcription of Interviews. *Contemporary Nurse*. Vol. 11. N°2–3. Pp. 1–80–186.

Wellisch, D., and Walz, U. (1998): Why do Rich Countries Prefer Free Trade Over Free Migration? The Role of the Modern Welfare State. *European Economic Review*. Vol. 42. Issue 8. Pp. 1–595–1612.

Wendt, A. (1992): Anarchy is What States Make of It. The Social Construction of Power Politics. *International Organization.* Vol. 46. Issue 2. Pp. 3–91–425.

Wendt, A.E. (1987): The Agent-Structure Problem in International Relations Theory. *International Organization.* Vol. 41. Issue 3. Pp. 3–35–370.

Wesseling, H.L. (2002): France, Germany and Europe. *European Review.* Vol. 10. N°3. Pp. 302–314.

White, G.W. (2007): Sovereignty and International Labour Migration: The 'Security Mentality' in Spanish-Moroccan Relations as an Assertion of Sovereignty. *Review of International Political Economy.* Vol. 14. Issue 4. Pp. 6–90–718.

Whitman, R., and Thomas, G. (2006): Two Cheers for the UK's EU Presidency. *Chatham House, European Research.* EPBP/06/01.

Williams, M.C., and Neumann, I.B. (2000): From Alliance to Security Community: NATO, Russia and the Power of Identity. *Millennium, Journal of International Studies.* Vol. 29. N°2. Pp. 3–57–387.

Wood, P.C. (1998): Chirac's "New Arab Policy" and Middle East Challenges: The Arab-Israeli Conflict in Iraq-Iran. *Middle East Journal.* Vol. 52. N°4. Pp. 5–63–580.

Woodworth, P. (2004): Spain Changes Course: Aznar's Legacy, Zapatero's Prospects. *World Policy Journal.* N°21. Pp. 7–26.

Woodworth, P. (2005): Spain's "Second Transition". Reforming Zeal and Dire Omens. *World Policy Journal.* Vol. 22. N°3. Pp. 6–9–80.

Yanci González, M.P. (1995): Algunas Consideraciones Sobre la Inmigración de Maghrebíes en España y su Incierto Futuro. *Espacio, Tiempo y Forma.* Serie VI. Geografía. T.8. Pp. 1–67–192.

Youngs, R. (1999): The Barcelona Process after the UK Presidency: The Need for Prioritization. *Mediterranean Politics.* Vol. 4. Issue 1. Pp. 1–24

Youngs, R. (2005): Ten Years of the Barcelona Process: A Model for Supporting Arab Reform? *Fride.* Working Paper, 2. P. 4–5.

Zapata Barrero, R., and De Witte, N. (2007): The Spanish Governance of EU Borders: Normative Questions. *Mediterranean Politics.* Vol. 12. Issue 1. Pp. 8–5–90.

Zapata, R. (2008): Policies and Public Opinion Toward Inmigrants. The Spanish Case. *Ethnic and Racial Studies.* N°32. Pp. 1–20.

Zelinsky, W. (1971): The Hypothesis of Mobility Transition. *The Geographical Review.* LX1. Pp. 219–249.

Zisser, E. (2009): Syria's Diplomatic Comeback: What Next? *Mediterranean Politics*. Vol. 14. N°1. Pp. 1–07–113.

Zoubir, H.Y. (1996): Algerian Islamits' Conception of Democracy. *Arab Studies Quarterly*. Vol. 18.

# D Internet Sources

## D.1 Electronic Newspapers

Abian, A. (2010): "Hablar los quintos". *La Vanguardia*. 20 June of 2010. Available at: http://www.lavanguardia.com/politica/20100620/53949261273/hablar-los-quintos.html

Aizpeolea, L.R. (2004): "El nuevo pacto antiterrorista propone mayor colaboración entre occidente y países islámicos". *El País*. 12 December. Available at: http://elpais.com/diario/2004/12/12/espana/1102806002_850215.html

Anon. (1996): "Aznar Quiere Impulsar las Relaciones con Marruecos en su Primer Viaje Oficial". *El País*. 7 May. Available at: http://elpais.com/diario/1996/05/27/portada/833148003_850215.html (Retrieved 15 March 2012).

Anon. (2001): "Bush Warns Europe of 'New Threats'". *CNN*. 12 June 2012. Available at: http://archives.cnn.com/2001/WORLD/europe/06/12/bush.visit.03/ (Retrieved 1 February 2012).

Anon. (2004): "Zapatero Anuncia la Retirada Inmediata de las Tropas de Irak" *El Mundo*. 19 April. Available at: http://www.elmundo.es/elmundo/2004/04/18/espana/1082303152.html (Retrieved 13 July 2013).

Anon. (2007): "La France et la Libye Signent un Accord Sur le Nucléaire Civil". *Le Figaro*. 25 June 2007. Available at: http://www.lefigaro.fr/international/2007/07/25/01003-20070725ARTWWW90355-la_france_et_la_libye_signent_un_accord_sur_le_nucleaire_civil.php (Retrieved 7 June 2012).

Anon. (2009): "Landaburu, El Poderoso Afable". *El Mundo*. 13 May 2009. Available at: http://www.elmundo.es/elmundo/2009/03/01/union_europea/1235927278.html (Retrieved 15 February 2012).

Anon. (2009): "Zapatero Ofrece que la Alianza de las Civilizaciones Colabore con la OTAN Para Reducir Conflictos". *El País*. 7 April. Available at: http://elpais.com/diario/2009/04/07/internacional/1239055210_850215.html (Retrieved 10 June 2012).

Anon. (2011): "L'Union pour la Méditerranée Décapitée'". *Le Nouvel Observateur*. Available at: http://tempsreel.nouvelobs.com/monde/20110126.OBS6993/l-union-pour-la-mediterranee-decapitee.html (Retrieved 22 August 2012).

Anon. (2011): El Conflicto en Libia Encarece el Crudo Pero No Afecta El Suministro Mundial. *El País*. 21 March 2011. Available at: http://economia.elpais.com/economia/2011/03/21/actualidad/1300696383_850215.html#despiece1

Anon. (2012): "Water Desalinization Projects to Solve Gaza's Problems: A Wolf in Sheep's Clothing?" *The Electronic Intifada*. Available at: http://electronicintifada.net/content/water-desalination-projects-solve-gazas-problems-wolf-sheeps-clothing/11370 (Retrieved 25 August 2012).

Bourdet, C. (1955): "Y-a-t-il une Gestapo algérienne". *L'Observateur*. 13 January. Available at http://jacques.morel67.pagesperso-orange.fr/ccfo/crimcol/node12.html (Retrieved 1 May 2011).

Cembrero, I. (2011): "Aznar, Ese Buen Amigo". *El País*. 27 February 2011. Available at: http://elpais.com/diario/2011/02/27/domingo/1298782356_850215.html (Retrieved 12 January 2012).

Claret, A. (2005): "Zapatero y el Mediterráneo". *El País*. 2 February. Available at: http://www.almendron.com/politica/pdf/2005/spain/spain_1965.pdf (Retrieved 2 March 2012).

Cornet, C. (2007): "Is the 'Mediterranean Union' Suffering From Amnesia?" *Babelmed Network*. Available at: http://eng.babelmed.net/cultura-e-societa/36-mediterraneo/2703-is-the-mediterranean-union-suffering-from-amnesia.html (Retrieved 23 August 2012).

Fernández Noguera, M. (2010a): "The UfM Budget Drops by 60% and Member State Experts Have not been Sent". In *Catalan News Agency*. Available at: http://www.catalannewsagency.com/news/politics/union-mediterranean-budget-drops-60-and-member-state-experts-have-not-yet-been-sent (Retrieved 12 August 2012).

Fernández Noguera, M. (2010b): "The Union for the Mediterranean Cannot Function Without the Members State Commitment". Interview to the UfM's Secretary General Ahmed Masa'deh. *Catalan News Agency*. Available at: http://www.catalannewsagency.com/news/politics/union-mediterranean-cannot-function-without-member-states-commitment-states-its-secret (Retrieved 12 August 2012).

Fernández Noguera, M. (2011): "The Secretary General Resigns". *Catalan News Agency*. Available at: http://www.catalannewsagency.com/news/politics/secretary-general-union-mediterranean-resigns (Retrieved 22 August 2012).

Girard, Q. (2011): "Fin 2010, La France Voulait Toujours Vendre du Nucléaire à la Libye". *Liberation*. 21 March 2011. Available at: http://www.liberation.fr/monde/01012326917-fin-2010-la-france-voulait-toujours-vendre-du-nucleaire-a-la-libye (Retrieved 7 June 2012).

González, M. (2008): "España Defiende de las Críticas de París el Proceso de Barcelona". 2 May. Available at: http://elpais.com/diario/2008/05/02/internacional/1209679206_850215.html (Retrieved 27 October 2011).

González, R. (2010): "Zapatero … y Quién es Ese?" *El Mundo*. 4 February. Available at: http://www.elmundo.es/america/2010/02/04/estados_unidos/1265313851.html (Retrieved 13 July 2013).

Jauregui, F. (1985): "Las Presiones Internacionales no Pudieron Frenar los Cinco Fusilamientos del 27 de Septiembre de 1975". *Periódico El País*. 27/09/1985. Available at: http://www.elpais.com/articulo/espana/FRANCO/_FRANCISCO/ESPANA/FRAP/ETA/FRANQUISMO/presiones/internacionales/pudieron/frenar/fusilamientos/27/septiembre/1975/elpepiesp/19850927elpepinac_8/Tes?print=1 (Retrieved 25 January 2011).

Kamen, H. (2004): "¿Qué Alianza? ¿Qué Civilizaciones?" *El Mundo*. 10 December 2004. Available at: http://viaforastore2004.blogspot.ch/2004/12/kamen-qu-alianza-qu-civilizaciones.html (Retrieved 1 May 2012).

Laurent, S. (2008): "Nucléaire Libyen: Des Documents Officieles Démentement la Version de Sarkozy". *Le Monde*. 18 April 2012. Available at: http://www.lemonde.fr/election-presidentielle-2012/article/2012/04/18/nucleaire-libyen-des-documents-officiels-dementent-la-version-de-sarkozy_1687018_1471069.html (Retrieved 7 June 2012).

Levi Julian, H. (2010): "US Joins Pro-Muslim 'Alliance of Civilizations' ". *Arutz Sheva*. 20 May. Available at: http://www.israelnationalnews.com/News/News.aspx/137610#.UiOkKT-rxzc (Retrieved 13 November 2012).

Marti Font, J.M. (2008): "Sarkozy Descalifica el Proceso de Barcelona de la Unión Europea". *El País*. 1 May. Available at: http://elpais.com/diario/2008/05/01/internacional/1209592805_850215.html (Retrieved 27 October 2011).

Naïr, S. (2005): "Alianza de Civilizaciones y Diálogo para la Modernidad". *El País*. 15 March. Available at: http://www.almendron.com/politica/pdf/2005/reflexion/reflexion_0591.pdf (Retrieved 15 May 2013).

Navas, J.A., and García, A. (2008): "Zapatero Anuncia Tiempos Duros y Presume de Dar la Cara en el Congreso". *El Mundo.* 10 September. Available at: http://www.elmundo.es/elmundo/2008/09/10/espana/1221039317.html (Retrieved 10 June 2012).

Simons, S. (2008): "Nicolas Sarkozy's New Club Med". *Spiegel Online International.* 7 December 2008. Available at: http://www.spiegel.de/international/europe/union-for-the-mediterranean-nicolas-sarkozy-s-new-club-med-a-565667.html (Retrieved 12 August 2012).

Tremlett, G. (2001): "US Offers to Spy on ETA for Spain". *The Guardian.* 15 June 2001. Available at: http://www.guardian.co.uk/world/2001/jun/15/spain.usa (Retrieved 1 February 2012).

## D.2 European Union

Anon. (1999): Presidency Conclusions: Tampere European Council. 15–16 October 1999. Available at: http://www.europarl.europa.eu/summits/tam_en.htm (Retrieved 5 February 2010).

Anon. (2011): Tunisia: PACE Calls on Political Forces to Start Democratic Reforms Without Delay. *Parliamentary Assembly Council of Europe.* Winter Session. Resolution 27/01/11. Available at: http://assembly.coe.int/ASP/NewsManager/EMB_NewsManagerView.asp?ID=6307 (Retrieved 29 January 2011).

EMP. (2005): Conclusions for the Seventh Euro-Mediterranean Conference of Ministers of Foreign Affairs. Luxembourg, 30–31 May. Available at: http://www.eu2005.lu/en/actualites/conseil/2005/05/31euromed/euromed.pdf (Retrieved 12 June 2012). P. 1.

EU. (2005): The Hague Programme: Strengthening Freedom, Security and Justice in the European Union. *Official Journal of the European Union.* C53/1. Pp. 5–7. Available at: http://eur-lex.europa.eu/LexUriServ/LexUriServ.do?uri=OJ:C:2005:053:0001:0014:EN:PDF (Retrieved 12 December 2011).

EU. (1997): European Union Enlargement. Presidency Conclusions. European Council. 12 and 13 December 1997. Available at: http://www.consilium.europa.eu/uedocs/cms_data/docs/pressdata/en/ec/032a0008.htm (Retrieved 1 September 2012).

EU. (2004): *Presidency Conclusions for the Euro-Mediterranean Meeting of Ministers of Foreign Affairs.* The Hague. 29 and 30 November 2004. Available at: http://www.consilium.europa.eu/ueDocs/cms_Data/docs/pressData/en/er/82876.pdf (Retrieved 4 April 2012).

EU. (2008): Barcelona Process; Union for the Mediterranean Ministerial Conference. Final Declaration. *Council of the European Union.*

Marseille 3–4 November. P. 2. Available at: http://www.consilium.europa.eu/ueDocs/cms_Data/docs/pressData/en/misc/103733.pdf (Retrieved 1 August 2012).

European Commission. (2013): European Neighbourhood Policy. Available at: http://ec.europa.eu/world/enp/policy_en.htm (Retrieved 20 May 2013).

European Council. (1997): Conclusions of the Presidency. Amsterdam. Available at: http://www.consilium.europa.eu/ueDocs/cms_Data/docs/pressData/en/ec/032a0006.htm (Retrieved 10 June 2013).

European Council. (1998): Conclusions of the Presidency. Vienna. Available at: http://www.europarl.europa.eu/summits/wie1_en.htm (Retrieved 10 June 2013).

European Council. (1999): Conclusions of the Presidency. Cologne. Available at: http://www.europarl.europa.eu/summits/kol1_en.htm (Retrieved 1 June 2013).

European Council. (1999): Conclusions of the Presidency. Helsinki. Available at: http://www.europarl.europa.eu/summits/hel1_en.htm (Retrieved 1 June 2013).

European Council. (2000): Conclusions of the Presidency. Santa María. Available at: http://www.europarl.europa.eu/summits/fei1_en.htm (Retrieved 1 June 2013).

European Council. (2001): Conclusions of the Presidency. Brussels. Available at: http://www.consilium.europa.eu/uedocs/cms_data/docs/pressdata/en/ec/140.en.pdf (Retrieved 1 July 2013).

European Council. (2001): Conclusions of the Presidency. Laeken. Available at: http://ec.europa.eu/governance/impact/background/docs/laeken_concl_en.pdf (Retrieved 1 July 2013).

European Council. (2002): Conclusions of the Presidency. Seville. Available at: http://www.europarl.europa.eu/summits/pdf/sev1_en.pdf (Retrieved 1 July 2013).

European Council. (2003): Conclusions of the Presidency. Brussels, 2nd Council. Available at: http://www.consilium.europa.eu/uedocs/cms_data/docs/pressdata/en/ec/75136.pdf (Retrieved 1 July 2013).

European Council. (2003): Conclusions of the Presidency. Brussels, 1st Council. Available at: http://www.consilium.europa.eu/uedocs/cms_data/docs/pressdata/en/ec/75136.pdf (Retrieved 1 July 2013).

European Council. (2003): Conclusions of the Presidency. Thessaloniki. Available at: http://www.consilium.europa.eu/uedocs/cms_data/docs/pressdata/en/ec/76279.pdf (Retrieved 1 July 2013).

European Council. (2003): Conclusions of the Presidency. Brussels. 3rd Meeting. Available at: http://www.consilium.europa.eu/uedocs/cms_data/docs/pressdata/en/ec/78364.pdf (Retrieved 1 June 2013).

European Council. (2004): Conclusions of the Presidency. Brussels. 1st Meeting. Available at: http://www.consilium.europa.eu/uedocs/cms_data/docs/pressdata/en/ec/79637.pdf (Retrieved 1 June 2013).

European Council. (2004): Conclusions of the Presidency. Brussels. 3rd Meeting. Available at: http://www.consilium.europa.eu/uedocs/cms_data/docs/pressdata/en/ec/82534.pdf (Retrieved 1 June 2013).

European Council. (2005): Conclusions of the Presidency. Third Meeting. Available at: http://www.consilium.europa.eu/ueDocs/cms_Data/docs/pressData/en/ec/87642.pdf (Retrieved 1 August 2013).

European Council. (2005): EU Strategic Partnership with the Mediterranean and the Middle East. Available at: http://www.consilium.europa.eu/uedocs/cmsUpload/Partnership%20Mediterranean%20and%20Middle%20East.pdf (Retrieved 13 July 2012).

European Council. (2006): European Council. Conclusions of the Presidency. Third. Available at: http://www.consilium.europa.eu/ueDocs/cms_Data/docs/pressData/en/ec/89013.pdf (Retrieved 1 August 2013).

European Council. (2007): European Council. Conclusions of the Presidency. Third. Available at: http://www.consilium.europa.eu/ueDocs/cms_Data/docs/pressData/en/ec/97669.pdf (Retrieved 1 August 2013).

European Council. (2011): Conclusions of the Presidency. EU. Third Meeting. Brussels. Available at: http://www.consilium.europa.eu/uedocs/cms_data/docs/pressdata/en/ec/126714.pdf (Retrieve 1 September 2013)

European Council. (2005): European Council. Conclusions of the Presidency. June 2005. Available at: http://www.consilium.europa.eu/uedocs/cms_data/docs/pressdata/en/ec/85349.pdf (Retrieved 1 August 2013).

European Parliament. (2008): European Parliament Resolution of 5 June 2008 on the Barcelona Process: Union for the Mediterranean. European Parliament. P6_TA(2008)0257. Available at: http://www.europarl.europa.eu/meetdocs/2009_2014/documents/afet/dv/p6_ta(2008)0257_/p6_ta(2008)0257_en.pdf (Retrieved 1 August 2012). Pp. 1–2.

European Union. (1994): Bulletin of the European Commission. Council of Corfu. N°6/1994. P.1 and 12. Available at http://aei.pitt.edu/1444/01/corfu_june_1994.pdf (Retrieved 21 November 2010).

European Union. (1994): Bulletin of the European Commission. Council of Essen. N°12/1994. Available at http://aei.pitt.edu/1447/01/Essen_Dec_1994.pdf (Retrieved 21 November 2010).

Ferrero-Waldmer, B. (2007): European Neighbourhood Policy. *Baltic Rim Economies.* N°148. P. 11. Available at: http://www3.tse.fi/FI/yksikot/erillislaitokset/pei/Documents/bre/expert_article148_62007.pdf (Retrieved 20 May 2013).

FRONTEX, Current Situation at the External Borders of the EU (Jan-Sept). Available at: http://www.frontex.europa.eu/situation_at_the_external_border/art18.html (Retrieved 4 December 2010).

## D.3 Electronic Journals and Working Papers

Anon. Dialogue 5+5 Western Mediterranean. *European Institute for Research on Euro-Arab Cooperation.* Brussels. Available at: http://www.medea.be/en/themes/euro-mediterranean-cooperation/dialogue-55-western-mediterranean/ (Retrieved 11 March 2012).

Anon. (2013): France-Morocco Economic Relations. *France Diplomatie.* Available at: www.diplomatie.gouv.fr/en/country-files/morocco-285/france-and-morocco/economic-relations6307 (Retrieved 14 May 2014).

Balfour, R., and Schmid, D. (2008): Union for the Mediterranean, Disunity for the EU. *European Policy Centre.* Policy Brief. Available at: http://www.epc.eu/documents/uploads/235206674_Union%20for%20the%20Mediterranean.pdf (Retrieved 15 March 2012).

Bardají, R.L. (2005): La Alianza de las Civilizaciones. Elementos Para una Crítica. *Grupo de Estudios Estratégicos. GEES.* FAES. Análisis N°77. Available at: http://www.almendron.com/politica/pdf/2005/spain/spain_2217.pdf (Retrieved 1 May 2012).

Calleya, S. (2003): The Euro-Med Partnership and Sub-Regionalism: A Case of Region Building? IPRI 4, Working Paper. Berkeley. Available at: http://ies.berkeley.edu/pubs/workingpapers/PRI-4-Euro-Med_Partnership.pdf (Retrieved 8 March 2012).

Carnero, A. (2007): Foreign Policy without an Idea of Spain. *FAES Papers.* N°60. P. 1. Available at: http://www.fundacionfaes.org/record_file/filename/1566/papeles60_ingles.indd.pdf (Retrieved 1 March 2012).

Daoud, A. (2012): France's New President: Foreign Policy and Where North Africa Stands. *The North African Journal.* Available at: http://www.north-africa.com/premium/opinions/2012/05/09/frances-new-president-foreign-policy-and-where-north-africa-stands/ (Retrieved 21 July 2012).

Daoud, A. (2012): France's New President: Foreign Policy and Where North Africa Stands. *The North African Journal.* Available at: http://www.north-africa.com/premium/opinions/2012/05/09/frances-new-president-foreign-policy-and-where-north-africa-stands/ (Retrieved 21 July 2012).

De Haas, H. (2005b): Morocco: From emigration country to Africa's migration passage to Europe. Country profile Morocco. Migration Information Source. Available at: http://www.migrationinformation.org/Profiles/display.cfm?ID=339 (Retrieved 1 May 2011).

De Haas, H. (2009): The Moroccan Emigrant Population. Bundeszentrale für Politische Bildung. Available at : http://www.bpb.de/themen/K0W40E,0,The_Moroccan_Emigrant_Population.html (Retrieved 22 November 2010).

Hardt-Mautner, G. (1995): Only Connect: Critical Discourse Analysis and Corpus Linguistics. Technical Paper, N°6. University of Lancaster. Available at: http://www.comp.lancs.ac.uk/ucrel/tech-papers.html (Retrieved 13 July 2013).

Hearthfield, J. (2006): *The Death of the Subject Explained.* Books Surge Publishing. Chapter 6 available at: http://www.marxists.org/reference/subject/philosophy/works/fr/defeat-french-humanism.htm (Retrieved 5 May 2011).

Kausch, K., and Barreñada, I. (2005): Alliance of Civilizations: International Security and Cosmopolitan Democracy. *FRIDE Foundation.* Available at: http://eprints.ucm.es/10533/1/WP_03-05.pdf (Retrieved 2 March 2012)

Keating, J. (2010): Bad Exes. *Foreign Policy.* 1 October 2010. Available at: http://www.foreignpolicy.com/articles/2010/10/01/bad_exes?page=0,1 (Retrieved 12 Feburary 2012).

Kilgarrif, A., and Grefenstette, G. (2003): Introduction to the Special Issue on Web as a Corpus. *Computational Linguistics.* Vol. 29. Issue 3. Available at: http://www.kilgarriff.co.uk/Publications/2003-KilgGrefenstette-WACIntro.pdf (Retrieved 13 July 2013).

Martin, J.P. (2008): Migration and the Global Economy. OECD. Pp. 1–3. Available at: http://www.oecd.org/migration/internationalmigrationpoliciesanddata/40196342.pdf (Retrieved 1 March 2010).

Prat I Coll, J. (2004): La Institucionalización del Espacio Euro-Mediterráneo. *Revista Valenciana d'Estudis Autonómics*. N°. 45/46. Pp. 1–27–137. Available at: http://www.pre.gva.es/argos/filead min/argos/datos/RVEA/libro_45_46/127-45_46.pdf (Retrieved 4 March 2012).

Schumacher, T. (2009): A Fading Mediterranean Dream. *European Voice*. Available at: http://www.europeanvoice.com/article/imported/a-fading-mediterranean-dream/65512.aspx

Suzan, B. (2002): The Barcelona Process and the European Union Approach to Fighting Terrorism. *Brookings Institution*. Available at: http://www.brookings.edu/fp/cusf/analysis/suzan.pdf (Retrieved 21 May 2013).

Tayfur, F. (2000): Security and Co-Operation in the Mediterranean. Working Paper. University of Ankara. Avvailable at: http://sam.gov.tr/wp-content/uploads/2012/01/FatihTayfur.pdf (Retrieved 5 May 2013).

Torreblanca, J.I. (2008): Sarkozy's Foreign Policy: Where Do European Interests and Values Stand? *Fride, Comments*. February. Available at: http://ecfr.eu/page/-/documents/Torreblanca-Sarkozy-Foreign-Pol icy.pdf (Retrieved 29 February 2012).

## D.4 Speeches

Aznar, J.M. (2000): Discourse. Official Visit to Iran. Available at: http://www.jmaznar.es/file_upload/discursos/pdfs/01045A1045.pdf (Retrieved 1 August 2013).

Aznar, J.M. (2001): Speech during Hosni Mubarak's visit to Spain. http://www.jmaznar.es/file_upload/discursos/pdfs/01275A1275.pdf (Retrieved 1 August 2013).

Aznar, J.M. (2001): Speech, Congress of Deputies. 18 October. Available at: http://www.jmaznar.es/file_upload/discursos/pdfs/01250A1250.pdf (Retrieved 1 August 2013).

Aznar, J.M. (2002): Discurso del Presidente del Gobierno, José María Aznar, Para Presentar el Programa de la Presidencia Española de la Unión Europea. Intervenciones Institucionales. Available at: http://www.jmaznar.es/discursos/pdfs/01317A1317.pdf (Retrieved 25 April 2012).

Aznar, J.M. (2003): Azores Summit, Intervention. Available at: http://www.jmaznar.es/file_upload/discursos/pdfs/01659A1659.pdf (Retrieved 1 August 2013).

Aznar, J.M. (2003): Conference during the Seminar on Terrorism and Democracy Organised by the PP New Generations. Available at: http://www.jmaznar.es/file_upload/discursos/pdfs/02081A2081.pdf (Retrieved 1 August 2013).

Aznar, J.M. (2003): Discurso del Presidente del Gobierno, José María Aznar en la Academy of Achievements. Intervenciones Institucionales. Official trip to the US. 8 May 2003. Available at: http://www.jmaznar.es/discursos/pdfs/01695A1695.pdf (Retrieved 1 January 2012).

Aznar, J.M. (2003): Speech. Deputies Congress. 2 December 2003. Available at: http://www.jmaznar.es/file_upload/discursos/pdfs/01841A1841.pdf (Retrieved 12 July 2013).

Aznar, J.M. (2004): Conference. Seminar from Yalta to the 9/11. Siena. Available at: http://www.jmaznar.es/file_upload/discursos/pdfs/2004%2007%2009%20DE%20YALTA%20AL%2011-S.pdf (Retrieved 1 July 2013).

Chirac, J. (1996): Discourse sur la Cooperation Culturelle, Economique, et Technologique avec l'Egypt, sur la Politique Arabe de la France. 8 April. Available at : http://discours.vie-publique.fr/notices/967005600.html (Retrieved 1 August 2013).

De Gaulle, C. (1940): Appel à la Résistence. Available at: http://www.charles-de-gaulle.org/pages/l-homme/accueil/discours/pendant-la-guerre-1940-1946/appel-du-18-juin-1940.php (Retrieved 5 May 2011).

Rodríguez Zapatero, J.L. (2004): Discurso de Investidura. PSOE. Available at: http://estaticos.elmundo.es/documentos/2004/04/15/discurso.pdf (Retrieved 3 March 2012).

Rodríguez Zapatero, J.L. (2008): Discurso del Presidente del Gobierno en el Pleno del Congreso de los Diputados para Informar de las Medidas del Gobierno Ante la Situación Económica y en Relación con la Creación de Empleo. Available at: http://estaticos.elmundo.es/documentos/2008/09/10/zapatero.pdf (Retrieved 10 June 2012). P.1.

Sarkozy, N. (2007): Discourse, Toulon. Available at: http://mouveuropeprovence.free.fr/serendipity/index.php?/archives/17-Discours-Nicolas-Sarkozy-a-Toulon,-Mercredi-7-fevrier-2007.html (Retrieved 4 December 2010).

Zapatero, J.L. (2004): Discurso de Investidura ante el Congreso de los Diputados. PSOE. Available at: http://estaticos.elmundo.es/documentos/2004/04/15/discurso.pdf (Retrieved 9 November 2012).

## D.5 Miscellanea

Charlemagne. (2010): Obama, Breaker of European Hearts. *The Economist*. 2 February. Available at: http://www.economist.com/blogs/charlemagne/2010/02/obama_snubs_eu (Retrieved 13 July 2013).

Database: *Observatory of Economic Complexity*. Massachusetts Institute of Technology. MIT. Available at: http://atlas.media.mit.edu/explore/tree_map/export/usa/all/show/2010/ (Retrieved 1–5 August 2013).

French Ministry of Foreign Affairs. (2007): Appel de Rome pour l'Union pour la Méditerranée. *French Embassy to Rome*. Available at: http://www.ambafrance-it.org/spip.php?article2721 (Retrieved 2 January 2012).

Grant, C. (2005): Variable Geometry. *Prospect Magazine*. Centre for European Reform. Available at : http://www.cer.org.uk/articles/grant_prospect_july05.html (Retrieved 6 December 2010).

Guerrero, C. (2001): El III Foro Formentor Impulsa el Proceso de Paz En Oriente Próximo. *La Semana*. 4 November 2001. Available at: http://www.lasemana.es/periodico/noticia.php?cod=1545 (Retrieved 12 February 2012).

Hassan II. (1985): Interview to King Hassan II by RTE. Available at : http://www.rtve.es/mediateca/videos/20091001/informe-semanal-entrevista-hassan/601716.shtml (Retrieved 25 November 2010).

Lara, R. (2010): EEUU se Desinteresó Pronto de la Hipótesis ETA/11M. Available at: http://www.laproximaguerra.com/2010/12/eeuu-se-desinntereso-pronto-de-la.html (Retrieved 1 August 2013).

MAEC. (2013): Alianza de Civilizaciones. Ministry of Foreign Affairs and Cooperation. Spain. Available at: http://www.exteriores.gob.es/Portal/es/PoliticaExteriorCooperacion/NacionesUnidas/Paginas/AlianzaCivilizaciones.aspx (Retrieved 10 June 2013).

Marticorena, A. (2012): Felipe González, El Último Líder en Quien Confió Gadafi. Available at: http://es.noticias.yahoo.com/blogs/episodios-nacionales/felipe-gonzález-el-último-líder-en-quien-confió-212329450.html (Retrieved 11 March 2012).

Martínez, L.F. (2009): 'Spain and China in the Age of Globalization'. Available at: www.theglobalist.com/storyid.aspx?StoryId=7813 (Retrieved 1 June 2009).

Ministry of Foreign Affairs. (2001): Brief Summary of the Proceedings of the OIC-EU Joint Forum. Republic of Turkey. Available at: www.google.ch/url?sa=t&rct=j&q=&esrc=s&source=web&cd=1&ved=0CCwQFjAA&url=http%3A%2F%2Fwww.mfa.gov.tr%2Fbrief-summary-of-the-proceedings-of-the-oic-eu-joint-forum.en.mfa&ei=28gdUqHAN-WA7Qau2YDgDg&usg=AFQjCNErRafhxE02JI OVSAQEmHKdv-0csg&bvm=bv.51156542,d.ZGU (Retrieved 2 March 2012).

Nafie, I. (2000): Interview to José María Aznar. *Al Ahram*. Available at: http://www.jmaznar.es/file_upload/discursos/pdfs/01162A1162.pdf (Retrieved 1 August 2013).

NATO. (2009): Declaration on Alliance Security. NATO Declaration Strassbourg/Khel. 4 April. Available at: http://www.nato.int/cps/en/SID-CA112F05-4BEF0170/natolive/news_52838.htm (Retrieved 13 June 2012).

Obama, B.H. (2009): A New Beginning. Speech in Cairo. 4 June. The White House. Available at: http://www.whitehouse.gov/issues/foreign-policy/presidents-speech-cairo-a-new-beginning (Retrieved 13 November 2012).

Partido Popular. (1993): *Ahora, Programa de Gobierno Para Todos. Partido Popular*. P. 114. Available at: http://www.pp.es/file_upload/recursos/pdf/20090915092057_349537285.pdf (Retrieved 25 February 2012).

Partido Popular. (1996): Programa Electoral: Con la Nueva Mayoría. *Partido Popular*. Available at: http://www.pp.es/file_upload/recursos/pdf/20090915093224_127951152.pdf (Retrieved 12 March 2012).

Partido Popular. (2004): Programa Electoral. Avanzamos Juntos. *Partido Popular*. Pp. 3–08–309. Available at: http://www.pp.es/file_upload/recursos/pdf/20090915095704_1630412855.pdf (Retrieved 2 February 2012).

Pérez-Maura, R. (2005): El Gobierno Deja Desaparecer el Foro Formentor Tras 6 Ediciones Exitosas. *ABC*. 25th of May 2005. Available at: http://www.abc.es/hemeroteca/historico-20-05-2005/abc/Nacional/el-gobierno-deja-desaparecer-el-foro-formentor-tras-seis-ediciones-exitosas_202591020506.html (Retrieved 1 February 2012).

Press conference, José María Aznar, and George Bush. Crawford, USA. 22 February 2003. Available at: http://www.jmaznar.es/discursos/pdfs/01613A1613.pdf (Retrieved 25 April 2012).

Prodi, R. (2002): A Wider Europe – A Proximity Policy as the Key to Stability. 6th ECSA World Conference. Brussels, 5–6 December. Available at: http://europa.eu/rapid/press-release_SPEECH-02-619_en.htm (Retrieved 15 May 2013).

PSOE. (2004): *Merecemos una España Mejor. Programa Electoral 2004. Elecciones Generales*. PSOE. P. 24. Available at: http://www.cadenaser.com/comunes/2004/elecciones2004/programas/psoe_programa.pdf (Retrieved 5 May 2012).

PSOE. (2008): *Motivos Para Crecer. Programa Electoral 2008–2011*. PSOE. Available at: http://www.psoe.es/source-media/000000118500/000000118784.pdf (Retrieved 10 June 2012).

Sanz Roldán, F. (Ed.) (2009): Del Desencuentro Entre Las Culturas a la Alianza de Civilizaciones: Nuevas Aportaciones Para la Seguridad en el Mediterráneo. *Cuadernos de Estrategia*. N°142. Dirección General de Relaciones Institucionales. Instituto Español de Estudios Estratégicos. Ministerio de Defensa. Available at: http://www.portalcultura.mde.es/Galerias/publicaciones/fichero/CE_142.pdf (Retrieved 14 April 2012).

Spanish Ministry of Foreign Affairs. (1965): Information Note Drafted by the Spanish Embassy to Paris on the New Europeanist Direction of Spanish Foreign Policy since the Arrival of Fernando Maria Castiella at the Spanish Foreign Ministry. P.5. Available at: www.cvce.eu/recherche/unit-content/-/unit/en/87c372a8-360d-4846-876e-d9d64705a918/30935d10-9431-42d9-a29c-3b23d72cc6f5/Resources#f6ec5a99-dba6-415c-bf58-f3cded9cf18d_en&overlay (Retrieved 1 June 2012).

UfM. (2008): Ministerial Conference on Water. A Calendar of Concrete Projects from 2009. UFM. Jordan, 22 December. Available at: http://www.medaquaministerial2008.net/ (Retrieved 15 August 2012).

UN. (2009): Resolution Adopted by the General Assembly. A/Res/64/14. Available at: http://www.worldlii.org/int/other/UNGArsn/2009/65.pdf (Retrieved 10 June 2013).

UN. (2011): Letter Dated 11 August 2011 from the Secretary-General Addressed to the President of the General Assembly. UN General Assembly, A/66/305. P. 7. Available at: http://www.unaoc.org/wp-content/uploads/Report-Published_English-copy.pdf (Retrieved 10 June 2013).

UN. (2001): Resolution 56/6. Global Agenda for Dialogue among Civilizations. New York. 21 November. Available at: http://www.elmundo.es/elmundo/2004/04/18/espana/1082303152.html (Retrieved 2 March 2012).

UN. (2008): Trends in International Migrant Stock: The 2008 Revision. *United Nations Department of Economic and Social Affairs*. Available at: http://esa.un.org/migration/index.asp?panel=1 (Retrieved 1 March 2011).

UNAOC. (2008): *First Alliance of Civilizations Global Forum. Madrid*. Alliance of Civilizations Secretariat. New York. Available at: http://www.unaoc.org/images/aoc%20forum%20report%20madrid%20complete.pdf (Retrieved 1 August 2013).

UNAOC. (2009): *Second Alliance of Civilizations Global Forum. Istanbul*. Alliance of Civilizations Secretariat. New York. Available at: http://www.unaoc.org/docs/AoC_Istanbul-09web.pdf (Retrieved 1 August 2013).

Vallespín, F. (2005): Alianza de Civilizaciones. *Claves de Razón Práctica*. N°157. Pp. 4–8. Available at: http://www.hugoperezidiart.com.ar/sigloXXI-cl2012/vallespin-1999.pdf (Retrieved 1 May 2012).

WWF. (2011): 'WWF Insta a los Países Miembros de la Unión por el Mediterráneo a que se Reúnan y Aporten Soluciones para los Retos Ambientales de la Región'. Observatorio de la Sostenibilidad en España. OSE. Available at: http://www.sostenibilidad-es.org/es/plataformas-de-comunicacion/agua-y-sostenibilidad/noticias/wwf-insta-a-los-paises-miembros-de-la-union-por-el-mediterraneo-a-que (Retrieved 25 August 2012).

## E Printed Newspapers

Anon. (1978): "La Longue Marche du Douzième Etat Membre de la CEE". *La Libre de Belgique*. 21 December. N. 335. P.D1.

Anon. (2004): "Exito de la Diplomacia Española: Mongolia es el Primer País que Apoya la Alianza de Civilizaciones de Zapatero". *La Razón*. 15 October 2004.

Kergorlay, H. (1977): "Espagne: Demande d'adhésion à la C.E.E". *Le Figaro*. 20 July.

Lajoine, A. (1977): "Empêcher le Mauvais Coup". *L'Humanité*. 30 July 1977.

Leparmentier, A.. and Zecchini, L. (2002): "Pour ou Contre L'Adhesion de la Turquie a l'Union Europeenne". *Le Monde*. 8 November.

Moratinos, M.A. (2007): "Del Proceso de Barcelona a la Unión Mediterránea". *El País*. 2 August 2007.

Ortega y Gasset, J. (1917): "La España Invertebrada". *Diario El Sol*. Madrid.

Palmer, J. (1978): "Getting Ready for EEC". *The Guardian*. 14 November.

Silve, R. (1964): "Les Régimes Passent, Les Peuples Restent". *Journal de Genève*. http://www.monde-diplomatique.fr/1999/11/B_/3409 10 May 1964.

Souske, A. (1977): "Marché Commun: La Question Espagnole". *L'Express*. 8 August 1977.

Wilhelmus Burger, J.A. (1962): "Démocratie et Désintegration: L'Espagne Membre de la CEE?" *Courrier Socialist Européen*. 2 April 1962.

# Appendix

## Interviews

1. Mr. Abel Matutes. Former Spanish Minister of Foreign Affairs (Aznar era) and Member of the European Parliament. (Madrid, 14 December 2011).
2. Mr. Alberto Carnero. Spanish Diplomat. Advisor of Jose María Aznar. (Madrid, 10 January 2012).
3. Mr. Alberto Navarro. Spanish Ambassador to Morocco. Former Secretary of State, EU. (Rabat, 1 July 2011).
4. Mr. Andreu Bassols. Director General of IEMED. Former Deputy Head of the Unit EuroMed and Regional Affairs Directorate General of Foreign Affairs of the European Commission. (Barcelona, 26 October 2011).
5. Mr. Andreu Claret. Executive Director of Anna Lindh Foundation. (Barcelona, 25 October 2011).
6. Mr. Carlos Westendorp. Former Spanish Minister of Foreign Affairs, 1995–1996 and Negotiator or the Spanish Accession to the European Community. (Madrid, 30 December 2012).
7. Mr. Cristina Gallach. Spokeperson of the Office of the Secretaty-General of the Council of the European Union. Former Spokeperson of Mr. Javier Solana at NATO and EU. (Brussels, 12 March 2010). Not recorded.
8. Mr. Eneko Landaburu. EU Ambassador to Morocco. Former Director General of the EU Foreign Policy and Director General of Committee of the Regions. (Rabat, 30 June 2011).
9. Mr. Fernando Jauregui. Political Journalist. (Madrid, 6 July 2010).
10. Mr. Fidel Sendagorta. EU Ambassador to Egypt. Former EU Director General for the Mediterranean, Maghreb and the Middle East. Not recorded.
11. Mr. Ibrahim Kraishi. Ambassador of Palestine (Geneva, 6 September 2012). Not recorded.
12. Mr. Jordi Pujol. Former President of Catalonia. (Barcelona, 25 January 2012).

13. Mr. José Luis Rodríguez Zapatero. Former President of Spain. (Madrid, 28 January 2011).
14. Mr. Oguz Demiralp. Ambassador of Turkey to the UN (Geneva, 30 August 2012).
15. Mr. Romain Nadal. Spoke person of the Elysèe. (Paris, 29 October 2012).
16. Ms. Anna Terrón. Secretary of State of Immigration and Emigration, Spain. Former Secretary for the European Union and Spanish Delegate to the EU. (Madrid, 29 June 2011).
17. Mr. Paolo Bergamaschi. Political Expert and Parliamentarian. The Green Party (Brussels, 15 May 2012). Not recorded.
18. Ms. Michelle Rieu. Parliamentarian. The Green Party. (Brussels, 15 May 2012) Not recorded.
19. Ms. Monica Frassoni. Parliamentarian. The Green Party. (Barcelona, 26 October 2011) Not recorded.
20. Mr. Jean Louis Guigou. Director General, IPEMED. (Paris, 19 November 2012).

www.ingramcontent.com/pod-product-compliance
Ingram Content Group UK Ltd.
Pitfield, Milton Keynes, MK11 3LW, UK
UKHW022236230426
12048UKWH00018BA/1292